DISCOVER THE UPSIDE OF DOWN

DISCOVER THE UPSIDE OF DOWN

INVESTMENT STRATEGIES FOR VOLATILE TIMES

Ron Coby
The Short-Side Strategist

John Wiley & Sons, Inc.

Published by John Wiley & Sons, Inc., Hoboken, New Jersey.
Published simultaneously in Canada.

For general information on our other products and services or for technical support, please contact our Customer Care Department within the United States at (800) 762-2974, outside the United States at (317) 572-3993, or fax (317) 572-4002.

Wiley also publishes its books in a variety of electronic formats. Some content that appears in print may not be available in electronic formats. For more information about Wiley products, visit our Web site at www.wiley.com.

Library of Congress Cataloging-in-Publication Data:

Coby, Ron (Ronald J.)
Discover the upside of down : investment strategies for volatile times / Ron Coby.
p. cm.
ISBN 978-0-470-41972-4 (cloth)
1. Investment analysis. I. Title.
HG4529.C62 2009
332.6—dc22

2008038655

Printed in the United States of America

10 9 8 7 6 5 4 3 2 1

Dedicated to

my beautiful wife, Susan
and our three wonderful children,
Anna, Grace, and Joseph

CONTENTS

ACKNOWLEDGMENTS

I had a ton of help and input in finishing this book. I would like to thank my in-laws, Pat and Bob Hautala, for all their time in helping me with the initial editing. I'd like to thank my wife for her keen insights along the way. I want to thank my dad for his encouragement and his words of inspiration that helped to push me forward to completing this book.

I want to especially thank Alan Morasch for his total dedication and creative marketing input, insightful suggestions and additions, and for making this book the final product it needed to be. Without his help this book would never have made it to completion. Alan and I had quite an adventure together—one we'll never forget.

Additional thanks to: Will Reishman, Wally Pistor, Richard Petralia, the EWI organization, Bill Smith, Denny Lamson, Bob Scott, and, finally, I'd like to thank my mom for being a role model to me in the areas of tenacity, resilience, and street smarts. Hi, Mom!

INTRODUCTION

A fierce economic battle is raging, and the Federal Reserve is fighting twin enemies on your behalf, both of which could destroy your investments. To secure your financial future, it is critical that you understand these two enemies. Today, more than ever, you must have a "profit and protection" investment strategy to safely cross the minefields that could cause the stocks in your portfolio to be blown up. This economic battle is between the forces of deflation and the forces of inflation, both attacking and devaluing your investments. The Federal Reserve is fighting these enemies on both sides but has been in a losing battle, as battling one only fuels the other.

The Federal Reserve's most frightening enemy is deflation, where debt contraction could risk the New Depression of the twenty-first century. The Fed is fighting this most fierce nemesis with all its power and might with multiple "emergency rate cuts" and even more creative and desperate means to keep the financial system from collapsing.

The Federal Reserve's biggest fear is the memory of a similar war that was fought and lost in 1929. The commander-in-chief of the current Federal Reserve is Ben Bernanke, a student of the Great Depression era of the 1930s. Bernanke knows all too well the mistakes that led to the stock market crash, which left mass casualties in the United States and around the globe. You need to know, as the Fed currently does, that some wars must be fought for the safety of "the many." Winning this war will be *very* difficult, because it is a war that has two equally dangerous outcomes, should it be lost.

The second enemy is inflation, which has gathered steam as the Fed fights deflation. This new opponent's leader is oil, and the allies are commodities of all kinds, which have gained domination alongside gold, intensifying price pressures in the economy and in your pocketbook. Gold is the leading defender of investors against the enemy of inflation. Gold has gained great power for the first several years of the new century. In fact, gold reached the height of its leadership and strength in 2008 as the Federal Reserve cut interest rates in an attempt to defeat asset deflation.

These two very difficult battles being fought by the Federal Reserve are a united force called *stagflation.* On one side of the struggle, Americans are faced with falling stocks and real estate prices. On the other side of the war zone, they are being hit by soaring prices for energy, food, tuition, and housing. This is putting the financial squeeze on families across the nation and around the world.

The Federal Reserve is throwing massive amounts of money at the deflation problem at the risk of creating a hyper-inflationary disaster. In *Discover the Upside of Down,* you will read about these powerful forces that could truly annihilate your portfolio and your future financial well-being if you are not prepared. The first half of the book explores gold, the U.S. dollar, oil, and the profit opportunities on their upside, as well as their inevitable downside movements.

The second half of the book is a detailed war plan with an investment strategy for protection and profits from the mine-fields created by the forces of deflation and inflation. This investment strategy will help you to know when it is time to retreat from the battle (sell stocks) and run for cover. It is critical to know when the war drums start beating so you can take action before calamity strikes. By recognizing these early warning signs, you will have the opportunity to jump into a foxhole, hunker down, and "cover your assets." This "eyes wide open" crash protection strategy will both help you recognize when this current battle is over and enable you to have plenty of asset ammunition when it is time to go back on the offensive in search of capital gains.

As a battle-scarred veteran, I have learned plenty to help me build this nearly bulletproof investment strategy. I have fought in many frightening market battles, like the 1987 crash and the Nasdaq 2000 meltdown. In *Discover the Upside of Down,* I share invaluable market knowledge I have acquired from experience along with relevant stories of success and defeat so you can be victorious throughout what I believe will be a very long war on stagflation. As a stockbroker, investment banker, syndicate manager, Wall Street market strategist, analyst, venture capitalist, and, most recently, a hedge fund manager, I consider myself a market veteran who has earned his stripes.

I am known as the "Short-Side Strategist," deploying a strategy for profits and protection. It is an appropriate strategy for this new economic environment that not only addresses the downside but sees profit opportunities in the downside as well. It is the right strategy because it addresses these two equally powerful and opposing destructive forces and deals with each accordingly.

I believe that *Discover the Upside of Down*, full of war stories, can be your profit protection gear as you fight the good fight to secure your future retirement needs. In the future, I believe there will once again be times of safety and prosperity. That is what most of us desire and have all experienced during this long and glorious productivity-led boom in stocks, bonds, and real estate. However, turbulent economic times are now upon us, and this book can be your investment guide as you attempt to navigate the tremendous market volatility that lies ahead for the United States and the global economy. This economic storm will eventually pass, and my short-side strategy of protection and profits will help you recognize that passing and prepare you to take full advantage of a shining new bull market as it rises like the phoenix to move the global economy forward once again.

BULLS VERSUS BEARS, AND THE WINNER IS . . .

Bulls debating bears has almost become a pastime sport on CNBC, or as I have heard it called, "the bull parade." Every day you can see the talking heads on TV argue their bullish or bearish cases. So many market prognosticators display their diametrically opposing viewpoints that they all sound equally convincing. One view is the prediction of a U.S. economic collapse, like Peter Schiff's in *Crash Proof* (John Wiley & Sons, 2007). Others, like the well-known market timing strategist Don Hays, predict "the greatest economic boom in world history" far ahead into the future. These equally convincing viewpoints leave most investors completely confused, less confident, and often misguided. To add to the confusion of the market prognostications, market gurus, traders, and investors alike are usually way too bullish at the top and too bearish at the bottom.

In this book, you'll learn how to navigate your financial future in what is shaping up to be the market roller-coaster ride of a lifetime ahead for U.S. and world markets. To wisely position your finances for the boom and bust periods that are ahead, let's look back to the past market debates in one of the biggest boom and bust period of this generation, 1995 through early 2008. Understanding the past psychology versus the actual realties will help you better position your investments for the future.

In the bull market run that started in early 1995, Oppenheimer's bearish chief investment strategist, the late

Michael Metz, advised clients to be cautious and raise cash right when they should have been buying stocks with both fists. At the same time, Elaine Garzarelli, chief market strategist of Lehman Brothers, debated the exact opposite. Elaine was so bullish in 1995 that she was fired because her views seemed so outrageous and contrary to the consensus sentiment after a very difficult 1994 market. However, the more bearish Michael Metz became on the stock market, the more airtime he received. As stocks rallied ahead, Elaine's bullish views were vindicated and she was granted celebrity status on Wall Street. When Michael Metz showed up at the floor of the New York Stock Exchange with his full bear suit on, he was most likely avoided as though he had some kind of transmittable disease because of his wrong bearish stock market calls.

At the very height of Elaine's fame, she had a change of fortune. On July 26, 1996, Elaine issued her widely advertised "Sell All Stocks Now" call right as stocks again launch-padded to new all-time highs. She ultimately had to reverse her bearish call after missing a huge bullish move by "making new changes" to her market timing model.

Probably the most advertised bullish market call early in the bull market came from Ralph Acampora in June 1995 as the Dow Jones Industrial Average (DJIA) was approaching 5,000. Ralph was the chief technical strategist for Prudential Securities, and he put out a detailed report titled "DOW 7,000." Ralph made a great call and caused quite a stir when he issued that report.

As the bull market was preparing to turn bearish in 2000, the three biggest bullish talking heads were Al Goldman, chief strategist of A.G. Edwards; Abby Joseph Cohen, chief market strategist of Goldman Sachs; and Joe Battipaglia, head of investment policy at Gruntel. These three famous bulls—Al, Abby, and Joe—had incredible airtime, and each became famous as a result. To their credit, they were correct on being bullish in the previous bull market run. To their detriment, they overstayed their welcome.

Another bull that received major airtime at the top was Brian Finnerty, head of Nasdaq trading, C.E. Unterberg, Towbin. I remember watching Brian on CNNfn on January 27, 2000, recommending JDS Uniphase (JDSU). In his very gruff voice, Brian said, "JDSU gave us a great number yesterday . . . JDSU is trading at 200 times earnings. But is that overvalued? I don't know." Shortly thereafter, JDSU then went on a slide from $155 to $1.55, only a small decimal change, but an enormous price change!

Also on CNNfn we had the famous Liz Ann Sonders, then managing director of Campbell, Cowperthwait (currently chief investment strategist of Charles Schwab and Co., Inc.) say this regarding JDSU, "Love it both long term and short term." She, too, loved the stock market and went on to recommend AOL, CSCO, Enron, and Broadcade before those stocks imploded 70 to 100 percent.

My personal favorite example of watching a talking head on the TV getting humbled was Ned Riley, chief investment strategist at State Street Global Advisors. Ned was a "perma-bull," and to prove it he was quoted as saying, "I'll be recommending the QQQ (Nasdaq 100) until the day I die." (*Sources:* CNN, *Moneyline Weekend*) He not only was married to the market, but to individual stocks as well. He was strongly recommending Elan Pharmaceuticals (ELN) in late 2001 on CNBC. This was his favorite pick, and he still loved it all the way down from the 60s, where he recommended it, to the mid-20s. ELN continued to head down, and the stock was one of *the* biggest losers in terms of the pure speed and pain of its fall. The stock bottomed at $1.03—so much for the experts.

In 2000, Al, Abby, and Joe's bullishness was diametrically opposed to the bearish outlook Don Hays, chief investment strategist of Wheat First Butcher Singer, had at the time. Don was calling for a big smash in stocks after being a long-running bull. As turmoil was sweeping through the world financial markets like an uncontrolled maelstrom in 2000, Al, Abby, and Joe were table-pounding bullish all the way down. On each big bear market rally in Nasdaq 2000, these three strategists were immediately paraded all over CNBC spewing the only action they understood to take—*buy, buy, buy.* Investors who listened to their advice saw their equity go bye-bye in the market devastation that followed.

Don Hays, however, kept his clients out of harm's way, albeit early on his bearish market call. After the Nasdaq 100 had collapsed 83 percent, Al, Abby, and Joe were avoided like the plague by the media. Don Hays—or as I like to call him, "Big Daddy Don"—then came out of his bear cave with his full bull suit on right at the bottom. Don has remained a bull, looking for "a new golden era of prosperity" for the United States even as stocks have been getting crushed in 2008.

Is It Doom or Boom?

Don Hays sees a new golden era of opportunity with low inflation ahead for the United States. He sees the market as the "most undervalued in 29 years." This outlook is greatly contrasted with Peter Schiff of Euro Pacific Capital. Peter is a stockbroker and controversial author of *Crash Proof.* At one time he was on the TV almost weekly debating any bull that came his way on why the U.S. economy is about to get annihilated. You can see Peter's past debates on his web site at www.europac.net. They are very lively and entertaining to watch. Peter sees the U.S. dollar on the verge of a complete and utter collapse.

He is still advising all his clients to get all their money out of the now rising U.S. dollar to buy high-dividend-paying foreign stocks, even as markets world wide implode.

Don Hays, however, thinks the United States is in the "second wave of the technological revolution." He sees a long and mighty boom coming on as new consumers and workers in India and China will keep demand high and wage inflation low. Peter is 100 percent out of U.S. stocks and dollars and sees mass inflation and financial destruction for U.S. assets ahead. Don Hays is 100 percent invested in U.S. stocks and sees great times ahead for U.S. stocks, bonds, and the U.S. economy. Peter points out that the huge trade and budget imbalances in the United States and the zero savings rate are leading to a U.S. economic meltdown. The bulls, conversely, see all the newly created wealth in investors' retirement and Keogh accounts as evidence of U.S. economic strength and power.

Personally, I can see both arguments having some credibility and possibilities. This is why it is imperative to have a strategy to protect *and* profit regardless of the boom or doom market calls you are hearing professed so loudly. I refer to this as having a short-side strategy. A short-side strategy employs stocks long *and* short for bull or bear markets ahead. It is a strategy that addresses the twin forces of inflation and deflation, which is called stagflation. It is an easy-to-understand commonsense strategy, regardless of your level of sophistication in the market.

Discover the Upside of Down provides you with proven indicators for spotting major market direction changes. My short-side strategy will help you recognize warning signs so that you are ahead of boom or bust times and positioned properly for both. I will share personal stories of triumph and failure that will be both educational and entertaining. You will see why most investors should deploy some form of a short-side strategy today and for the foreseeable future. Later in the book I will also share with you an incredible market timing indicator I discovered to help you execute on this short-side strategy.

Bulls and Bears in Ojai

In 2005, I went to an enlightening stock market conference for professional investors and traders in Ojai, California, called "Minyans in the Mountain Retreat." Minyanville is a very cool interactive web site (www.minyanville.com) where great minds share their keen market views. This Ojai conference had some brilliant strategists and forecasters all sharing their outlook, mostly on the U.S. stock market.

I was highly impressed but amazed at how such successful market forecasters could have such deep convictions so opposite each other. Tony Dyer, a market strategist of excellent insight, predicted a rip-roaring bull market to come. He showed how undervalued the markets were and his argument was very sound. John Succo, a proven and brilliant hedge fund manager of Vicis Capital, envisioned a coming economic hurricane to wipe this country off the face of the economic map. His views stem from how many additional dollars of debt are now required to generate a single dollar of gross domestic product (GDP). In John's own words, "In 1980 it took $1 of new debt created by the Fed to generate $1 of GDP. In 2000, it was $4 of new debt for $1 of GDP. In 2007, it takes $6." John goes on to say, "So as liquidity grows (inflation), the forces of liquidity reduction (deflation) grow as well. At some point, the probabilities of deflation (debt reduction) will become manifest."

John sums this up well with, "So as things look better, they are actually getting worse." I quote John here because *Discover the Upside of Down* explores the possibility of an economic collapse in detail.

This is important for you as an investor today to understand because of the potential consequences to your portfolio, as well as our country, which could develop if this deflation thesis is in fact correct. We will thoroughly explore the global ramifications in this book. Most importantly, you will need a well-defined strategy for protection, then profit, if such a dire forecast were to materialize. What if this global economic boom were in fact built on reckless amounts of debt taken on by the U.S. government and real estate speculators? What if this asset inflation in stocks and real estate were to suffer a collapse resulting in forced debt reduction? Are you fully prepared with a strategy to protect and profit if such a dire scenario were to unfold? Will you recognize the proven and dependable signs to get out before calamity strikes?

The Ojai conference had many roaring bulls and growling bears of equal stature and intelligence standing at polar opposites. One of my favorite presentations at the Ojai conference was from Steve Shobin. Even as a technical strategist, Steve believes that fundamental analysis is just as important as the technical side of the market. Steve Shobin is not only one of the most brilliant market technicians, but he is also one of the all-time great human beings. Steve's strategy is not to live or die on a big market call. Steve looks at both sides of the market and trades on both sides of the tape.

My sense at the time in Ojai was that the audience and the guest panelist were overall bearish, which was a short-term bullish signal for the market from a contrarian's point of view. This was an outstanding and very educational conference that brought me home asking the question, "What if? . . ."

You should ask yourself this same question, *What if the market bears are right and financial destruction lies dead ahead?* The bullish and bearish forecasts all had a ring of truth to them. The irony was that both John's bearish views and Tony's bullish views had equal merit. With the combination of low interest rates and a flowing river of liquidity, how can the market and the economy fail to boom again like the bulls predict?

There's a flip side to that bullish coin, however. If the combination of prolific money supply growth and chronic twin deficits in the United States continues, how can the dollar possibly avoid an outright collapse, or, at the very least, a currency crisis of some kind? The real question is: How does one safely trade or invest in an environment where you can protect and profit if a boom or bust lies immediately ahead? Throughout this book I will be emphasizing just such a strategy.

My contention is that if asset prices can stay elevated, then the prodigious net worth of U.S. investors will result in manageable levels of debt. If the U.S. dollar or bonds don't collapse and foreign central banks and investors choose to finance our debts and deficits, then we can avoid the financial catastrophe of stagflation.

The other side is that eventually this debt-induced boom will prove largely false as stocks, bonds, or real estate experiences an outright price collapse. If this happens, the U.S. economic boom will go *ka-boom,* just as the bears are forecasting.

Here's where I come down on all of this after 21 years of studying markets. I have seen flash-in-the-pan strategists come and go, and they all have one thing in common. They have made a big market call, bullish or bearish, at the wrong time and their fame was short-lived. The short-side strategy that I describe is flexible and positions your portfolio for protection and profits on both sides of the market in domestic and global stocks as well as in noncorrelated markets.

The Bad News Bears

The bears have taken the biggest beating in this respect by looking foolish with end-of-the-world market calls at the wrong times. I'd have to say that Robert Prechter wins as the number one Bad News Bear in terms of bad timing. Robert put out two books looking for market devastation. Both of these books called for the end of the bull market right as the bull was ready to run like never before. His first book, *At the Crest of the Tidal Wave* (New Classic Library, 1995), came out literally at the bottom of the stock market in early 1995. His second book, *Conquer the Crash* (John Wiley & Sons, 2002), came out at the next bottom in 2002. This is horrible stock market timing, but a perfect time to market these books as fear gripped investors at the bottom.

Peter Schiff is now by far the most vocal bear and is often featured by the media. Investors have seen Peter on TV because of his daunting comments of a currency collapse coming in the U.S. dollar. To his followers, this call appears to be slowly playing out as the dollar in 2008 hit all-time lows on the U.S. Dollar Index. Peter's call on gold was right on the mark as gold went to new highs. His calls on a collapsing U.S. economy and stock market have many of Peter's followers waiting in great anticipation. Could Peter Schiff of 2008 be what Michael Metz was in 1995, or could Peter be correctly bearish right in front of a market collapse?

Peter is advising his clients to put all their money in foreign stocks and gold. However, foreign stocks closely follow the U.S. market in terms of direction, as is widely evidenced by recent and historic bull and bear market moves in U.S. stocks. Peter is buying high-dividend-paying stocks as his strategy for client protection but even high-dividend-paying stocks can crash.

A short-side strategy addresses both sides of the market and depends solely on neither. Only time will tell if Peter's dire U.S. economic call is correct. One thing is correct: Peter may or may not be a market genius, but based on his successful media recognition, he is a marketing genius.

The other bear who took it on the chin in the late 1990s was Gail Dudack, market strategist of UBS securities at the time. She was one of the "Elves" on the Louis Rukeyser show, *Wall Street Week.* I personally thought the show was the best, and it was truly one of the all-time great shows to watch on the stock market. The "Elves Index" was created by the late Lou Rukeyser in 1989 and it had a very poor track record of market timing results. He had 10 panelists voting on the market's direction. The index was so bad that it became a contrary indicator, so when the Elves were bullish on the stock market, that was the signal to start getting cautious. He was getting pretty upset with Gail Dudack on his TV show because she had a long-running bearish stock market call. As the Nasdaq bubble train was gaining a full head of steam, Gail dug her feet in even more and stayed true to her bearish outlook. You could see the frustration on Rukeyser's face as he resorted to mocking her bear market calls live on the show. In November 1999, right near the all-time climactic top in Nasdaq, he replaced her with Alan Bond. The "Elves" then became almost uniformly bullish right at the top in March 2000. I spoke to Gail right after that firing and told her that redemption was shortly coming on her early, but correct, market call. Of course, the dot-com bust began just a few months later!

What about the long-term outlook espoused by today's popular market forecasters? In the bull's corner, you have Don Hays, who thinks gold, oil, and commodities of all kinds have built up potential bubbles like that of Nasdaq 2000. Don sees a continued long-running U.S. economic boom like the world has never seen. This view is 100 percent diametrically opposed to Peter Schiff, who is calling for a U.S. economic apocalypse. Whom can you believe and which judgment can you trust?

What if you are a bear only shorting stocks, or are in cash and Don Hays is right and stocks resume their boom higher and higher? What if Peter Schiff is right and a severe crash is right around the corner and you are 100 percent long stocks in your 401(k)? This is why, in this new era of volatility, that *both* sides of the market need to be addressed even by the most bullish or bearish of investors.

Because you, and everyone else, do not know for sure if a protracted decline is ahead, you must first position yourself for protection, then profit. Your strategy should provide you stock market crash insurance in case the U.S. stock market is a gigantic house of cards ready to collapse. Because you don't know if a boom is to resume once again, you must also be in a position to profit if Don's new golden age of prosperity were in fact to happen. You must learn how to be prepared with crash protection for either future scenario. In this new era of market volatility I see ahead, you must be willing to look at both sides of the marketplace, long and short.

No one can see the future—absolutely no one. If an unexpected event like the U.S. or Israel attacking Iran occurs, as some have predicted, then stocks will implode and the bulls will be wrong. If the dollar reverses and money continues to flood into U.S. assets, then the bears will have egg on their faces. The fact is that the credit buildup in the United States has never been so incredibly high. The other side is the fact that huge amounts of net worth have also built up in stocks and real estate in this long and mighty boom.

I will help you recognize the many classic signs of a market top so that you can make wise and timely adjustments to your portfolio. These signs often present themselves after the Fed has been cutting interest rates and bullish sentiment rises to an extreme like the stock market top in late 2007. I will also show you how bull markets climb a "wall of worry" and die in an atmosphere of euphoria, and how to easily recognize both.

From a long-term viewpoint, stocks are perched up very high and there is precedent that a long-term bearish or sideways trend is likely. Any unexpected outside event like a dollar collapse, an interest rate crisis, or a surprise attack on Iran could send stocks into a great and mighty crash. If one of these scenarios were to happen, it would create a giant global margin call where assets fall below all the massive amounts of debt stacked up against stocks and real estate. This giant global margin call would negatively impact stocks and economies around the world. The exposure to stocks and real estate has never been higher, as evidenced by the largest percentage of U.S. household ownership of stocks and real estate in the new century. The affinity for stocks and real estate is further evidenced by the record high levels of margin and mortgage debt so investors have the highest exposure possible to these two major asset classes.

From a cyclical point of view, the bullish case could very well take place whenever the Fed is aggressively cutting interest rates and flooding money into the system. From a long-term secular point of view, the warnings made by the bears should convince investors to be prudent regardless of which side of the fence they are on. Most believe that Peter Schiff's nihilistic viewpoint of getting all your money out of the country is over the top, but the warnings cannot be ignored. He was correct on his call of a falling U.S. dollar. What if Schiff is right about the U.S. economy and stock market devastation is yet to come? Are you prepared, or are you a long-only investor?

Don Hays is one of the better investment strategists I witnessed from 1987 to 2007, so bears must also beware. With all these confusing and conflicting, but convincing arguments, you must position your portfolio with a safe and sensible strategy to protect and profit in future boom or bust, bull or bear markets. My philosophy is not to be a hero on a big market call, but to present a flexible strategy to make money with some peace of mind regardless of what scenario the talking heads on TV say will happen. *There is the bull side, the bear side, and money to be made on both sides.* Learn to focus on keeping your portfolio most heavily on the right side but positioned on both sides of the market. As the legendary trader Jesse Livermore once said, "There's only one side of the market that counts and that's the right side."

The Bull Parade

I truly never thought we would see the kind of market hysteria with the bullish gang on CNBC like we saw in 1999, but I was wrong. A new member was added to the bullish gang, and you can hear him screaming stuff like "The Bull is alive" and "BUY, BUY, BUY" or "SELL, SELL, SELL" every single day. Jim Cramer has now become the leader in the bull parade, fully equipped with loud horns and crazy sound effects used during his daily market show. Jim has become a larger-than-life symbol to investors worldwide because of his keen insights and his crazed antics. He is a former successful hedge fund manager who gained his fame when *60 Minutes* did a piece on Jim trading stocks for his hedge fund. It was a great piece to watch, and at the time I thought Jim was just some wild man day trading stocks. Then, to my amazement, CNBC hired him and gave him his own TV show.

Jim is very sharp and a well-liked guy. He has been able to wisely capitalize on the general state of bullishness and excitement that exists in the stock market. The truth is that Jim has become the face of the market. As he has become Mr. Market himself, people all want to know, "What does Cramer think?"

Cramer has become so big that *BusinessWeek* featured him on the front cover of the September 2005 issue. When I saw this article, it gave me great pause as I remembered the now infamous *BusinessWeek* cover titled "The Death of Equities" in 1979. It took a couple of years after that cover story before the market reached its final secular bottom and then roared ahead. That article put a long-term secular bottom in for the stock market as stocks eventually went on to the longest bull market run in U.S. history. Stocks went on to become a table-pounding buy-and-hold for decades.

I have to wonder if *BusinessWeek* positively featuring Mr. Market himself on the cover in 2005 isn't also setting up for a new secular move, this time putting in a long-term secular market top. Again, it took a couple years before stocks reversed course from the 1979 article. Having Mr. Market himself featured positively on the front cover of *BusinessWeek* in 2005 could be as contrarian as "The Death of Equities" front cover was in 1979. If the *BusinessWeek* contrarian indicator holds true, then we saw the top in 2007 and we are on the cusp of the best time to deploy the short-side strategy presented in this book. A front cover article in *BusinessWeek* is a great indicator of the nation's emotions near the peak or bottom of a long business cycle.

I will say this about Jim Cramer and the power of CNBC. Jim's TV show has made him so popular that he could become the next president of CNBC. If the DJIA goes to 39,000, like Japan did in the 1980s, then Jim even has a chance of being elected president of the United States—he is that famous. Personally, I admire the guy for what he has accomplished and, given the current and likely future state of U.S. politics, I'll be Jim's first vote if he runs for president.

If It Looks Like a Bubble . . .

The Bond Bubble

Bonds have been in a long bull market since the early 1980s. Bond prices collapsed in the 1970s as oil exploded and inflation ripped through the economy. The Fed pumped too much money under Presidents Nixon and Johnson, which led to rip-roaring inflation, resulting in crashing stocks and bonds. A prudent investor should note some eerie similarities between the present and the 1970s period of stagflation.

As I write, we are having a similar crisis, yet yields on bonds have stayed low. The Fed has been inflating the money supply as it did in the 1970s, yet bond prices are stable and rising, as bonds are responding more to the deflation side of the stagflation equation.

Commodities of all kinds also raced to new all-time highs in the big 2001 through 2008 run. This can be seen in the Commodity Research Bureau (CRB) index, which is a basket of commodities that comprise the index. The CRB posted record highs as oil exploded to triple digits in 2008. This put the 2001 through 2008 upside move well ahead of the 1971 through 1974 146.7 percent gain in the CRB index.

Gold touched $1,000 an ounce in 2008 and registered new cycle highs like in the 1970s, yet all we hear about is that there is "little to no inflation." The bond market has been ignoring these traditional inflationary warnings, which has many economists and bond bears raising their eyebrows. To add to all of these bearish bond indicators, the U.S. Dollar Index has been weak for the first several years of the new century. To top it all off, the Federal Reserve cut interest rates in 2007, and aggressively in 2008. These rate cuts are like pouring gas on a slow-burning fire. A wild fire of inflation could spread and eventually send bond yields through the roof and bond prices into the abyss. If inflation does spiral out of control, then interest rates will likely double or triple, like they did in the 1970s. This is when the Federal Reserve will need to follow the proven formula for fighting inflation, which is cutting the money supply and hiking interest rates.

A simple way to play the downside in bonds is to put money into the Rydex Juno Fund (RYJUX). If the 30-year Treasury bond is to fall 10 percent, then the Juno Fund is designed to go up 10 percent. (Go to www.rydexfunds.com for more information.) The market professionals short bond futures to hedge against rising interest rates, but the futures market is no place for novice investors. When the charts on bonds finally do top out and line up with the fundamentals, get short. As bonds reverse course, the 25-year bull market will be over and a generational bear market will begin.

Paul Volcker fought 1970s inflation by cutting the money supply, forcing up interest rates. Once the inflation fight begins, bonds will fall out of bed as interest rates rise. More recently, the huge money supply buildup in the Greenspan and Bernanke era has been the lifeblood of stocks, real estate, and debt creation. If the money supply is ever to be cut, then the current slow-motion real estate decline will move into fast forward. This would kill consumer spending, which would take the economy and stocks down like in the 1930s, creating a daisy chain of destruction, where one negative event feeds upon the other. This would result in what will likely be coined "The New Great Depression of the Twenty-first Century." The difference this time is that it will feel more like the New Great Depression but combined with inflationary pressures in a New Era of Stagflation.

The forces of deflation in a stagnant economy combined with rising inflationary pressures is what I call the Stagflation Equation (Stagnation + Inflation = Stagflation). Deflation is what happened to Japan when its economic miracle turned into a nightmare. Interest rates dropped to low levels, but Japanese investors had no desire to borrow and take on additional debt, no matter how low interest rates went. As the U.S. mortgage debt bomb explodes, debt will be shunned once again, especially for highly speculative purposes.

Bonds are currently setting up to be one of the great short opportunities eventually leading to one of the great long-term buying opportunities in the future, once the Fed fights inflation rather than igniting it. This is important to know as bond prices typically fall first, leading to severe stock market reversals within 6 to 12 months. In the new environment of stagflation, stocks can go down even as bond prices hold up. Bonds can suddenly reverse as the Fed starts to cut money growth as it focuses on reducing inflation from the dramatic rise of costs for goods and services in the economy. That will be the loud bang that pushes U.S stock momentum down the mountainside like a cascading avalanche.

This is why I named Chapter 6 "Nothing but Downside." When these events come to pass, there will be nothing but downside in stocks, bonds, and real estate for quite some time in the future. This will most certainly happen once the Fed is forced to cut the money supply and hike interest rates. Another reason for the chapter title is that investors who buy at the top experience nothing but downside, and investors who sell at the bottom see nothing but downside.

The Real Estate Bubble

Real estate has been in a bull market for 50 years, but hit a serious bump in the road in 2005. This bump is looking more like a major pothole based on all the negative news concerning the state of real estate in 2006, 2007, and 2008. The question to ask is, "What if the pothole is the Grand Canyon—then how significant is the downside yet to come in real estate?" We will explore that question in the book with interesting stories and real life experiences.

The fact is that this real estate bubble is not a domestic one, it is a global phenomenon. At the top in 2005, *The Economist* magazine called the housing boom "the biggest bubble in history," with "world residential real estate values escalating from $40 trillion to over $70 trillion" in the last decade's bull market run. The article pointed out that the $30 trillion increase in world residential real estate values is just about equal to the GDP of the entire advanced world. Housing prices in the United States, Australia, Spain, Ireland, and the United Kingdom exploded in price during the 1995 to 2005 bull market run. *If it looks like a bubble, acts like a bubble, and feels like a bubble, then it must be a bubble!* The evidence of the air slowly coming out has been seen on a weekly basis since that article came out. You know this is a serious concern of the Federal Reserve by the Fed's aggressive policy actions. The Fed cut interest rates in 2007 and 2008, which is exactly what they did in 2001 when they tried to slow down the Nasdaq crash. Nasdaq fell over 80 percent before the bottom finally hit. How far can real estate prices fall before they reach their ultimate long-term bottom? Again, read on as I explore a 1929 downside scenario to come from a debt contraction cycle that has begun. The problem with bubbles is that when they burst, they typically overdo it to a downside extreme like they overdid it on the upside explosion.

The Commodity Bubble

The CRB posted a high in 2008 exceeding its best move ever of 146 percent from 2001. Speculative momentum buying sent gold, oil, copper, silver, platinum, and almost every other commodity to dizzying heights. The U.S. dollar hit its lowest level ever and that boosted the price of real assets that are priced in terms of depreciated dollars. The commodity bulls believe that the combination of a continued weak dollar and the apparent insatiable appetite from China and India for energy and metals will propel prices much higher far into the future. The famous commodity investor, Jimmy Rodgers, has come out with another book that encourages investors to buy China and commodities. Jimmy was interviewed on Bloomberg TV in November 2007, saying he is getting all of his assets out of the United States and out of U.S. dollars. He said we have "a lunatic Fed chairman" that is going to blow up the U.S. currency with his reckless Fed policies. He sees the commodity run as early in its bull market. With the price of oil and oil stocks running wild both up and down so violently, one has to wonder if we aren't once again seeing another price bubble like Nasdaq 2000.

Regardless of what the commodity bulls think, the easy money has most likely been made in commodities. If the U.S. dollar does have a currency crisis, then commodities will have another blow-off-like run before putting in a final top. As the China bubble blows, the perceived insatiable demand for commodities is withering and the commodity bubble appears to be popping. More details on this later in the book, but suffice it to say that looking ahead, investors and traders will also need a short-side strategy in commodities. Long-only investing in commodities will no longer work because, as they say on Wall Street, "trees don't grow to the sky."

The Stock Market Bubble

The secular boom in stocks has been a very long one indeed. Stock prices have enjoyed the best of all worlds in the "Goldilocks" economy, not too hot and not too cold. As real estate has its "perfect storm," investors continue to pour money into stocks even as prices fall. Stocks are competing with weak real estate and unattractive bonds. In 2007, stocks experienced a merger and acquisition boom that lowered the supply of stocks outstanding. This propelled the DJIA and the Standard & Poor's (S&P) 500 to all-time record highs in 2007 right before they severely corrected into bear market territory in 2008. Money goes where it feels the safest and is treated the best, and over the long haul that has been in stocks. The concern of many investors, including myself, is how bad will the economy and stocks get if real estate weakens considerably or interest rates finally start to rise?

From a wide-angle viewpoint, stocks, bonds, commodities and real estate still look very high and overvalued. This does not mean that certain stocks in hot sectors or the market cannot rise substantially. It also doesn't mean the real estate market can't have a mild recovery and quite possibly, yet unlikely, boom ahead. With bond yields so low, many see stocks as undervalued relative to bonds, and mortgage rates favorably disposed to future gains in home prices. If I am correct about the coming substantial rise in interest rates, then stocks and real estate will not look as cheap or desirable as the economy falls and jobs are lost. The other concern is that the first two years of a new presidency can be very difficult and volatile for the stock market.

How does everything seem to you? Do you think stock prices are attractive and cheap? Do you think real estate prices are low, undervalued, and affordable? Do interest rates look attractive to you with low, single-digit yields? There is a case to be made that from a long-term secular point of view, there could be nothing but downside pressure in stocks, bonds, and real estate.

This book is not intended to be pessimistic, but a realistic explanation why most investors should have a short-side strategy to counter the new economic force of stagflation. More importantly, this is a strategy to deploy no matter which camp you fall into, bull or bear. So let's *Discover the Upside of Down* with my message summarized in nine words: Bull or Bear, Boom or Bust, Long *and* Short.

CHAPTER 2

BOOMTOWN TO GHOST TOWN

Of the three main asset classes—stocks, bonds, and real estate—real estate had been by far the most loved and overvalued. In the real estate market, I see a scenario that could play out a lot like 1929, which led to the Great Depression of the 1930s. In the 1920s, stock investors were able to buy stocks for 10 percent down on margin. A stock owner could control $100,000 worth of stock with only 10 percent margin, or $10,000. This left an incredible amount of leverage against an overvalued asset class. When those overvalued stocks crashed, all the debt had to be paid through the liquidation of those stocks. One could easily see this situation developing in today's real estate market and that it could lead the United States into a new depression.

An enormous amount of real estate has been purchased in the new century with little or no money down. Homeowners and speculators have controlled real estate with 10 percent down payments, just like stocks in 1929. Many home prices have dropped well below that 10 percent payment, so homeowners are left with negative equity where the debt is greater than the deflated equity in the home. This negative equity in homes is like the negative equity in stocks in 1929 that created margin calls. The monthly mortgage payments would be like a margin call that a stock speculator had to meet without having to sell. If real estate has a price collapse, then homeowners will be faced with huge losses on their homes. This would cripple the U.S. economy. Extremely low interest rates led to excess credit creation that spilled over to the real estate market in a spectacular way. This is very similar to the credit explosion that

Table 2.1 Greenspan's Analysis vs. Coby's Comparisons

Greenspan's Analysis of 1929	Comparisons of 1929 to the Modern Era
"When business in the United States underwent a mild contraction . . .	Post Nasdaq 2000 bubble burst, and the economy underwent a mild contraction.
. . . the Federal Reserve created more paper reserves in the hope of forestalling any possible bank reserve shortage. The Fed succeeded . . . but it nearly destroyed the economies of the world, in the process. The excess credit which the Fed pumped into the economy spilled over into the stock market, triggering a fantastic boom . . .	The Fed cut interest rates to Depression-era lows of 1%, which spilled over into the real estate market, creating a tremendous speculative boom!
. . . Belatedly, Federal Reserve officials attempted to sop up the excess reserves and finally succeeded in breaking the boom. But it was too late . . .	Greenspan raises interest rates in 2005 to slow down the real estate bubble's expansion.
. . . The speculative imbalances had become so overwhelming that the attempt precipitated a sharp retrenching and a consequent demoralizing of business confidence . . .	Bernanke's emergency rate cuts in late 2007 into 2008 to stave off the credit crisis from the enormous debt against the declining real estate prices.
. . . As a result, the American economy collapsed."	Real estate correction turns into a crash and economy collapses for the New Great Depression of the Twenty-first Century

led stocks into a giant boom, and its subsequent price collapse in the 1929 Dow Jones Industrial Average (DJIA), and more recently the Nasdaq 2000 crash.

The left side of Table 2.1 contains a direct quote from Alan Greenspan describing what happened in 1929. (The quote appeared in "Gold and Economic Freedom," *The Objectivist,*

1996, and was reprinted in Ayn Rand's *Capitalism: The Unknown Ideal,* New York: Penguin, 1987). To get a sense of what is happening today, just replace "stocks" in his quote with "real estate" to fully appreciate 1929's comparison to today.

Greenspan repeated these mistakes on both accounts and in two asset classes. He exploded the money supply in the late 1990s, which created the Nasdaq bubble peak in 2000 that collapsed after the Fed hiked rates in 1999. Nasdaq crashed close to the 89 percent drop in the 1929 DJIA. Then he exploded the money supply after 9/11. He cut interest rates to 1929 lows of 1 percent as well. This fueled a 1929-like explosion in real estate that peaked in 2005. That explosion will become an implosion if the Fed uses all its monetary magic bullets without a significant recovery.

In 2008, the Fed resorted to emergency interest rate cuts and revolutionary liquidity creation tools, as it feared another 1929-like collapse. This time the collapse was started by declining real estate values. It took until early 2008 to finally infect the stock market. If the Fed revives real estate and stocks with more easy credit, then we will only put off the crash for a later date. I call this the Fed's "short-term gain for long-term pain" monetary strategy.

Many would argue that, unlike with stocks, homeowners aren't forced to sell. As long as they can make their mortgage payments, they won't care about declining values or be forced to sell at a loss. This is true unless jobs are lost from a stagnant U.S. and global economy. Here is how that has happened and will happen if the debt contraction cycle accelerates:

- Homeowners who used their homes as ATMs can no longer borrow from the rising equity in their homes.
- They continue to read all the bad news in the papers and see it firsthand from their neighborhood's declining home prices.
- They feel poorer. As a result, they start to tighten their belts financially.
- The real estate weakness spreads to every state in the nation.
- When enough people pull back on their spending, the economy will start to decline.

- As the economy declines, the newspapers will highlight the possibilities of a recession.
- Once the economy heads into a recession, jobs will be lost.
- As jobs are lost, more homes will come on the market for sale.
- As supply increases, prices will decline. People will feel even more nervous about spending money, so the economy will decline even further.
- This will force companies to cut further back on production, which leads to more layoffs.
- These further layoffs will lead to more contraction until the "D" word gets thrown around in the media.
- Once investors fear a depression, consumption and production will continue to fall and more jobs will be lost.
- As homeowners sell their homes that have dropped 50 percent, they will be responsible for all the mortgage debt borrowed on the home.
- This will lead to massive numbers of bankruptcies and the New Great Depression of the Twenty-first Century will unfold.
- As jobs are lost, and the mortgage payment can't be met, forced liquidation of homes on a nationwide scale will be the end result.

Instead of imploding stocks like in 1929, this time it is real estate that is sending the U.S economy into a depression. The cause will be forced liquidation due to the same enormous debt from a rapidly declining asset class.

Let me express this in terms of a baseball team. The game is real estate and the players are real estate speculators. From 2003 to 2005, the real estate team had a huge winning streak. The real estate team has had a great long-term track record for the last 50 years or so as real estate prices have gone up dramatically over that time span. The last three baseball seasons, 2006 to 2008, have been a disaster. This seemingly unbeatable team is in a major slump and losing badly. Fans are disgruntled and no longer desire to own their season tickets. They are upset because they paid good money for their seats (houses) and now they can't sell them for what they paid—even though in past years, the excitement of the team caused a significant increase in ticket prices and value. The owner of the team (the government) is doing everything it can to turn things around—giving additional tax rebates, building hope, giving incentives, and promising the ticket owners who made bad purchasing decisions that they'll rescue them from their despair.

This real estate down cycle only completed its third inning in 2008. This is a losing team, and this down cycle is going to go into extra innings of decline. A nine-inning ball game going to extra innings means that this real estate down cycle could last for 7 to 10 more years. Yes, the team can have a couple of good innings in a losing effort, but the end result will be the same—LOSS.

Let's take this down cycle and bring it to a personal real-life level so you can better understand and prepare. In mid 2007, I drove around the country, from Winthrop, Washington, to Darien, Connecticut, to work for Peter Schiff. I did this because I had come to the dire conclusion that the U.S. dollar was on the verge of a major breakdown (which happened) with the potential of a future currency crisis (yet to happen). Peter and I shared similar beliefs, so I thought it would be interesting to be around some like-minded guys at his firm. After four weeks I quit Euro Pacific Capital, so my trip wound up taking me in a complete driving loop around the country.

On my cross-country trip I learned quite a bit about the current and likely future health of the real estate market. From Minnesota to Ohio, Florida, California, and Oregon and back to Washington, I heard stories of the rapidly rising number of foreclosures, as well as the number of homes coming to the market for sale. In August 2007 for example, the number of unsold homes hit a 16-year high. On November 1, 2007, the number of foreclosures went up 100 percent on a year-over-year basis, and foreclosures were up in 48 of 50 states. According to Jim Rokakis, the county treasurer for Cleveland's Cuyahoga County in November 2007, "Wall Street strategies that made the cycle of 'no money down,' 'no questions asked' lending have sucked the life out of my city." A similar sentiment existed in 1929 when Wall Street strategies of 10 percent down sucked the life out of the U.S. economy as prices in stocks collapsed.

When I left Euro Pacific Capital I headed south to see my Mom, who got slightly trapped in this real estate mess. She was in Venice, Florida, where she had purchased a small but very nice second home, apparently at the top of the market. As I walked around her neighborhood of similar-looking houses, I noticed they were selling for about $100,000 less than the $300,000 my Mom had paid two years earlier. Fortunately for my Mom, she owns a house in Myrtle Beach, South Carolina, which she bought several years ago, and it has retained much of the escalated value, so she is still way ahead of the game. Like my Mom, most real estate investors still have considerable equity in their homes even though the market is currently weak. This cushion has kept real estate investors from panicking and the U.S. economy from tanking. In 2008, those homes in my Mom's Florida neighborhood are now cut in half from their 2005 highs. Chances are, you also have a relative or a friend stuck with overpriced real estate.

On my way down the East Coast, I drove through South Carolina and called my cousin Dave, who is a successful real estate agent in Myrtle Beach, and asked him how the real estate market was there. He told me it was extremely weak, yet the home builders mysteriously kept building homes, only adding to the current excess supply on the market. He also mentioned all the "flippers" (people who speculated on a quick turnover for profit) were trapped in their houses and faced the prospects of foreclosure. The market was so weak that many realtors like my cousin Dave are getting night jobs to make ends meet until the real estate market turns around.

While driving around Venice, Florida, I saw a number of bikini-clad young women holding up giant signs stating, "$1 billion in savings on homes this weekend." The home builders were giving away everything, including the kitchen sink with granite counter tops, for free. Initially, the giveaways were not reflected in the price declines in Florida, or around the country. The discounted home prices originally came in the form of freebies given away to entice folks to buy those homes. Falling prices are finally starting to show in the real estate statistics, so the true weakness across the country is being more accurately exposed.

On my way westward across the country I continued to see, hear, and read the same things in the newspapers, in conversations and through general observations. It appeared to me that California was another bubble deflating, similar to Florida. As I drove up the West Coast, I arrived in Medford, Oregon, which is a perfect example of the weakness in housing that I believe is going to happen to real estate all across the nation. Medford is one hour north of the California border and is greatly affected by the economy in California. This is a town of about 80,000 people, and the place where I relocated my family and my business. What I noticed was astonishing—homes for sale everywhere. I wondered if there were some kind of "Three Mile Island" fallout because it looked as if everyone was trying to get out of Dodge.

I called a local realtor and was shown some rental properties. I was not looking to buy a home because I believed real estate prices had nothing but downside. I asked him what was going on in the Medford real estate market. He told me that there is a "daily growing number of homes on the market and there is several years' worth of supply." I asked why. He gave me the example of the lady who was trying to rent the house he was showing me. She is a real estate speculator who attempted a "nothing-down flip" where a person buys a house with no money down, hopefully on the cheap, and then immediately tries to sell it to someone else and make a quick profit. This is a Ponzi-like scheme where you don't want to be the last person holding the bag, or in this case the mortgage. Unfortunately, the flip, flopped, and she had not been able to sell the house flip for over one year. She was forced to rent the failed flip instead. Her broker also said, to my surprise, that if she can't rent it, she will be forced to sell it below what she paid, for a sizeable loss.

I investigated further and checked numerous home-for-sale fliers in Medford, Oregon, and found consistent overpricing. Modest, ill-maintained houses for over $300,000! It looked to me like speculators bought crummy little homes and thought that with a new roof and a fresh paint job they could make huge profits. I noticed extreme overvaluation throughout the area on homes for sale at all price levels. Apparently, these sellers really think their homes are worth such inflated prices. This overwhelming confidence persisted in spite of the fact that the supply of homes on the market in Medford had exploded, while demand was down and homes were slow to move.

A Lesson from Nasdaq

This experience in Medford, and around the nation, reminded me of the same confidence I saw in Nasdaq 2000 even as prices were falling. This is why I see real estate most likely playing out like the Nasdaq 2000 crash in stocks, but in a very slow-motion-like decline. I am convinced that a major part of the problem is the total faith of realtors and investors that "real estate prices always go up," even in a slow market. As a result, home and property sellers stubbornly maintain their inflated prices, only prolonging the problem. This psychology reminded me of the Nasdaq investors in 2000 who put limit orders on their stocks at prices substantially above falling prices. They were waiting for the rally that never came. When the margin calls did come, they were forced to sell at substantially depressed prices. It was only then that the illusion of quick and easy riches was finally shattered. This is happening in the stock market, and will happen to real estate speculators and homeowners as reality has finally set in.

Remember how the bubble started? Homeowners saw neighbors sell their houses near the peak at very high prices and calculated how much their own houses must be worth. They believed they had discovered a huge cash deposit in their bank accounts, so they went out and sold their house, bought a bigger house, and took on even larger amounts of debt. Both real estate investors and speculators saw home prices rise spectacularly, so they took on even more debt. It's a sad story that will end very badly because this newly created paper equity caused real estate investors to do foolish things. Outrageous amounts of extra equity were taken in the form of home equity lines of credit (HELOCs) or second mortgages. Many referred to this phenomenon as their house being used as an ATM machine. This equity extraction has left homeowners burdened with enormous amounts of mortgage debt. This debt overhang will impact the U.S. economy for many years to come. If real estate prices collapse, this will be the biggest story of the new century as the economy will sink into a depression.

This equity-extracted cash from homes was used for reinvestment in other real estate, remodeling, and stock purchases, sending asset prices up. A fictitious boom built on such prodigious levels of debt is similar to a Ponzi scheme ready to fall. In the "Roaring 20s," speculators bought stocks with little money down, using 90 percent margin like real estate speculators did in the roaring 2000s. When the inevitable reversal came in 1929, stocks collapsed, but the debt remained. This is precisely what will happen in the U.S. real estate market as homes that were bought with little or "no money down" experience a severe price reversal.

I remember going to my favorite pub in Bend, Oregon, for a beer in late 2004, right at the top of the market. There I was reminded of the stories about shoeshine boys giving out stock tips in 1929 right before the great market crash. While I was at the bar, a soccer buddy of mine was the bartender and handed me a business card with my beer. I asked him, "John, since when do bartenders hand out business cards?" He laughed and told me to read the card. He was doing real estate part time for a small firm in Bend. I looked at my friend, smiled, and calmly instructed him, "Don't quit your night job." I took my beer and wished him well and went back to the table and told my wife that we had to sell our house before the Bend real estate market came crashing down. That story gave me the thought that the Bend real estate market was like a red-hot technology stock at the top of Nasdaq 2000. I'll bet there were bartenders-turned-real-estate-agents in your town or city as well. This real estate bubble had the whole nation caught up in excitement. This is evident by all the money investors borrowed and spent against the ever-rising prices of their homes.

By late 2007, the supply of existing homes on the market hit a 15-year high and the supply of new homes on the market hit a 16-year high. In 2008, the real estate market only accelerated its fall. By 2009–2010, we could see prices collapse if interest rates rise or massive numbers of jobs are lost as the economy tanks. We are in a severe mortgage crisis from all the nonsensical loans made in the real estate bubble. This has resulted in tighter mortgage lending conditions, which are further dampening the demand side of the real estate market. Even with the rising supply and falling demand, most real estate agents I speak to tell me that they are not worried because "real estate always rises in the long run." This is one reason why I believe 2008 will only complete the third inning of a declining real estate market that could go well into extra innings if interest rates rise or the economy sinks.

Eventually, real estate speculators and homeowners will realize that something is seriously wrong. Like Nasdaq speculators before them, fear will take hold and the real estate market will continue to fall and eventually collapse. *When homeowners see their neighbors sell at a steep discount, this will be like the last price tick in a stock. All of a sudden, a price shock will set in across the nation and a plethora of homes with reduced price signs will be the sign of the bad times ahead for real estate.*

However, there is a simple and effective way to make money in falling markets, and that's by having what I call a short-side strategy. There are many real estate–related stocks to sell short as well as to buy. As the Fed cuts interest rates, these stocks could have spectacular bear market rallies to buy for trades before they resume their long decline. We call these trades "dead cat bounces" or "bear market rallies." The market doesn't go straight in one direction. If it did, then all the home-builder stocks would soon be zero at the pace they have fallen from 2006 through 2008. Remember, there are two sides of all markets to make money in—the long side and the short side. We will be exploring both sides and show you how to make money long and short for any market environment and in any asset class. Later in the book I will share with you a price pattern recognition indicator for the identification of tops and bottoms that I discovered when I arrived in Medford.

Boomtown Bend, USA

I lived in Bend, Oregon, for 10 years and, according to the March 1, 2007, Dow Jones Newswire, "Bend was the number-one fastest growing housing market in the United States from fourth quarter 2005 to fourth quarter 2006." I saw spectacular growth in the short time I lived there. Bend is a very cool place. It is less than an hour away from Mount Bachelor Ski Resort, and has many attractions, such as great hiking trails, on- and off-road biking, river rafting, fishing, golf, and national parks and forests. Californians have been selling their steeply overvalued homes and moving to Bend by the droves, which accelerated the boom.

I am a perfect example of the dangerous psychology of real estate speculators around the nation. When my wife and I bought our first Bend house in 1996, we paid $100 per square foot, eventually selling that house six years later for an approximate 70 percent gain. Then we did what everyone else seemed to be doing, which was to buy a much bigger house. We paid $795,000 for the second house, and then two years later we decided to sell, trying to catch the top of the real estate market. Before we listed that second home, an excited neighbor ran across the yard to tell me a lesser house in the area sold for $1.1 million. He advised me that my house must be worth "at least $1.3 million." Enamored by the easy paper profit gain, we listed our house for that illusionary price of $1.3 million. After we listed, I noticed many of my neighbors had the same idea and they were listing their homes for big prices as well. This continued until I realized that the supply of homes was rising rapidly, along with the competition.

Here's an example of how so much supply can saturate and quickly depress a market. Against my better instincts, my wife and I held an open house (I thought nosy neighbors would come to nitpick our pluses and minuses). It was a typical gorgeous sunny day this particular Saturday in Bend. The house and grounds were in immaculate condition, yet not one person showed up—not even a nosy neighbor. Reality quickly sunk in: The market was weakening rapidly and prices were declining even faster. This was shocking as our home listing price was way out of whack. In order to sell, I was forced to lower the price of the house not once but three times. I finally got an offer for $1 million with no contingencies and I happily accepted. This "solid buyer" measured rooms, took photos, and said how happy he was to be buying this "beautiful home." His exuberance quickly faded when he couldn't sell his home and he backed out of the deal in the final hour. This is a prime example of what happens when the real estate market gets weak. In fact, according to the CEOs of the major home builders, cancellation rates have skyrocketed, a clear sign of rising fear among speculators in real estate across the country.

We were devastated when we lost this buyer because the Bend real estate market was getting weaker. Fortunately for us, four months later, we sold for $975,000. We were lucky to sell our home because inventories kept increasing in Bend. According to my Bend realtor, the original potential buyer who backed out had not sold his home two years after he walked away from his offer. His decision to not buy my house was the right one because he would have been stuck with two giant mortgages. This very thing is what happened to homeowners and speculators across the nation.

Interestingly enough, this buyer who backed out of buying my house was a real estate agent. Realtors and speculators tend to rely too heavily on continual growth of home values so they are full of confidence on real estate. This is because most real estate brokers and investors have experienced only steadily rising prices. Home sellers thought that because their neighbor got some absurd price for his home, they could too. The reverse happens when neighbors eventually drop their selling prices. All of a sudden, the market values for homes go down, but the new debt they borrowed with HELOC loans against their overpriced home remains.

In summary, I sold that second house in Bend for $273 per square foot versus the $100 per square foot I paid for my first house 10 years earlier. Recently, my Bend real estate agent sent me an e-mail telling me, "Ron, you got out just in time, the market in Bend continues to be weighed down by increasing amounts of new supply with few buyers. Prices are heading down." She also said that "unsuccessful sellers are remaining stubborn by not lowering their prices enough and sales have fallen 48 percent." Another longtime friend and successful Bend real estate investor wrote the following, "Not much going on here in Bend, Oregon, besides the real estate turndown, which shows no sign of ending anytime soon. In fact, some believe it might be 2010 before the Bend real estate market even attempts to make a comeback." Here is the question to ask yourself: What if a 48 percent sales drop turns into a 48 percent drop in home prices in Bend and around the country?

Paper Gains Are Just Numbers on Paper

The paper gains that real estate investors and speculators thought they had at the peak in 2004 was only an illusion. Let me illustrate what I mean. A friend, who has been a long-time real estate investor in Bend, told me he was worried. He could go bankrupt because of the weight of debt he has against his portfolio of properties. Two years earlier he was a real estate paper multimillionaire and now he is concerned he will lose it all because of the debt against those paper gains. I know that Bend will always be a desirable place to live. It won't surprise me if prices continue to drop, and, if my wife and I choose, I'll bet we can move back to a house similar to the one we sold, substantially below $275 per square foot at the final secular bottom of the market. At that point, Boomtown Bend will feel a lot like Ghost Town Bend.

As real estate sinks, "price reduced," "motivated seller," "slashed prices," and "priced to sell" signs will become the new sign of the times for real estate. Millions of investors bought homes with very little money down ("nothing down" real estate) and used their apparent increased equity to spend, speculate in stocks or worse yet, purchase even more real estate. This has led me to believe that the current real estate speculation could lead us into the New Great Depression of the Twenty-first Century as prices collapse and the enormous debt against that real estate remains.

Bank Your Profits

It is possible that the Fed's heroic efforts may revive the real estate market temporarily, with the predictable cutting of interest rates and explosion of the money supply. If this happens, I would advise readers to bank the profits and reduce their debt. I can hear you saying, "But I've got to live somewhere, so I will just wind up buying another overpriced house."

I have two suggestions. First, if you can bank your home equity and call it a profit, you can buy a smaller home, so when prices do collapse your loss will be diminished and your debt reduced. Second, do what my wife and I did—rent. For two years after we sold our Bend home, we lived in a home of similar size and quality as the home we sold for $975,000 and paid rent of only $1,100 per month. This compares with our former mortgage payment of $4,000 a month. Each month I sent our rent check with a big smile on my face, knowing that as the real estate market was weakening across the country, I was not losing money and saddled with enormous debt.

I regularly hear from real estate bulls that renting is stupid—like throwing money away. Homeowners in the states of Florida, California, and much of the country since the 2005 peak must feel like they are flushing much of their money down the toilet in real estate as prices fall. On April 11, 2007, the *New York Times* did an analysis on buying versus renting in every metropolitan area. It found that "the costs associated with buying a home, e.g., mortgage payments, property taxes, fees to real estate agents, etc., remain a lot higher than the cost of renting." For now, I am confident that renting may be a wise strategy as prices around the nation come crashing back to more realistic and affordable price levels.

Leverage Also Works in Reverse

Real estate and leverage have worked together beautifully throughout this long and mighty real estate boom. My case is a perfect example. I borrowed 80 percent from the bank to buy my first home in Boomtown Bend. Then I was able to sell that first house and use the gains to go buy a much larger house, again borrowing 80 percent from the bank. This leverage looked great on paper, but in reality all I was doing was trading one overpriced asset for another. I was lucky and able to sell that second house at a nice bankable profit because the market immediately soured after I sold it. After I bought the second house, I was carrying about $635,000 in mortgage debt.

About one year after I bought the house, and with prices screaming, I decided to get a home equity loan against the increased home price. I wound up spending that money, not unlike other Americans, on vacations, furniture, consumer goods, and to keep up with the rising costs of living associated with raising a family of five. When I applied for the loan, the bank asked me to put a value on my home. The higher I valued the house meant the more I could borrow, so I put down $1.1 million as the value of my house. The bank didn't even question the amount, which allowed me to unwisely borrow an additional $225,000 on my home. At this point I am up to my ears in debt, but I have no worries because housing is "booming in Boomtown." In reality, I have $860,000 in debt, but in my mind I believe my house is worth $1.3 million dollars, or $440,000 in paper equity. Of course, when I sold my house for $975,000, that hypothetical profit disappeared. Homeowners in 2008 are starting to get a nasty taste of this kind of reality. When you take out the commissions I paid to my broker, I came away with little more than the relief that I had eliminated a massive amount of mortgage debt.

What if my Bend home were still on the market and I needed to sell, but real estate prices had dropped 30 percent? CNN's *Market Watch* reported that the Bend real estate market was "50 percent overvalued" so a 30 percent drop isn't much of a stretch. With a 30 percent drop I would have a house valued at $686,000, with $860,000 of mortgage debt stacked against it. Now the debt is no longer my friend and the leverage has worked in reverse. I now have what is effectively a margin call and negative equity. If I were forced to sell my home at the reduced price, I would then owe the bank over $174,000. What if Bend real estate values do fall 50 percent like many are predicting? Bend real estate will look like a dot-com stock in Nasdaq 2000.

What if I didn't have that money to give to the bank? I went from thinking I had $440,000 in my paper gains to over $174,000 in realized losses on that 30 percent estimated fall. This is how the math will work for homeowners once real estate prices crash back to earth. The additional debt, and the math will only work if prices keep rising. Otherwise, as prices fall, reverse leverage will nearly wipe U.S. real estate values off the face of the Earth.

As a side note, I'd like to mention that the March 2007 Dow Jones newswire also mentioned Wenatchee, Washington, as the number two best-performing real estate market in America from 2005 to 2006. In the *Wenatchee World* newspaper on November 2, 2007, the front-page headline read, "Sept. Home Sales Take Year's Steepest Drop." The paper went on to say, "Home sales took the biggest drop of the year—a 28% decline over September 2006." The paper continued with, "Foreclosures in Okanogan County increased 117% in line with the current national averages of 100% foreclosure rates." The two best-performing markets in America remind me of the stocks JDSU (JDS Uniphase) and CSCO (Cisco Systems, Inc.) at the top of Nasdaq. When prices go straight up in a parabolic increase, the inevitable fall is just that much more severe.

What every real estate investor, homeowner, and speculator needs to ask himself is, "What if real estate is Nasdaq 2000, but in a slow-motion downward spiral? What if the economy turns down and massive unemployment results?" Instead of hocking your house and buying products made in China, maybe you should do the opposite. As the boom goes bust, aggressive investors are hocking their houses and shorting the world, especially China.

Home Sweet Home

When the real estate market does finally hit bottom, a house will be viewed as a place to live in rather than a place to speculate in. In recent years, real estate investors have been like the technology investors of 1999. Both were able to trade one overpriced asset for another inflated asset and feel wealthier as a result. In the market mania of 1999, investors would sell stocks like Microsoft and use the proceeds to buy other ridiculously overpriced stocks like Cisco or Amazon.com. In real estate, a speculator trades up to a nicer home or does a 1031 tax-free exchange rollover. This type of speculative activity reminds me of the boy who one day excitedly told his dad that he just sold his dog for $50,000. The father asked, "Son, how in the world did you sell your dog for $50,000?" The son said, "It was really quite simple, Dad. I just traded him for two $25,000 cats."

If prices have a severe reversal like I expect, then let me ask the question: Was this trading up activity really a wise idea? Of course not, but it sure felt like it at the time. If you take on too much debt and are forced to sell into a weak market, then your American dream can quickly turn into your own personal nightmare.

On April 4, 2007, Bloomberg reported that the all-time top-performing real estate fund manager, Kenneth Heebner, gave this assessment on the future of real estate: "The biggest housing decline since the Great Depression is coming" and "prices may fall by a fifth in some markets around the country before it finally bottoms." In 2008, pending new home sales hit "all-time lows," so we may well be on our way to this successful real estate manager's prediction. *If the bears are correct, then buying a house will be viewed like that of buying a brand new car. The minute you turn the key, you'll be losing money.*

Robert Shiller, a Yale University professor, who called the top in Nasdaq 2000, was on Bloomberg TV saying, "Sharp drops are coming in real estate." He went on to say "the bigger the boom, the bigger the bust" and that the "home price decline has just started." He noted that from 1890 to 1990 home prices increased approximately "3 percent per year," but that real estate prices had "doubled" in the first five years of the new century and that this was an "anomaly." He also thinks "some markets will fall by 50 percent." I couldn't agree more. Again, speculators are in the early innings of a long-term real estate market decline. However, U.S. stocks have only recently completed extra innings of a long-running bullish game. *The Federal Reserve's policy of short-term gain for long-term pain may only temporarily help a recovery in the U.S. real estate market and help the stock market to boom again. This will only delay the painful debt liquidation that ultimately lies ahead.*

The flip side of the bearish coin is that the new Federal Reserve chairman, Ben Bernanke, is a student of the 1929 Great Depression. Bernanke was quoted as saying, "I am a Great Depression buff, the way some folks are Civil War buffs." This is good news for the economy because the Fed chairman knows that it was the 1927 housing weakness that preceded the 1929 stock market collapse and the ensuing Great Depression. Bernanke is creating new money out of thin air and is cutting interest rates in an attempt to prevent such a calamity from happening while he is at the helm. He understands how severely declining asset prices would devastate the net worth investors have built up in the U.S. stock market and real estate market boom. In 1929, crashing asset prices weakened banks, which choked off new lending and depressed the economy. In 2007 and 2008, as the mortgage crisis took hold, banks raised their credit standards as delinquencies mounted. This has greatly reduced the number of consumers and speculators able to obtain a mortgage.

On November 8, 2007, Bernanke gave his testimony to Congress on real estate's "intensifying weakness" and the outlook for the economy. Congresswoman Loretta Sanchez of California stated in her testimony that the real estate crisis is "far worse" than Bernanke thinks. She stated that "one third of the homes in Anaheim, California, have for-sale signs on them and most are in, or soon to be in, foreclosure." She stated that she went out to buy a house one week earlier with a "perfect credit score, lots of assets, and no debt." Yet she was quoted by her bank a mortgage loan "100 basis points above what is quoted in the papers." She went on to say that if she experienced the credit crunch, then America is really in a bad credit crisis. She scolded Bernanke about bad Fed policy decisions today and in the past and implied that easy credit policies are at the heart of this mortgage crisis. Bernanke understands this well and is fighting the housing decline with emergency interest rate cuts and a rapid expansion of the money supply (short-term gain). Gold investors anticipate rapidly rising inflationary pressures and an impending currency crisis, especially after the U.S. dollar hit all-time lows in 2008. This combination of falling asset prices with rising inflationary pressures is called stagflation. Simply put, the Fed is fueling inflation as it desperately fights deflating asset prices in this new era of stagflation.

The good news for the economy is that real estate prices are still very elevated. This wealth effect from high real estate prices has kept the economy from a sharp contraction. Bernanke knows he must keep investor balance sheets healthy or he risks a severe recession or an outright depression. The stock market has cast its vote on the eventual outcome for real estate. Homebuilder stocks and mortgage lending stocks have been sinking hard and fast. Many mortgage companies like Fannie Mae (FNM) have gone up in a giant puff of smoke and many others no longer exist. Banks and brokerage stocks have huge exposure to failing mortgages and the stock market has given many of those stocks two big thumbs down as well. The financial stocks that have a high degree of exposure to risky mortgages appear to have a long way to go on the downside when you look at the long-term stock charts. The good news is that when these stocks bottom, they will give advance notice that fortunes are about to change in the real estate market, even if it's just a temporary rebound like I suspect.

The bottom line is that both the real estate market and the U.S. economy are skating on very thin ice. The real estate market is sinking through the cracks, but the real question is: Will it pull the economy down with it? My best guess is that it will, so I expect that the U.S. and global economies will go from red hot to icy cold. The next question is: Are you on thin ice? No matter what happens in the future of the real estate market, the lesson is clear—do not heavily speculate in real estate because housing prices don't always go up as so many speculators were led to believe.

CHAPTER 3

TODAY'S DOLLAR IS WORTH LESS, TOMORROW'S DOLLAR COULD BE WORTHLESS

"U.S. Investors in Denial—U.S. Dollar Is Collapsing"

"The Stock Market Is in a Steep and Steady Decline"

"The United States, Once the World's Most Prosperous Country, Is in an Economic Free Fall—Dragging Down Most of the World Stock Markets with It"

Headlines like these came out of Hong Kong during the Indonesian currency collapse on January 9, 1998. By changing a few words and substituting the United States for Indonesia, these headlines could soon be ours. If the Fed doesn't slow the pace of money growth and the U.S. government doesn't get control of its twin deficits (budget and trade), then a U.S. dollar crisis is entirely possible. Odds keep getting higher that the United States ultimately faces a coming economic hurricane exacerbated by the explosion of personal debt and the U.S. government's national debt. The storm clouds are on the horizon as this devastating economic tsunami is rapidly approaching.

The United States has gone from being the greatest creditor nation to the greatest debtor nation on a level that is unfathomable to the rational mind. The U.S. government and its citizens have been very lucky and blessed with a long-running bull market in stocks, bonds, and real estate that has kept alive this illusion of "deficits don't matter." If the long-running bull market and economic boom collapses, we face potential economic extinction like that of past fallen empires.

Foreign central banks and investors have helped finance this great debt-induced economic boom. If this same group gets nervous that the economic party is ending, then the U.S. dollar will collapse at a level similar to the dollar crashes we experienced in the 1970s. The run on the dollar this time could be even deeper and faster simply because our country's finances have never been this unstable.

The United States has become too deeply dependent on foreign nations to buy our debt to fund our growing imbalances. If foreign central banks and foreign investors don't see a reversal of the steady decline of the U.S. dollar we have had in the new millennium, foreign central banks may start to flee all U.S. assets. Then the U.S. dollar would overshoot to the downside. That would send inflation soaring and lead to asset price declines across the board. With interest payments already such a heavy burden for both individuals and our government, we risk sinking into a period of economic decline combined with inflation, a toxic mix called stagflation.

Our heavy debt burden combined with the heavy dependence on foreign capital could create an economic event that real estate and stock investors have only read about in history books. When bonds fall as interest rates rise, all those adjustable-rate mortgages will just continue to reset to higher rates. At some point, even the U.S. government will be unable to rescue all of the homeowners whose payments have exceeded their ability to pay. The result will be an even larger number of homeowners facing foreclosure.

The Economic Snowball

Here is what we risk if our government doesn't get its economic house in order:

- The overburdened economy weakens and the U.S. dollar heads lower, causing inflation.
- Stocks fall and the economy just continues to get worse and enters a severe inflationary recession.

- As real estate sinks lower, corporate America and consumers cut back on spending and gross domestic product (GDP) declines for six quarters in a row, resulting in an official depression.
- The long-running consumption boom ends as stocks fall, inflation rises, and a new period of stagflation unfolds.

Each negative event feeds on the other like a giant snowball rolling down the mountainside. This economic snowball grows larger and larger as the problems get bigger and bigger until a great and mighty crash drives the U.S. economy to the bottom.

A U.S. collapse like this would be disastrous for the rest of the world. To the countries that own our stocks and bonds, the crashing dollar will be like multiple financial atomic bombs reverberating throughout the world in what will likely be called "The Great Global Depression of the Twenty-First Century." This action will start with massive inflation as the dollar's purchasing power erodes sharply. *What we risk more than the dollar's being worth less is the U.S. dollar's being altogether worthless.* Once the confidence in our full faith and credit backing is lost, then the dollar will be looked upon as just a green piece of paper with a dead president's picture on it.

Since President Nixon's elimination of the gold standard in 1971, the U.S. dollar has nothing backing it but our government's "full faith and credit." If the value of this commitment vanishes, then so does the value of our fiat currency.

Think about this for a minute. The United States has built up enormous amounts of debt, with its citizens heavily speculating that overpriced stocks and real estate have nowhere to go but up in the long run. The U.S. economy has been like a giant casino with speculators gambling wildly on stocks and real estate with easily available credit.

How the Giant Casino Grew So Large

We need to go back in history to the end of World War II for a key lesson. In 1944, the leading nations were concerned about the new money created by governments around the globe to finance the war. These nations worried that the new money created would lead to rampant inflation spiraling out of control. A world money summit was held in Bretton Woods, New Hampshire. The participating nations came up with a plan to foster postwar trade and stability to prevent governments from printing excessive amounts of newly created money. The plan was ratified by 44 nations around the globe, and it was at this time that the International Monetary Fund (IMF) and the World Bank were created. Since the United States held much of the world's gold reserves, the dollar was designated the world's "reserve currency."

To ensure that no government would print excessive amounts of their respective currencies, the United States agreed to make its own money convertible into gold. The IMF member countries knew that excess new money creation would be like pouring gasoline on a raging fire of inflation. In 1967, President Lyndon B. Johnson (LBJ) and the Federal Reserve printed enormous amounts of money as the economy headed into a very steep and painful recession. LBJ unleashed a torrent of spending to create "A Great Society" and to fight a war without raising taxes. As LBJ was fighting the Vietnam War, he declared another war—the "War on Poverty." The U.S. government repeatedly issued new bonds, and the Federal Reserve created new money to buy the bonds to help the government finance these two wars. Banks across America were bursting at the seams with new money, so runaway inflation started to take hold and interest rates started to explode.

After LBJ, President Nixon pressured then–Federal Reserve chairman Arthur Burns to crank up the printing press to help rescue the economy from Nixon's failed fiscal policy actions. This started to overheat the economy; Nixon imposed price controls and slammed the gold window shut, ending the dollar's convertibility to gold. This nullified the Bretton Woods Agreement. Inflation erupted several times in the 1970s, and oil prices exploded exactly like they have been doing in the early years of the twenty-first century. With oil and commodity prices becoming incredibly volatile in 2008, 2009 is shaping up to look similar to the late 1970s. This is the last time stagflation gripped America and is what people from around the globe are starting to get a taste of as inflation rises and world economies stagnate.

The Fed Becomes an "Engine of Inflation"

During Jimmy Carter's presidency, inflation and the problem economy got worse. When it was understood that the Bretton Woods Agreement essentially went up in flames, there was no way to prevent the Fed from printing limitless amounts of dollars. This is when the Federal Reserve became what many back then termed an "engine of inflation." The Fed basically buys bonds from the banks and leaves them with piles of greenbacks (dollars) to go lend. This excess money initially finds its way into speculative assets, eventually making its way into the general economy. The result is the potential for runaway inflation like we saw in the 1970s.

Early in the Reagan years, then–Fed chairman Paul Volcker took on the fight against inflation. He needed to restore confidence in our weakening currency, so he cut the money supply and aggressively hiked interest rates. This is the exact opposite of what Ben Bernanke has been doing in 2007 and 2008. Ben cut short-term rates as the weakening dollar hit new all-time lows and oil was hitting all-time highs. This action would likely be viewed as pure insanity by past responsible Fed chairmen like Paul Volcker. The country owes a great debt of gratitude to Paul Volcker for killing inflation during the Reagan years. He took a lot of political heat as the economy sank, but it was the right thing to do. It's very unfortunate, but the only way Ben Bernanke can save the U.S. dollar from an outright collapse is to raise interest rates like Paul Volcker did, and the best way for the Fed to do that is to cut the money supply.

The Start of a New Boom

Alan Greenspan did a great disservice to America by creating two of the biggest asset bubbles in American history. He did it first in Nasdaq 2000, then again in real estate, the latter being a deadly bubble that has led to economic destruction looming on our horizon. If the mortgage crisis of 2008 turns into a crashing real estate market in 2009 or 2010, then Greenspan will go down as the most reckless Fed chairman in U.S. history. Greenspan's and Bernanke's fate will be set in the history books. The records will show that their easy money policies led to 1970s-like inflation early on in the twenty-first century.

Once Paul Volcker broke the back of inflation in the early 1980s, the U.S. went on to enjoy 25 years of a mighty boom. Alan Greenspan entered the picture, becoming the new Fed chairman in 1987, and raised rates following in the footsteps of Paul Volcker. This was not needed as the inflation war had already been fought and won. The financial markets quickly responded with a crash. This is the point when Greenspan became a pro–Wall Street Fed chairman.

If you study the money supply figures, Greenspan started to aggressively expand the money supply in 1996 with only one brief interruption in 2000. In 2001, he reverted to his old ways. All of this Monopoly-like money has created a giant economic casino. This economic casino was primarily created by Greenspan's choosing to print limitless amount of dollars "out of thin air," providing all the chips needed for the casino-minded investors and speculators. Whenever the speculators lost money and their chips were down, the Fed's response was to just print more Monopoly money. The Fed couldn't have the speculators lose too many of their chips (dollars) so they always resupplied (printed) them to keep the whole speculative game alive.

In 1987, we saw this happen when Greenspan provided the money to help meet redemptions from panicked mutual fund investors. At the time of the savings-and-loan crisis, he artificially suppressed interest rates to allow major banks to heal, contributing significantly to the moral hazard at a later date. We saw it again in both the 1997 and 1998 global currency crisis events in Asia and Russia and the Long-Term Capital Management blowup that followed. Greenspan was a former computer programmer, and he became alarmed about Y2K. He primed the pump in anticipation of the year 2000 problem, fearing that banks would not have enough money to meet redemptions as the predicted January 1, 2000, doomsday approached. This erroneous new explosion of the money supply led to a speculative boom not seen since the late 1920s as Internet and dot-com stocks went wild. The most pessimistic of today's bears believe that the Nasdaq 2000 bubble burst was the preview to the coming main economic event when stocks, bonds, real estate, and the U.S. dollar all fall simultaneously.

When Greenspan saw the obvious technology bubble in 1999, he started to hike interest rates to take the punch bowl away from the party in Nasdaq. It wasn't working, so when he finally started to cut the money supply in 2000, that was all that was needed to prick the biggest bubble since the 1929 market top. Even before 9/11, Greenspan reversed this policy and started to cut interest rates. After 9/11, there was another burst of the money supply as Greenspan saw his role as savior by preventing a severe recession. The public's faith in Greenspan, often referred to as "The Maestro," was high while he slashed interest rates aggressively to the very low levels seen in the Great Depression.

Whenever the economy would try to cleanse itself from speculative excesses, Greenspan resorted to the Fed's winning strategy of printing funny money from their bottomless checkbook. This did the trick and stocks hit their ultimate bottom in March 2003, with something most interesting taking place. The severely discounted rates by the Fed created a whole new and even bigger, more dangerous bubble, one that is slowly deflating now and could, in fact, cripple the nation. Greenspan realized that he had created a new bubble in real estate and started to hike interest rates in 2005 just like he did in 1999 to slow down Nasdaq. This time he needed to let some air out of the real estate market, hopefully without a collapse like that of Nasdaq. With mortgage rates so low and the banks flush with all the cash supplied by the Fed, this new boom in real estate had taken on similar speculative characteristics to Nasdaq in 2000. *What Greenspan didn't fully realize at the time of cutting rates so low was that investors would just take their chips from one casino (stocks) and go play at another one (real estate).*

After Nasdaq 2000 through 2002, technology speculators licked their wounds and started a whole new form of gambling, this time in housing. The Nasdaq bubble, which burst in 2000, impacted only stock investors. This real estate bubble, however, has impacted the whole nation—and in fact the entire world—as it collapses in very slow motion. I say slow motion because the Fed, after tightening interest rates in 2005, sent tremors throughout the real estate market in 2006 through 2008. Fearing a collapse, the Fed started cutting interest rates and exploding the money supply once again. This easy money is the lifeblood of real estate, so this will be a slow-motion decline filled with mild and temporary recoveries. *Easy money is keeping a very sick real estate patient alive. Over the longer term, the patient's prognosis appears to be terminal.* The long-term real estate bulls are looking for a new boom to resume with lower interest rates and a rising money supply. This is the basis for confidence among the real estate bulls.

The Credit Bubble

There is no doubt that the real estate bubble was built on easy money and readily available credit. This easy money policy by "Easy Al" led investors and speculators to take on more debt than ever before, and why not? The debt was so cheap with rates so low, how could they refuse? The best part was that the assets they were buying increased in value much faster than the debt that was being created. As real estate prices continued to rise exponentially, so did these investors' paper equity and their willingness and deepening desire to accumulate more of this debt-created wealth.

To add to the excitement of visions of increasing wealth, homeowners decided that they wanted a vacation home or a newer, more expensive home, and real estate speculators could make two times as much as before. Not only was the American homeowner merely trying to keep up with the Joneses; now they wanted to buy the house the Joneses lived in. In the process, they took on higher levels of mortgage debt.

Spectacular levels of debt continued to be piled on real estate owners and speculators around the nation. As if this level of speculation was not enough, new exotic mortgage products like "interest only" payments and "no money down" were created by the banks and mortgage companies to inflate prices to even more absurd levels. This easy money fueled yet more speculation, and a new breed of speculator was born—the "flipper." *Like the day trader cousin before him in stocks, the flipper has become an extinct breed as the real estate market repeats Nasdaq 2000.*

Real estate's speculative fever hit its climax in 2005, just like its sister bubble Nasdaq did in early 2000. As the Nasdaq bubble went pop, so too is the real estate bubble in its very slow-motion-like decline. When the stock market actually started to correct on fears of a real estate crash, along came our new Fed chairman, Ben Bernanke, to the rescue. Like his predecessor, he resorted to the printing presses to save the day. How creative!

While some called Greenspan Alan "Bubble Blowing" Greenspan, so too does Ben Bernanke have his own nickname. Many refer to him as "Helicopter Ben." Interestingly enough, Helicopter Ben was a self-created name, as he is a helicopter pilot, and mostly because of his famous speech before the National Economists Club in Washington, D.C., on November 1, 2002. Ben was quoted as saying that he would "helicopter drop" bales of dollar bills if asset deflation ever took hold in America—in other words, create new money from the U.S. government's bottomless checkbook.

This leads many dollar bears to a dire conclusion. The most vocal of these bears see an impending U.S. dollar crisis resulting in hyperinflation. This possibility is why investors need to consider gold and a short-side component to their portfolios.

The Goal-Line Stand

The U.S. Dollar Index, which is the U.S. dollar as measured against a basket of the world's other major currencies, has historically found significant levels of support in the 79–80 area. In 2008, the U.S. dollar continued to break down to new all-time lows before staging a meaningful rally. These were fresh new 41-year lows since the U.S. Dollar Index was created in 1967, as shown in Figure 3.1.

These new all-time lows happened partly because Bernanke cut interest rates to prevent the mortgage crisis from spilling over to real estate prices.

The U.S. dollar faces a potential currency crisis. However, central banks around the world will find a spot and make a goal-line stand to support the dollar, at least temporarily. The reason is that most of the world's central banks have been sellers of gold, and they are all hocked up to their eyeballs in U.S. dollars and dollar-denominated assets like bonds. It is simply

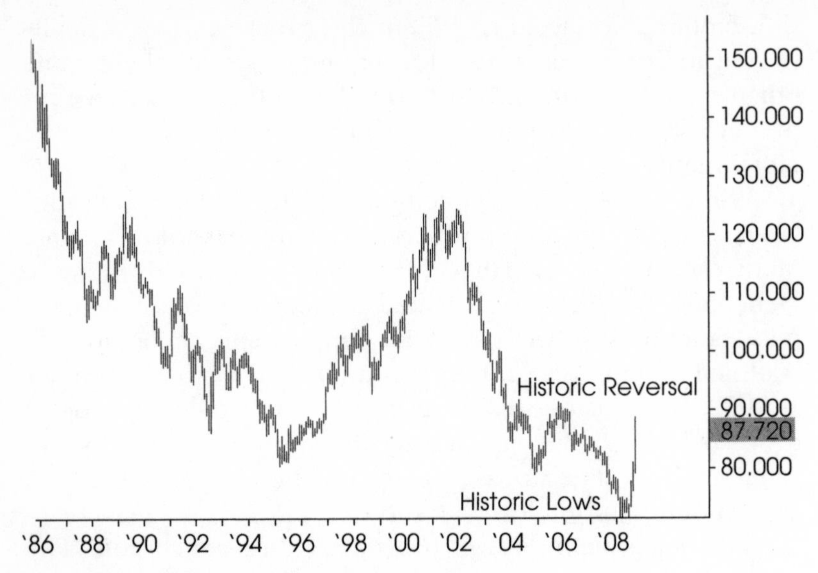

Figure 3.1 US Dollar Index 1986–2008
Created with TradeStation

not in their best interest, or that of the world, to have the U.S. currency collapse.

In 1999, as gold was touching $253, daily reports of central banks from around the globe selling gold made headline news. I had never played the gold futures market, but based on what I could tell, gold couldn't get any lower because gold mines had been closing, which meant supply was very low. More importantly, the disdain for gold by investors and traders was so high that nobody could say anything good about the yellow metal, so I dove in and played the futures market.

Technically, gold was also tracing out a short-term double bottom in the charts. I called a commodities broker, opened an account, and sent him $30,000 to put into gold contracts. He advised me not to put it all in at once but to do several stair-step investments at a time. Since I was the futures novice and he was the supposed expert, I listened to him and put $6,000 into gold futures. I wish I hadn't listened because gold went limit-up in the commodity pits a few days after I bought because of news about world central banks controlling their selling of gold. I had only invested the first $6,000 in the futures contract when gold exploded to $330 an ounce on news of the Washington Accord. I then put my sell order in at the market. There was so much activity in the gold futures pits that it took several days for me to get a confirm ticket back with the sell price. When the confirm ticket came back, I had a fantastic gain in just three days. Although I was sad I hadn't listened to my gut and put the whole $30,000 in, I was excited with my gain.

The point here is that central banks have been selling gold for years from the low of $253 all the way up. Now central banks worldwide are loaded with U.S. dollars and dollar-denominated assets like stocks, mortgage-backed securities and government bonds. The U.S. dollar has been falling for several years against just about every world currency, except for countries like Zimbabwe, of course. As a result of the dollar's selling crescendo, gold has zoomed higher. In effect, many foreign central banks have been selling low in gold and buying high in falling greenbacks. They will do everything in their power to save and protect the U.S. greenback as long as they can. (By the way, who are "they"?)

The Dollar's Dive in '95

Let's go back to 1995 when the dollar was in another crisis mode. The dollar was making post–World War II lows in early 1995. On May 31, 1995, multiple central banks launched waves of dollar purchases that lifted the wobbly greenback. This was a well-coordinated effort by central banks in Germany, Japan, England, France, Austria, Switzerland, Sweden, Italy, Belgium, and the Netherlands. "They" stepped in and made a goal-line stand. This action preempted an expected slide. Everyone in the currency markets incorrectly agreed that this massive action would have only a short-term effect. In reality, this intervention had a huge psychological effect because the large short-side speculators betting on a continued slide in the dollar got their heads handed to them. These central banks also made it clear that they would step in again on any major weakness in the dollar.

At the time, Treasury Secretary Robert Rubin was quoted as saying, "We are prepared to continue to cooperate in exchange markets as appropriate." This created a perceived floor on the dollar and kept speculators from getting short. This also created upward pressure on the dollar as the shorts ran for cover and closed out their positions and long players got confident enough to buy the dollar.

In 2008, the U.S. dollar continued to hit all-time lows. If you took a poll, 9 out of 10 currency speculators would tell you that the dollar has nothing but downside. The sentiment in 2008 is similar to 1995, so another attempt by the G-8 nations could postpone the dollar's day of reckoning. Unfortunately, they will abandon the effort if the U.S. money stock continues to balloon, overwhelming central bank buying. The bears argue that central banks will throw in the towel on U.S. dollars and dollar-denominated assets like stocks and bonds, especially if dollar intervention does not prevail and weakness persists.

If this anticipated day of reckoning by the most voracious of the dollar bears does in fact take place, then the U.S. boom will go over Niagara Falls in a barrel. Gold will cross $2,000 an ounce and stocks will give back all of their gains created by the Greenspan experiment. This has been a psychotic experiment of mass funny money creation. Since Greenspan's mass money creation experiment started in 1996, Bears believe assets will reverse all of the stock gains once the money supply is cut. That would take the Dow Jones Industrial Average (DJIA) back to 4,500, or nearly 10,000 points down from the 2007 high, and likely cut real estate values in half or maybe even by two-thirds. There's really only one way this could ever happen. It would take a forced debt contraction cycle from massive losses of jobs and asset liquidation on a grand scale to get these assets back to 1996 levels from whenever and wherever they ultimately top out.

The Future View from a Helicopter

It's not surprising that from the moment Bernanke made his comments on Fed policy recommendations, the U.S. dollar started to slide and gold prices started to rise. We can discern a lot about the future just by recalling Bernanke's reckless inflationary comments about dropping dollars from the sky. We can also compare the words from his infamous November

2002 speech with his policy responses to the credit crisis of 2007 and 2008.

Bernanke made the "helicopter drop" comments as stocks were falling and the markets feared deflation. This deflation fear resulted because of what Japan had experienced after its stock and real estate bubbles deflated in the 1990s. He was saying that the U.S. economy will never experience deflation like we saw in the Great Depression or Japan, where prices totally collapsed. Bernanke says this in great confidence because he knows the power of the printing press over which the Fed has control. Bernanke was a member of the Federal Reserve under Greenspan. He knew that that the Fed, with just the click of a mouse, could accelerate this flow of unrestricted credit into the asset markets, preventing such a deflationary event. Like a magician saying "abracadabra," all these new dollars created out of thin air would ultimately find their way into the economy.

What he apparently failed to see is the same thing his predecessor failed to see, and that was the undesirable effect of mass speculation fueled by easy access to credit. Greenspan and Bernanke didn't realize that a casino-like mentality of investors would take hold, where the appetite for risk would just grow and the fear of taking risk would evaporate. This happens when the head of the casino, the Federal Reserve, is handing out new free chips (new money) anytime the gamblers start to lose or get into trouble.

Investors and speculators bought stocks and real estate on borrowed money from banks, but they also borrowed money on their credit cards to buy homes and stocks. In recent years, credit card debt has exploded. In addition, record high levels of margin debt increased against overvalued and inflated stocks.

Unfortunately for us all, the Fed has created a giant debt monster. *If the Fed rescues the economy and stocks and real estate boom ahead again like the bulls believe, this will only make the debt monster hungrier for more debt-induced gains.* The Fed will create a monster so large that it will take an economic nuclear blast, and a very brave Fed chairman, to kill it. I don't know if this will happen, but I am confident that the end result would be economic pain and suffering. The Fed's cutting the money supply would be an event of biblical proportions and would bring on an economic hell where there will be plenty of anguish and gnashing of teeth.

The House of Cards Becomes a "House of Pain"

U.S. homeowners have taken on record high mortgage debt, which undoubtedly accounted for the spectacular rise in real estate prices. With prices in stocks and real estate so high, debt has been a speculator's best friend, as debt becomes less burdensome when prices continually rise. This is how paper millionaires in real estate created their wealth, on a giant house of debt. Recently prices have started to fall precipitously, and the foundation of debt on which those homes were built has begun to weaken. If prices in real estate continue to crash, then the real estate bubble, built on a mountain of debt, will become a giant house of cards. As the house of cards starts to crumble, so will stocks, dollars, and the world economy right along with it. Again, one asset's weakness will accelerate another asset's weakness, and on and on we go down the slippery slope of deflation.

As Bernanke cuts rates and pumps yet more money into the economy, the enormous supply of newly created dollars will likely create a severe dollar crisis in the future. In fact, after Bernanke's first Fed cut as Fed chairman, the U.S. Dollar Index sank to all-time lows. He will eventually learn that he cannot follow Greenspan's formula of creating endless amounts of dollars without finally seeing a dollar crisis unfold or inflation rip through the economy. Unfortunately for Bernanke, those monetary magic bullets were mostly used up by Greenspan during his extended term as Federal Reserve chairman. If the dollar falls to extreme lows and becomes a currency crisis, investors in the United States will, for the first time since 1979, care about the falling value of the dollar. But unlike Paul Volcker, who hiked interest rates to save the dollar, Bernanke is not expected to follow the Volcker inflation-fighting model. This is because of the severe financial fragility we find the U.S. economy in today.

Bernanke is a towering intellectual and a great student of the 1929 stock market crash and sees his role quite differently. He knows what happens to an economy overweighted in debt as asset prices are falling, and knows the kind of hardship the Great Depression caused our country, with the explosion of unemployment and homelessness. He knows that massive liquidity will be needed, and he will provide it in spades. The problem is that we cannot continue to increase the supply of anything without risking a collapse in the thing that has been oversupplied. Bernanke's thinking is that he already knows he will create an economic equivalent of Hiroshima if he hikes rates and cuts the money supply. If he does the opposite, maybe he will get lucky and create new asset bubbles and booms like Greenspan before him. It's a dangerous bet, but it's the only bet he can make, and he has Greenspan to thank for that.

Inflation First, Deflation Follows

The U.S. money supply accelerated spectacularly in the Greenspan era and again in 2007 and off the charts in 2008. The Fed manages the money supply by trading Treasuries in the open market. It buys or sells Treasuries to keep bank reserves consistent with its target for the Federal Funds Rate (what banks charge each other for overnight loans). The Fed sells Treasuries to drain reserves, as Paul Volcker did to win the inflation war. When the Fed sells Treasuries, the monetary base slows. When the money grows too slowly, economic activity tends to falter. When the money supply expands too rapidly, then the economy heats up and dangerous asset bubbles are the result.

Alan Greenspan single-handedly surpassed the combined money created by all previous Fed chairmen before him. This can be seen by looking at the enormous growth of the M3 money supply under Greenspan. Combine this with our trade deficits, and we have a huge supply of greenbacks sloshing not only around the United States, but around the globe as well. This seeps into asset prices and commodity prices and eventually sent the price of everything higher. As evidenced by the progressive annual new lows in the U.S. Dollar Index, the supply burden became very heavy. The best example I can give to investors today is Nasdaq 2000. If you look back to 1999, you will see enormous amounts of insider selling of stocks across the board, especially in technology and dot-coms.

You may recall a reporter on one of the financial networks who did her reporting from the floor of the New York Stock Exchange during the bubble days of 1999. I'd give anything to get my hands on those recordings. She would proclaim with such excitement about the new initial public offerings (IPOs) "skyrocketing 100 to 200 percent in a single day." She would excitedly yell something along the lines of this, "Folks, the voracious demand for stocks down here is intoxicating as companies issue new shares and investors bid them up 50 to 100 percent in minutes. It is so thrilling just being down here." Her state of euphoria stunned me. This nonsensical euphoric state was repeated on secondary stock offerings of new shares where companies would issue yet more shares to the public because demand for stocks was so high.

The point here is that the supply of stocks continued to grow until eventually it overwhelmed the demand for those stocks. Once demand peaked, the glut of supply meant that stock prices had to crash until demand returned. This is precisely what could take place in the U.S. dollar. The ongoing never-ending supply of dollars prompted Alan Abelson of *Barron's* newspaper to refer to Greenspan as "the king bubble blower" multiple times. Greenspan and his successor Bernanke will be guilty as charged when the dollar falls from the weight of supply.

An ivory tower student like Bernanke will look back to recent history and eventually be forced to do what has been done before. Kicking and screaming all the way, he will be forced to hike interest rates and cut the money supply to save the dollar and put out the inflationary wildfire. If Bernanke refuses to "get it," then the task will fall to his successor after he is replaced or quits. This is when the inflation fight will begin and the forces of deflation and credit contraction will take over. Just as the "wealth effect" has pumped up prices, the poverty effect will push prices down. One way or another, with all this unlimited, never-ending money supply, the long-term secular move on the dollar has only one way to go, and that is ultimately down. Of course, the market already knows this, and the U.S. dollar has been steadily falling for several years.

As we discussed earlier, there will be only a few ways to make money if there is a New Great Depression sprinkled with heavy doses of inflation. First, you must own gold as a pure hedge against inflation. As we enter a protracted period of stagflation, gold will have violent corrections along the way, but ultimately it will hit new all-time highs after highs and gold stocks will likely become the dot-coms of the future. The dollar will have big countertrend rallies as interest rates rise, but its long-term trend will be down.

The Flip Side of the Dollar Outlook

The dollar's reserve currency status has allowed the United States to avoid a collapse like that of Third World nations that had similar imbalances before collapsing. The advantage the U.S. dollar has is that being the main international reserve currency means that foreign governments keep billions of U.S. dollars on hand to settle their current account balances. The dollar is what economists call *numeraire* for trade in many goods. That means that many key commodities, most notably oil, are priced in dollars. Iran is trying to change that, and Iraq tried right before Bush invaded their country. When countries buy oil, they pay in dollars, so the dollar is a universal currency. Perhaps the biggest advantage of being the world's reserve currency is that America can settle its debts with its own currency.

In 1995, the Mexican peso crisis hit, and the United States was a leader in creating a rescue package to save Mexico. The reason for the crisis was that Mexico's supply of dollars on reserve to pay its debts dwindled to zero as investors sold peso-denominated assets to buy dollar-denominated assets. The U.S. government obviously has no such worries, as it just pays its debts in its own currency. However, the precipitous fall in the dollar has many questioning its reserve-currency status. Who wants to hold a currency that continually experiences attrition and weakening value? Prior to falling precipitously in the Fall of 2008, the Euro, the Canadian Dollar, the Swiss Franc, and the Australian Dollar all rose dramatically against the U.S. Dollar. As long as there is confidence that stocks will have renewed momentum to the upside, then this will be a magnet for foreign capital, and therefore a source of demand for dollars. With the 2008 stock and real estate market weakness, many around the world are starting to lose that confidence.

Investors have traditionally looked to the U.S. dollar as a safe haven when there is turmoil in the world. The United States has a stable and democratic government, and that is a big plus for the dollar. The United States has the most powerful military in the world, the economy has been strong, and these have been pluses for the dollar. However, the tide has shifted. Sentiment here at home and around the globe is decidedly negative about Bush's preemptive strike and invasion of Iraq. Regardless of how the Iraq war turns out, the United States now stands very isolated in pursuit of its foreign policy. The U.S. financial system is wracked by a deepening crisis and systemic rot throughout its banking system. The consumer is caving in, squeezed by stagnant earnings and soaring fuel and food prices. Real estate weakens, and as the air leaks out of that bubble, there seems to be no end in sight. The U.S. dollar hitting new record lows is evidence of the sentiment shift from dollars to other currencies like the Euro and to gold.

Let's go back to the last dollar crisis and compare the current situation to see if the dollar decline will bottom as it did in 1995. In 1995, stocks had come off of a stealth bear market and stocks were very cheap. Bond yields were testing 8 percent and bonds looked attractive, with high after-tax yields. In 1995, real estate was also very cheap. Since U.S. assets were undervalued at that time, money plowed into our stocks, bonds, and real estate. The dollar was able to rebound, having attractive dollar-denominated assets, and a sustained boom was launched.

This is not the case today. The DJIA and Standard & Poor's (S&P) 500 hit all-time highs in 2007, and the trends are pointing down in 2008 even as the Fed cuts interest rates. Bond yields are spectacularly low today, so bonds look like a bubble waiting to pop, or, at the very least, remain unattractive. Real estate is weakening but prices are still very high, even as the air comes out of this market. Mixing all of that in with the weak U.S. dollar is a highly explosive combination, and the slightest jolt can cause it to spontaneously detonate. If confidence in the long-term outlook for stocks, bonds, or real estate is shaken, then expect the U.S. economy to detonate and reverberations of that explosion to be felt worldwide.

Alan Greenspan's Future Legacy

As I watched Alan Greenspan on *60 Minutes* promoting his new book, *The Age of Turbulence* (Penguin Books, 2007), I had to shake my head in amazement. The TV showed real estate and stock investors running up to Alan in the street to thank him for all their wealth he created by his low interest rate/easy money policies. These fans had Greenspan autograph their dollar bills. Since he had created several trillion new dollars as Fed chairman, there were plenty of dollars to go around for him to sign. Greenspan also had the nickname of "Easy Al" on Wall Street, according to *60 Minutes,* because of his lowering of interest rates and easy money policies whenever stocks got into trouble. When the inevitable dollar crisis strikes, those excited investors will want to crumple up those autographed dollars and throw them back in Mr. Greenspan's face. *When the Queen of England knighted Greenspan "Sir Alan," the whole world took notice. When the dollar collapses, maybe investors worldwide will realize that instead of knighting him, the Queen should have clubbed him!*

As investors understand that this huge buildup of newly created money by Greenspan and Bernanke caused a dollar collapse, they will not look so kindly upon either of them. Just like Abraham Lincoln's mass issuance of money to pay for the Civil War, greenbacks will be avoided like the plague. Investors will come to understand that "fiat" money is money backed by nothing and has been created in excess, causing huge real estate and stock market bubbles. Just as when folks avoided greenbacks at the time of the Civil War, a day is coming when people will once again desire gold-backed money. People sarcastically called dollars greenbacks back then because they depreciated so much against gold and they were in such high supply. It got so bad that greenbacks were accepted only at deep discounts, and that's what can be expected in the future as well. The biggest buildup of Monopoly-like money has created the single biggest bubble the world has ever seen, and that is the credit bubble. As this credit bubble starts to deflate in 2008, look for the first depression of the twenty-first century to unfold.

Alan Greenspan's book *The Age of Turbulence* is a great read and one of the most informative business books I have read. The title of the book is reflective of what Greenspan experienced as Fed chairman and his part in creating all the turbulence in stocks, real estate, and the economy. He has the 1987 crash, the Nasdaq bubble and crash, and the 2005 real estate bubble and subprime mess all on his watch, and to his credit. At one time Greenspan's legacy appeared great because of the enormous wealth created in this country since he became Fed chairman. Housing and stock prices have exploded to incredible heights thanks to "Easy Al." The flip side of that coin is that household debt has also exploded. Margin debt, mortgage debt, and credit card debt are all at all-time highs. *The Fed has ingrained so much confidence in the minds of real estate and stock investors that to many, debt creation is equivalent to wealth creation.* Whenever asset prices get into serious jeopardy, the Fed will come and bail out investors. All investors have to do is sit tight and wait for stocks and real estate to recover and use that equity to go even farther into debt.

Banks, brokers, savings and loans, mortgage companies, and home builders have taken on incredible amounts of risk, all tied to excess speculation in one form or another. Interestingly enough, most of the stocks in these sectors got completely annihilated in 2006, 2007, and 2008. Citigroup and Bank of America fell like sinking torpedoes. Washington Mutual, the largest savings and loan got down to sixteen cents per share from a high of $45 per share. NVR Inc. (NVR), a leading home builder, has fallen from $851, where it put in a perfect double top chart, to as low as $400 per share. The Federal National Mortgage Association (Fannie Mae [FNM]), the nation's largest mortgage buyer, collapsed in 2008 from a high of $68.60 in 2007. Fannie Mae crashed 98 percent before the government announced bailout. Think of Fannie Mae as a liquid "futures" contract on the illiquid "physical" real estate market. In other words, "LOOK OUT BELOW!" for the future direction of real estate.

Merrill Lynch (MER) fell from $98 to $12 per share. This fall by MER is also directly tied to the subprime mess in 2007 and 2008. As a reward for doing such a lousy job for shareholders, the ousted CEO received a $216 million farewell paycheck.

The point is that excess speculation in stocks and real estate has left investors with significant debt. It has left the U.S. economy very vulnerable to any outside shock or unexpected event that could roil markets. The banking system, continually desperate to shore up its balance sheet, has limped along since the summer of 2007, and finally collapsed into a banking crisis that is shocking world markets. God help us all if real estate or stock prices completely collapse because this country will experience massive economic pain. This may well be one of the main reasons for such low interest rates in the face of very high commodity prices and a weak U.S. dollar.

The "bond ghouls" (the late Louis Rukeyser's term for bond traders) are bullish on bonds because they see the inevitable asset correction combined with mortgage and margin debt contraction and liquidation. All of this will lead to severe economic weakness and that usually leads to extremely low interest rates. Two other times that interest rates got this low were in times of economic trouble. The Great Depression of the last century as well as the dot-com bubble burst saw short-term rates drop to as low as 1 percent. If the Fed winds up cutting interest rates below 1 percent, bond speculators and investors are correct and bonds are still worth buying.

The message of the commodity market with persistently high oil and gold prices is that mass inflation will come on strong sometime in the future. We have already seen extreme asset inflation in stocks and real estate, and that's "good inflation." It's good only because investors feel good about rising stocks and real estate. It is also good in that it keeps high levels of debt manageable for households and speculators. Exploding gold, oil, commodities, and the falling greenback represent "bad inflation," and that is impoverishing the well-being of the American public. This is where prices rise across the board in the economy for goods and services and falling U.S. dollars are worth less in terms of their purchasing power. If and when bad inflation firmly takes hold, the Fed will be forced to reverse its 2007–2008 rate cut policy to that of rate hikes. If that happens, then the only game in town to make money will be on the short side, and Greenspan's legacy will be that of an asset bubble blower and asset bubble buster.

Derivative Exposure Is an Accident Waiting to Happen

Alan Greenspan let another monster-sized future problem grow so large that I am afraid it's going to be too late to stop this beast called derivatives. This could be the single most frightening investment animal ever created. Derivative contracts are options on steroids. Greenspan actually praised and encouraged their explosive growth as Fed chairman. The U.S. Treasury defines a derivative as "a financial contract whose value is derived from the performance of underlying market factors such as interest rates, currency exchange rates, and commodity/equity prices. Derivative transactions include a wide assortment of financial contracts, including structured debt obligations and deposits, swaps, futures, options, caps, floors, collars, forwards, and various combinations thereof."

Derivatives are an extremely high-risk bet on stocks, bonds, and foreign currencies. Growth in derivatives has absolutely exploded out of control, and it is infecting our banking system. While 986 U.S. banks trade in these risky instruments, 97 percent of the derivative activity comes from the top five banks. The exposure to these banks is astronomical relative to these banks' entire capital structure. According to the U.S. Treasury web site, there is a total of $152 trillion (that's not a misprint—$152 trillion) of derivative exposure at U.S. commercial banks and that figure is growing by the day.

The credit exposure is a function of movements in market rates. Banks do not know how much the value of a derivative contract might be at various points of time in the future. Measuring credit exposure in derivative contracts involves identifying those contracts where a bank would lose value if the counterparty to a contract defaulted.

What that all means is that these very complex derivative swaps and arrangements force these banks to depend entirely on each other's ability to pay. If conditions continue to erode, derivative-caused accidents like Lehman Brothers will be common among banks. Trouble in one bank would quickly spread to all financial firms everywhere. This systemic risk is that of a global financial meltdown. A derivative accident is the type of event that could send the United States and the most of the world into the New Great Global Depression of the Twenty-First Century. On November 7, 2007, a spokesperson of CNBC stated that there are "$750 trillion credit derivatives worldwide" so the implications are global in scale. According to Jim Sinclair of www.jsmindset.com, in June 2008, the notional value of all outstanding derivatives now totals approximately $1.144 QUADRILLION ($1,144,000,000,000,000) which sounds like a frightening number to me—how about to you?

The truth is that nobody really knows how dangerous these markets are until an abnormal event takes place. That abnormal event would likely be a serious drop in bond prices. Since 80 percent of the derivative exposure is tied to interest rate contracts, any abrupt spike in interest rates would likely be the fuse to light this powder keg. If interest rates do spike and a U.S. meltdown ensues, then the economy would have an outright collapse. Derivatives are the highest-risk and least understood kind of instrument ever invented, so we will only know the extent of the danger when a systemic meltdown takes place. If the economy booms and interest rates stay stable, then an accident is less likely. Banks can continue to profit from these transactions, and the derivative market can grow to even more absurd levels. If we get an unexpected disruption in the stock, bond, or currency markets, then a systemic meltdown will happen and derivatives will be to blame.

The flip side is that Greenspan believes derivatives are a good thing. He sees derivatives as a way to spread the risk around and as an important stabilizing force. He is half right as the derivative market will be stable until the bond, stock, or currency markets get extremely unstable. Look to the Bear Stearns collapse in 2008 for a preview of the coming potential collapse of the big banks from the perils of extreme leverage. In the wake of the Bear Stearns/JPMorgan bailout, we have learned how desperate the Fed has become. The Fed has now contaminated its balance sheet with lower-quality collateral extending even deeper to the purchase of bonds backed by student loans. The Bear Stearns collapse was a seminal event and a warning of things to come.

Everyone should pay very close attention to interest rates and the top five banks with the biggest derivative exposure. The best way to do that is to watch their stock charts. As we begin 2008, the banks stocks are getting clobbered, along with the homebuilders' and savings-and-loan stocks. In 2008, these five bank stocks look very bearish in the long term. Citibank (C) is down 80 percent from its highs and JPMorgan Chase (JPM) is also getting smoked in price and continues to hit new lows in 2008. Bank of America (BAC), HBSC (HBC), and Wachovia (WAB) all look like giant boulders rolling down from the top of a mountain. It is no surprise that the three banks with the greatest derivative exposure are being punished the most. From a longer-term chart, it would appear that these banks have nothing but downside for a very long time to come. In other words, this decline may only be at halftime of a very long, difficult, and losing game.

Remember, if one bank goes, then they can all fall like dominoes as the derivative accident spreads from one bank to another and then to another until all 986 banks that trade in derivatives are infected. These are extremely dangerous devices that could cause economic pain throughout the globe. This systemic risk must be looked at in terms of "what if"–type questions. What if interest rates suddenly spike? What if stocks crash overnight and become a 1929-style decline? What if the U.S. dollar goes from its long, slow decline to a rout and a crisis?

The answer to these questions should lead regulators to establish new rules to govern how traders buy and sell these derivative contracts. This is something that must be done by Bernanke and the Fed to protect the world from its first depression of the new century. The only guaranteed way to make money in a systemic meltdown is to short stocks and to have a short-side strategy. In the next chapter, I will show you how the falling greenback is contributing to a crisis that is a catalyst toward a coming price collapse in stocks, bonds, and real estate throughout the globe.

CHAPTER 4

BLACK GOLD: BOOM AND BUST PROFIT OPPORTUNITIES IN OIL STOCKS

The proverbial "powder keg" in the Middle East has been hanging over world markets for a very long time. As the new century rolls along, the sparks are close to setting off a combustible explosion. The fuse is getting shorter on this powder keg explosion, with fears of Iran becoming a nuclear power and a weapon possibly finding its way into the hands of terrorists. The fuse gets shorter by the day with the political instability of Pakistan, and even shorter as the United States continues the war in Iraq. With so much instability in this region, it's only logical to assume that the fuse is close to being lit and the explosion is set to incinerate global stock markets and economies. This persistent high price of oil is putting extreme pressure on the inflation side of the stagflation equation.

As the Federal Reserve frantically prints new dollars in the new century to stave off a Nasdaq 2000–like real estate implosion, the value of those dollars lessens and that affects the exchange rate against the other world major currencies. As the U.S. dollar fell in the first several years of the new millennium, some nasty repercussions resulted. Since oil is priced in U.S. dollars around the world, the Organization of Petroleum Exporting Countries (OPEC) dealt with the falling dollar with higher oil prices. OPEC keeps supplies tight to keep prices high. One reason they do this is to compensate for the reduced purchasing power of the falling dollar. While oil-producing countries could decide not to accept dollars, that would be not only the wrong economic decision, but also a very dangerous one as well. When Iraq stopped accepting U.S. dollars as payment for oil, it wasn't long before the U.S. military invaded and the leader who made that decision was roped and hung. Iran followed Iraq's lead in 2007 and stated that they "prefer the euro or yen" and no longer desire falling "worthless dollars." As a result of this, in combination with the increasing demand from China and India, oil prices soared to $145 per barrel in 2008.

A big part of the rise in oil prices has been related to traders' fears that an attack on Iran is coming from either the United States or Israel. This event would rock global markets and send the world into the economic dark ages. Any invasion of Iran would send oil prices quickly to $200 per barrel because 40 percent of the world's oil supplies transit the Strait of Hormuz. This very narrow area would be completely shut off if Iran is attacked. Traders in the oil pits must have thought that oil prices would initially escalate to $200 per barrel because activity in the December 2008 $200 oil contracts spiked up in volume in November 2007 and continued to do so through 2008. According to commodity traders interviewed on CNBC, this activity was directly related to fears of a surprise strike on Iran.

A few days later, in November 2007, Hugo Chavez of Venezuela was quoted as saying, "Oil prices will spike to $200 per barrel if the U.S. strikes Iran." Chavez was meeting with the president of Iran, who joined in by saying, "U.S. dollars are just worthless pieces of paper and the empire of the dollar is crashing." Some of these oil-producing countries are intentionally cutting supplies and using the high price of oil as a weapon against the United States. Their biggest oil customer is the United States, which accounts for 25 percent of world oil demand.

The bad news for stock and real estate investors is that oil spikes were at the heart of past recessions and bear markets, with the high price of oil giving advanced warnings of the recession to come. The recessions of 1973, 1979, and 1990 resulted primarily from energy price shocks. Obviously, with oil at such high levels in 2007 and 2008, many stock market bears expect an economic recession, which intuitively makes good sense. Fortunately, the residual strength from the long global boom has delayed the U.S. economy from entering a recession caused from the falling real estate market and persistently high oil prices.

The terrorists, and the rogue nations that fund those terrorist organizations, know that our economy is dependent on foreign capital and oil for survival. Without foreign capital and oil, the U.S. economy would crumble and the stagflation described earlier would follow. Unfortunately for the Federal Reserve, printing money cannot solve an oil crisis, nor can government rebates and bailouts.

The U.S. economy cannot afford even a mild recession when you think about the effect it will have on the already soft real estate market. Real estate got incredibly weak in a period of near record low unemployment, extremely low interest rates, and very high stocks. How bad will it get with an oil-induced recession or a rapidly rising interest rate environment? The answer is that the real estate market would face the very real possibility of a complete price collapse. This would then result in a New Great Depression.

The truth is that the reduced demand for oil from the bad news of a depression is about the only thing that could lead to the good news of an oil price crash. As fears of a recession took hold in 2008, oil stocks corrected and became a great short-term trading opportunity on the short side just like they were in 1998. Back then, the Asian currency crisis resulted in weak demand for oil, and oil stocks crashed. How much greater a short-selling opportunity could oil stocks become if fears of a depression take hold?

Let's face it: We are largely dependent on unfriendly countries like Saudi Arabia, Russia, Iraq, Iran, and Venezuela to meet our energy needs. This is not a comforting thought. Thank goodness we have friendly countries like Canada and Mexico as our number one and two suppliers of oil to the United States. Saudi Arabia is number three and Venezuela is our fourth largest supplier of oil. It is obvious that rising oil prices will have a devastating effect on the global economy. During the last energy crisis in the 1970s, inflation ripped out of control, interest rates went to unimaginable heights, and stocks became unglued in one of the worst secular bear markets in history.

After the stock market peaked in 1968, it took until 1982 to finally hit the bottom. How many long-term investors stayed the course through that entire 14-year secular bear market in stocks? How many will persevere in the coming secular bear market? *Fear is a powerful emotion that brings with it panic selling.* Mass liquidation of assets will have to happen just to service the debt that real estate and stock investors have taken on once jobs are lost and an oil-induced recession unfolds. It becomes more obvious daily that an economic alternative to oil must be developed as soon as possible. Demand for oil is far outstripping increases in oil production, and OPEC is setting higher prices to compensate for the falling dollar. The sad part is that most experts believe there is not enough time to avert an oil crisis before alternative energy or newly discovered supplies can free us from dependence on foreign oil.

Iran's Dangerous Chess Game

In President Bush's own words, "We will not permit the world's worst dictators to threaten us with the world's most dangerous weapons." This is known as the Bush Doctrine. This statement clearly shows that President Bush had Iran as a top priority in his "Axis of Evil." To get to Iran, Bush had to first attack Iraq and Afghanistan to surround Iran. In 2007 and again in 2008, President Bush sent multiple ships and carriers to perform military exercises in the Persian Gulf. Bush had his eyes on a surprise attack on Iran right from the beginning of the war on terrorism. The oil speculators believed that the odds increased that Bush would go ahead with his attack before he completed his second term as president in 2008. The stakes were much higher than the Iraq invasion because if he went directly to war with Iran, it would likely have started another world war. This goes for the new administration as well.

Unlike Iraq, Iran has vast amounts of weapons with very accurate guidance systems and real weapons of mass destruction. According to the *Jerusalem Post* on September 17, 2007, "Iran claims that 600 of its SHAHAB-3 medium-range missiles are available to target U.S. forces in Iraq." If Bush or the Obama administration were to attack, our soldiers would be like sitting ducks across the border in Iraq.

Former Secretary of State Colin Powell said that he had seen intelligence indicating that Iran was working hard to make the SHAHAB-3 missiles nuclear-tipped. The 2007 "surge" of additional troops in Iraq further suggested that President Bush still desired a surprise attack on Iran. President Bush labeled Iran as one of the three nations of an "Axis of Evil" in a landmark speech at the United Nations in New York in September 2002. As the president of Iran continued to thumb President Bush in the eye with belligerent rhetoric, he was pushing Bush and Congress toward such an event. This is a major reason why oil prices rose to almost $150 per barrel.

In September of 2007, President Bush stated that Tehran is putting the Middle East "under the shadow of a nuclear holocaust." This is a reality that future presidents will face as well if Bush wisely decides against pulling the trigger on the surprise attack on Iran. This "mushroom cloud" fear will likely push the United States or Israel to war with Iran before a nuclear bomb is developed. Most estimate that Iran is three to five years away from a nuclear bomb, so we should expect an attack from either the United States or, most likely, Israel against Iran before that time. If an attack happens, millions of people will die and the oil fields of the Middle East will get completely contaminated. This would most certainly bring on a global depression, as the world would enter the economic dark ages of crashing assets combined with rising inflation from rapidly rising oil prices. When unexpected events such as these happen, you will be supremely happy you had a short-side strategy that addresses these systemic risks.

A short-side strategy positions your portfolio for the current and future war on stagflation the Federal Reserve is and will continue to be fighting.

The leader of Iran, President Ahmadinejad, has been contentious in his defiance of the U.S. and UN demands of halting his nuclear development program. He insists Iran will move forward with "its peaceful intentions for energy purposes only." Iran is the fourth-largest producer of oil in the world and is sitting on vast reserves of petroleum and natural gas. To think the world would or even could believe the president of Iran's statement of using nuclear technology for "energy purposes only" is absurd.

The Iranian president shocked the world when it was reported that he said he would not only destroy Israel, but that the holocaust was a myth and threatened to wipe Israel off the map. Never has a UN leader of one country publicly called for the elimination of another UN country, so we are dealing with a situation that could become explosive. Nevertheless, the game of nuclear chicken that Iran is playing with the world could end badly and soon. Israel will attempt to destroy Iran's nuclear ambitions the way they did in Iraq with a surprise air strike on hidden nuclear sites. *If you don't have stocks on the short side as the market goes crashing down, then you are a long-only investor. You will not be able to benefit in any way from falling prices, nor will you enjoy the protection a short-side hedge affords.* President Bush was in no mood to stand around and have President Ahmadinejad poking his nuclear trigger finger into Bush's chest before a newly planned "Shock and Awe" campaign followed for Iran. Here's proof of what I mean. General Wesley Clark wrote the book *A Time to Lead* (Palgrave Macmillan, 2007). Here is what he has to say about Iraq and Iran shortly after the Twin Towers fell:

> When airline service resumed, I flew to Washington to check with my Pentagon friends. To that end, I dropped in on the Joint Staff. There, a senior general relayed some disturbing news: "We're going to attack Iraq. The decision has basically been made."

On page 231, he wrote:

> "But why?" I asked. "I had already caught indications that the Bush administration and some persons associated with the Israeli political right wing were seeking to pin the blame for the 9/11 attacks on Iraqi president Saddam Hussein. Based on everything I knew—and I'd followed the intelligence very closely while in uniform—this didn't seem likely. Saddam was a secular leader, and to the Islamic Al Qaeda, he was a sworn enemy." "Did they

> discover a linkage?" I asked. "No, it's nothing like that. It's just that they don't know what else to do. If the only tool you have is a hammer, then every problem has to be a nail, and we're no good against terrorists, but what we can do is attack governments."
>
> Certainly this was part of the explanation, but it wasn't all. When I returned to the Pentagon six weeks later, as we were striking Afghanistan and chasing off the Taliban, I asked the same general if there was still a plan to go after Iraq. "Oh, it's worse than that," he said, and held up a memo on his desk. Here's the paper from the Office of the Secretary of Defense outlining the strategy. We're going to take out seven countries in five years! . . . And he named them, starting with Iraq and Syria and ending with Iran. It was straight out of Paul Wolfowitz's 1991 playbook, dressed up as the search for weapons of mass destruction and the global war on terror.

I reprinted this mostly because these are the kind of unexpected events that rock world markets. The point is not to predict a future strike on Iran, but to emphasize that unknowable risks like this always exist. This is why you need to have a short-side strategy for crash insurance against these shocking catastrophic events. Major events will send our very vulnerable world economy into a severe asset decline with a forest fire of inflation in what everyone will recognize as a New Era of Stagflation. Is your portfolio properly protected from such an unexpected event? Then prepare your portfolio because the possibility of needing to prevent a nuclear Iran does exist.

Leaders from around the world know what the Iranian president's religious views are. President Ahmadinejad believes in the 12th Imam, who, according to legend, disappeared about 1,000 years ago and who requires an apocalyptic conflict of biblical proportions to usher back his return. This messianic view almost requires or at least encourages a nuclear conflict to spur on the 12th Imam's second coming. This is just one of many reasons why many around the world fear Iran's having nuclear weapons and also why a military strike is forthcoming.

Surprise Attack on Iran

The second Iraq war that started in the twenty-first century, and the possible military strike against Iran by the United States or Israel is as much about oil and settling old scores as it is about terrorism. We desperately need oil—the world is reportedly running low, and many countries that produce oil are our enemies. The financing that the United States needs to fight wars around the globe is precisely what our enemies see as the United States' future financial downfall along with our heavy dependence on oil. President Bush, a former Texas oil speculator, knows that we are totally dependent on foreign oil. He also realizes the effect of a tightening oil supply. This is a key reason why we invaded Iraq the second time, and the same reason why the United States may eventually attack Iran and put an even bigger U.S. footprint in the Middle East.

No matter how many ways you slice it, the U.S. economy faces some serious headwinds with rising oil prices, a weak real estate market, and exploding debts and deficits. Our Federal Reserve and elected leaders are aware that the asset value of stocks and real estate must not deflate to keep our huge debt burden from causing a complete collapse in our economy as happened in The Great Depression. The Federal Reserve will continue to print dollars and the government will continue to spend on wars around the globe to avoid such a catastrophe. This increases the odds that eventually the U.S dollar will eventually experience a severe crisis.

When a U.S. dollar crisis occurs, the flow of the monetary spigot will be tightened to cool inflation. Economists know the fundamental relationship that exists between the supply of money and the price of money—better understood as interest rates. If you shrink or cut the money supply, then interest rates will go up. This was most widely evident when Paul Volcker followed the monetarist's playbook and slashed the money supply. A monetarist holds to the economic theory that a well-controlled money supply is critical to a stable and balanced economy. This is in great contrast to the views of today's Federal Reserve, which appears to be trying to turn U.S. dollars into confetti. When Paul Volcker cut the money supply to crush inflation, interest rates took off. In the new century, the

Fed will not follow such a plan until inflation absolutely runs wild. The Fed hopes that debt-ridden U.S. citizens can grow their way out of their strangling debt burdens. They think the best way to do that is with controlled inflation, with the debts being repaid with depreciated dollars.

OPEC will continue to keep prices high as long as U.S. dollar–debasing tactics continue. This has gotten totally out of our control because U.S. oil production peaked in 1970 and since then has fallen to near all-time lows. Many oil-producing foreign nations think they have the United States where it hurts because the United States appears to them as a country running out of oil. If oil does go to $200 a barrel like the speculators believe, then spectacularly rising interest rates and damaging inflation will surely follow. Inflation has steadily been rising, and that makes bonds a sell now. Bonds are not only a sell, but are also setting up to become a fantastic short opportunity once they top out technically and reverse course.

The president and members of Congress need to get a loud and clear message from its citizens that the war we need to be fighting is to put the energy issue front and center and accelerate the development of our untapped conventional resources, while also aggressively pursuing alternative energy programs. The United States' economic future and well-being depends on the success of this battle. While a lot depends on whether our government moves away from a militaristic approach, there are steps we can take for inflation protection that I will soon highlight. *Protecting our finances is a first step toward fiscal responsibility.* Your own purchasing power can be protected from rising inflation by implementing a short-side strategy.

Looking Back at 1997–1999 Oil Stocks

In late 1997 and into 1998, as the Asian crisis unfolded, oil demand started to weaken and oil stocks collapsed. The "Asian flu" caused the Oil Service Index (OSX) to drop 43 percent in 1998. Unfortunately for me, I learned the hard way how fast the OSX can fall. Owning the oil service stocks in 1998 felt like getting a brick thrown at my head, a very painful learning experience. After three solid performance years, my hedge fund skidded on the oil patch for a big loss that year. Here's how it happened:

A good friend of mine, who was also a hugely successful hedge fund manager, was wildly bullish on the oil stocks. I knew little about the oil stocks at the time. I was not even interested in oil stocks until my hedge fund buddy explained the huge upside earnings leverage these stocks had to the rising price of oil. Remember, leverage works both ways, and I had to learn that lesson the hard way.

My hedge fund friend was extremely bullish on the oil tanker plays in the sector because they looked so cheap, with single-digit price-to-earnings ratios. The stocks he loved the most were TRICO Marine (TMAR) and HVIDE Marine (HMAR). I called these stocks the "Boat Guys" because they were marine transport stocks and they were a very hot group at the time. The analysts on Wall Street had fantastic earnings estimates and target prices on HMAR and TMAR, and I felt lucky buying these stocks in the mid $20s, down from the high $30s. I was "loading the boat" on these names (pardon the pun). Before I knew it, both of the Boat Guys slid to the high teens in price. I was getting destroyed in these stocks and fast. I literally found my head near the wastebasket, as I was sick to my stomach. When you feel this way, or are losing sleep, SELL.

After finally selling TMAR and HMAR around $17 to $18 per share, both stocks immediately went to single-digit prices on fears of reduced oil demand caused by the Asian flu. In the case of HMAR, a Q was added to the end of the symbol, and it became HMARQ. It was soon delisted and quickly went bankrupt. As I had read the analyst buy reports all the way down, I understood how the oil price leverage worked in reverse for these companies. The Boat Guys would sign fat contracts and expand their fleets when oil prices were high and demand was strong. When demand fell, so did the prices of their contracts. The boats built on debt became an oversupply burden. An oversupplied fleet of boats cannot be used with low contract prices, so the boats are dry-docked.

When oil prices were high, the debt taken on to build new boats was manageable. Once prices fell, the debt burden pushed them right into bankruptcy. Debt is a friend on the way up, resulting in exploding earnings for oils stocks. On the way down, the Boat Guys sank under a burden of debt. *When fortunes reverse, debt becomes enemy number one.* This kind of stock meltdown happened in every oil stock I owned in 1998. Be wary, as oil could pop on Iran or a terrorist attack on a Saudi pipeline and then quickly collapse on fears of a demand slowdown in the United States like the "Asian flu" caused in 1998.

In 2007, the Boat Guys performed exceptionally well in the market along with all the oil stocks. The leader Boat Guy is Tidewater (TDW). This stock hit $80 per share as oil was trying to test $100 per barrel. The market looked ahead to a drop in oil or the future oversupply of boats like in 1998. On top of that, the Boat Guys like TDW had very tough earnings comparisons to make year over year. As oil falls, boat prices drop and those earning comparisons get really ugly. TDW saw their earnings increase only 1 percent year over year for the third quarter of 2007, and that sent TDW and many of the Boat Guys stocks over the edge. TDW stock anticipated all of this and fell from $80 in mid-July to the mid-$40s in November 2007 as a result of the disappointing year-over-year third-quarter earnings comparison. The news was great at $80, but investors who bought near the peak did not feel so great a few months later at $40. *Those who buy at the top experience nothing but downside.* TDW then reversed course and raced back to over $70 from $40 as oil exploded to $140 per barrel before tanking once again. You can see why having a short-side strategy, looking at both sides of the market, makes complete sense in this new era of market volatility.

There was another Boat Guy that small investors went nuts over in 2008. Frontline Ltd. (FRO) had a stock price explosion as oil crossed $140 per barrel. FRO then set up a huge head-and-shoulders top, setting up for lower prices ahead. The interesting thing about FRO is that the high-dividend yield attracts investors of all kinds. With the stock climbing, as well as paying a big fat dividend, small investors thought that they could have their cake and eat it, too. The truth is that as oil prices drop, that dividend payout will likely get cut. As oil collapses, the dividend payment could be eliminated.

As the price of oil started to fall, the oil stocks severely corrected, like they did in 1998. The net result for savvy traders was a trading opportunity for shorting oil stocks even as the fundamentals appeared to look great. Oil stocks tend to have fantastic price reversals, and that's the short-side opportunity I'm talking about.

By the way, TMAR is now TRMA. After a reverse split and a new red-hot boat market, TRICO Marine got back to the $40s again and put in a big head-and-shoulder top just like FRO did. The other stocks in the boat group all looked the same as TDW and FRO, all in negative downtrends on the chart. Remember the saying, "birds of a feather...?" In the stock market this applies, and my saying is *stocks of a feather rise and fall together.* I don't recommend shorting stocks that pay big dividends. The biggest reason is that the big dividend keeps investors hopeful and not readily willing to sell. Shareholders can stubbornly keep the prices of dividend-paying stocks up for much longer than they could have if they didn't pay a dividend. If they set up perfectly on the charts like the Boat Guys did, then you can take a shot. Remember, all trades should have stop losses for risk control.

Canadian Oil Sands

There are some exciting investment opportunities to make money in the oil patch and areas where substantial additional undiscovered reserves can help keep a lid on oil prices. Canada, one of the few export-friendly countries, sits on the largest pool of oil reserves outside of Saudi Arabia. The Canadian oil sands are one of the most promising regions in the world to find such plays. The Canadian oil trusts are an interesting way to invest and get equity exposure to this oil play and region. The full cost of new production in these challenging oil fields is roughly $30 to $50 a barrel. If oil drops below $50, then drilling would cease and these stocks would tank that much further than from a mere fall in oil prices. Canadian oil trusts are oil and gas companies. Many of these trusts trade on U.S. exchanges and pay a substantial percentage of their cash flow out to shareholders. These shareholders, called unit holders, get paid monthly distributions or dividends.

These Canadian stocks first got blasted when the Canadian government said they were going to change the way they tax these trust companies. This proposed increase in taxes would result in lower dividends that can be paid out to the unit holders. This absolutely clobbered these stocks because of the uncertainty of the future tax legislation. This became a political football as the Canadian government hotly debated the tax proposal. All the uncertainty created a great opportunity to buy these stocks very cheaply in 2007, and they had very high dividends.

Like any stock or sector I mention, the fundamentals *and* the charts must line up positively on a stock before considering any investment, long or short. When they both line up and give the signal to buy, then and only then, consider buying. Never buy a stock on just getting a high dividend. If you get a 7 percent dividend but you bought the stock and it falls 10 percent, then your dividend benefit is lost. When the charts turn negative, you must sell even if the fundamentals still appear positive.

The benefit of stock charts is that they will give an advance warning as to when the fundamentals are likely to turn negative in any sector or commodity. The chart price will be a forward-looking indicator that will discount the future changes in fundamentals. If the forward six to nine month fundamental picture is good, then the stocks will stay in a bullish chart pattern. When the fundamentals are about to change, the stock patterns will turn negative and give advance warning of a crash to come. A great example was in 2008 as oil prices reversed from $145 and collapsed. The Canadian oil stocks gave back most of their 2003–2008 gains, becoming interesting buy candidates once again.

Oil Sand Symbols

In 2007, one of the best oil sand stock picks from a short-term technical perspective was PrimeWest Energy (PWI). At the time, PWI was yielding 13.7 percent and had a great fundamental story. The chart also looked great as it traced out a big inverse head-and-shoulder bottom. The stock was in the $30s before the Canadian tax hike speculation smoked this stock all the way down to $18.37 (left shoulder). The stock rallied to $22, and then more bad news hit and the stock found its ultimate low at $17.01 (the head). The stock then rallied to

$20 and fell back to $18.45 (right shoulder). From there, the stock moved up and then had a gap up to $28 on a proposed buyout announcement. To find stocks with a big dividend like 13.7 percent previous to a 27 percent capital gain is a great hit if you can get the timing right. This is where technical analysis using stock charts can help you identify the lowest-risk and highest-reward prices to buy or sell short any stock or market. Soon I will discuss technical analysis and my newly discovered timing indicator.

As I write, PWE (Penn West Energy), BTE (Baytex Energy), and, lastly, CNQ (Canadian Natural Resources) look to be the stocks traders are most focused on in this sector. The fact of the matter is that oil built a price bubble, as did most oil stocks as oil hit $145 a barrel. Now that these stocks have completely reversed, investors need to look for some nice buying opportunities in the Canadian oil sands. Remember, the charts and the fundamentals must line up positively before being purchased or shorted and then watched carefully along with sell stops placed.

Oil appeared to be racing toward $200 per barrel in price, and much of that price rise was the perceived unending demand from China as well as fears of a surprise attack on Iran. When it appeared that Bush wasn't going to strike Iran in 2008, then $50 came out of the price of oil quickly. When the world recognized what a polluted bubble China was, oil stocks fell hard. Once the air comes completely out of China.com like that of Nasdaq 2000, then another $50 could come out of the the price of oil, so be careful on investing on the long side of oil. That's the flip side to the gloomy outlook most investors have on ever-rising oil prices.

High Prices Eventually Cure High Prices

Whenever the price of anything goes up to extremely high levels, an adequate or substantial supply is usually not too far behind to meet all that demand. In Nasdaq 2000, stock prices rose to a point where every CEO and technology stock insider sold shares to meet the insatiable demand for dot-com stocks and to take full advantage of the high price. Once the overwhelmingly high supply of stock met the nonsensical speculative demand, prices stopped rising. Then, when the demand waned, stocks fell and supply greatly exceeded that demand. This lethal combination results in a price collapse. The extremely high commodity prices have a way of curing themselves by creating increased supply. This is why there is just as much opportunity to short oil stocks on the way down as there is to go long on the way up.

If you missed the boom in the oil stocks, don't worry. The ride down on the short side is just as exciting and rewarding and can last for many years as well. If crude prices spike up because of Iran or a terrorist attack on pipelines, then enormous amounts of supply will eventually be found to meet that demand. If global growth wanes as supplies proliferate, then a complete collapse can be expected. To keep things simple, just watch the OIH (NYSE exchange-traded fund [ETF]) and DIG (NYSE ETF) chart patterns for the future bullish or bearish trends to come in the oil patch. These charts will anticipate an Iran strike rise or a recession-induced fall in the future six- to nine-month outlook in oil.

The fundamentals of $145 a barrel of oil was not as promising as the table-pounding bulls on oil had proclaimed. According to British Petroleum (BP), worldwide demand grew modestly in 2006 and 2007, and when oil prices went to $145 a barrel, demand fell even further. ExxonMobil Corporation (XOM) as well as other oil companies cut their long-term forecast for oil consumption for this very reason. This is how price cures price. Prices get too high, and then demand slows just as supply is expanding rapidly to take advantage of the very high prices. Falling demand coupled with rapidly expanding supply leads to a collapse. This is true for any asset or commodity. Look to the rise and then the mighty fall of the S&P 500, global stock markets, Gold, China, and Silver in 2008 for evidence of what I'm talking about.

Part of the recent problem in the U.S. housing market is the growing monthly supply of the number of homes on the market (a record number in 2008 and still growing). Part of the reason for this is that prices got so high that the housing supply increased to take advantage of the ridiculously high real estate prices. This will happen in the oil patch as drilling activity in new regions like the Canadian oil sands increase and new alternatives are fully developed.

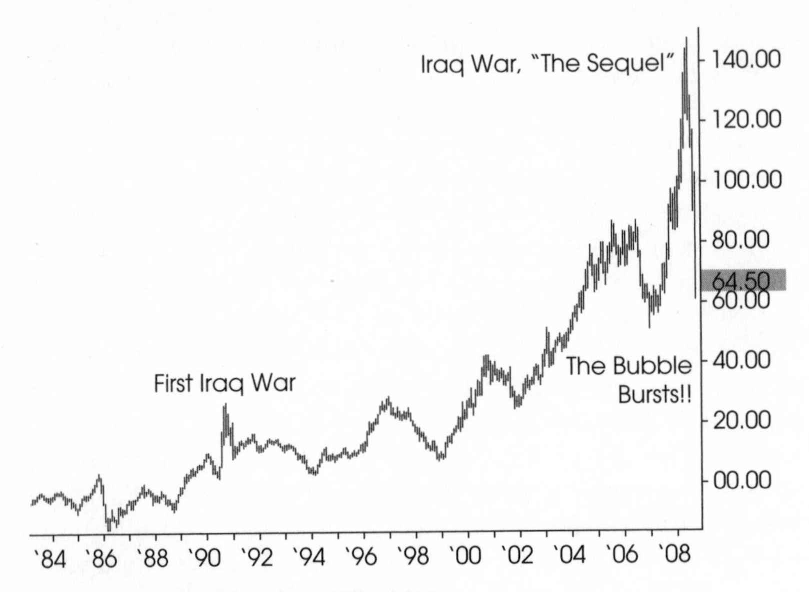

Figure 4.1 Crude Oil 1984–2008
Created with TradeStation

The other way that price cures price is through speculation. As prices rise dramatically, investors become wild speculators looking for a quick way to make easy money. We saw this in the real estate market with the birth of the "flipper." Shortly after, the flippers and flipper-wannabes died in the rising flames of speculation. In Nasdaq 1999, it was the Internet and dot-com day trader that went up in flames. In 2008, it was the oil speculators that followed the same downward path.

The speculative fever went wild in the price of oil right before the high prices reduced demand and collapsed the oil market. See Figure 4.1.

It takes only a few dollars of margin to make a highly leveraged bet on the price of oil in the futures markets. According to CNBC, speculators were buying December 2008 $200 oil futures. Open interest in crude oil contracts by financial speculators exploded as well. As prices fell, the option leverage worked in reverse. The speculative hot money turned cold as the momentum turned negative. Hedge funds switched gears in mid-2008 and pounced on the oil names, sending them down hard.

There is often so much excitement at the top of any market that small investors join the party right as the party is ready to be crashed by huge price declines. This is simply human nature. *The emotions of fear and greed cause investors to sell at the bottom and buy at the top.* This fact will never change. The good news is that the charts will put in top patterns, which will give you advance notice on when to "get short" and when to "go long" the oil stocks. When the China bubble burst, oil stocks came crashing down.

As President Bush leaves office and the fear of a U.S. surprise attack wanes, the price of oil could very well accelerate its fall. The supply of oil in storage tanks around the world hit all-time high numbers of barrels in 2007 and 2008. If supplies continue to grow as demand falls, then the price of oil will completely collapse. I saw this 1998 scenario play out before and still remember the financial spanking received from my oil stocks experiment. The painful memory of that experience haunts me still.

In summary, you can see that there is a flip side to every investment. *Enabling your investment strategy to allow you to go long and short is like saying, "Heads or tails, you can win!"* Sometimes the coin lands on heads for the bulls. Other times it lands on tails for the bears. Adhering to a short-side strategy can provide you with protection and profits on both sides of the market. Adhering to a short-side strategy opens up the opportunity to make money on both sides of any market versus being a long-only investor. In the coming war on stagflation, you will need some exposure to the short side of the marketplace.

CHAPTER 5

WHY GOLD? THE PROLIFERATION OF PAPER MONEY CREATION AND INFLATION

The wisest way to protect and profit from the coming inflation or deflation is gold and gold stocks. At this point, it doesn't matter whether we face a deflationary death spiral or a hyperinflationary global bubble. If, God forbid, we have a worst-case economic scenario of a combination of both, then gold will at worst hold its value and will most probably appreciate relative to all other asset classes that will come crashing down.

Ben Bernanke said on the day he was designated to be the new Fed chairman that he would carry on Greenspan's legacy and focus on "strong economic growth." To gold traders this meant that he would be committed to keeping markets very liquid, primarily through the rapid expansion of the money supply and emergency rate cuts. This also meant that "Helicopter Ben" would save the day when the economy sees the slightest bit of danger, as Alan Greenspan had done when he was Fed chairman. This was demonstrated in Ben's first crisis as Fed chairman; he cut the "emergency" Fed fund interest rates 0.75 percentage points to 4.5 percent in two meetings in an attempt to stave off the "subprime mortgage crisis" in 2007. The Fed followed with further sharp rate cuts before pausing 10 months later. This is extremely important to understand because it all but guarantees that gold will continue its bull market run from the secular lows seen in 2001, as Ben continues to plant the seeds for a crop of future inflation.

Boom/Bust Lesson

The Federal Reserve obviously believes that there is no longer any need to have recessions to clean out the excesses that economic booms create. Just as the Greenspan Fed did, the current Fed believes it can alter the natural business cycle by pumping more and more liquidity into the system on each sign of weakness. Of course, most free market economists know that staving off the economy's natural corrective course will only inflate asset prices and the economy to an unsustainable breaking point.

To see evidence of asset inflation, all you have to do is look at the China boom and the Chinese stock market *ka-boom!* China is awash in billions of U.S. dollars. This massive excess liquidity is a root cause of the hyperinflating Chinese stock market and economy. Rampant inflation, already running at double digits in 2008, threatens to destroy the Chinese economy. As it does, hot-money hedge funds will continue to flee its market and Chinese stocks will further implode. That market got out of control to the upside, and as the bubble continues to pop, China is learning a painful lesson in free-market capitalism. China will learn the way the United States did and that's by experiencing major stock market crashes and economic depressions prior to emerging as a dominant economic superpower.

The United States has learned this boom/bust lesson over and over in its history. Look at the inflationary 1970s to see the effects of printing too much money and then being forced to cut the money supply. Bernanke knows that recessions are not necessarily bad things, as they help cleanse the system of excess. Then, once repaired, the economy can lift off from a strong foundation for the next healthy boom. Bernanke and the Fed know that if you fight the economy's natural course, you risk a long, severe, and painful depression instead of much less painful periodic recessions. *By intervening in this way, it is clear that modern-day Federal Reserve chairmen, like Greenspan and Bernanke, see themselves as economic saviors to the world.*

Rising Gold Prices

The Fed behaves like a cartel, chopping off the market's "invisible hand." The invisible hand is a metaphor coined by the father of modern economics, Adam Smith. The term is used to describe the natural force that guides free-market capitalism through competition. *If individuals believe that the business cycle is altered by the Fed, then they will speculate wildly in stocks, real estate, or other asset markets in the belief that recessions are things of the past.* The Fed's new visible hand is seen as a hand that only gives and never takes away. Having the punch bowl always full has led to a moral hazard situation, dangerous speculation, and a bad economic hangover. For a preview of this risk, you only have to look to the China boom as it goes into what could be a catastrophic bust. The Federal Reserve's loose monetary policy may also create a hyperinflationary economy.

From a long-term perspective, gold can travel only one way with this kind of inflationary Fed policy, and that is up. Greenspan has been quoted as saying to Congress that "the price of gold is a meaningful tool to forecast inflation." He also went on to say that "the price of gold is one of the major indicators of inflation." I am sure that gold's enduring and persistent strength has not been comforting for the Federal Reserve as they cut interest rates in an unsuccessful attempt to fight a housing market correction and credit crisis. This kind of Fed action, in spite of the inflationary warning sign of rising gold prices, has given the green light to gold speculators and investors worldwide. It also gave U.S. stock and real estate market speculators a green light to go borrow every nickel they could get their hands on and speculate wildly in the inflationary Fed-induced liquidity boom and "new economy."

Gold, in many ways, is the ultimate commodity. Gold has had an uneven track record of performance, as evidenced by its relatively constant price from 1871 to 1971, followed by a boom decade, and its recent long secular bear market that didn't end until 2001. During most of the earlier 100-year time period, gold was fixed in price. It wasn't until 1968 when the price of gold was floated freely in the world's marketplace that the price started experiencing downward and upward movements. Gold's biggest bull move was from 1971 to 1981, where it skyrocketed from $42 an ounce to an intraday market peak of $875 an ounce. Gold made a 20-fold move in the inflationary decade of the 1970s as it was unleashed from government price control. Since that time, gold has had mini-bull and mini-bear market runs, but all in the context of a long secular bear market decline. That decline initially ended in 1999 and didn't resume a new uptrend until 2002.

In this new century, gold is poised to repeat the 1970s. It will again have mini-bull and mini-bear market moves along the way, but the long-term secular move will be up—way up. If we experience true hyperinflation, then gold will match the percentage gain we saw in 1971 to 1981. I do expect gold to easily top $1,500, and probably cross $2,000 per ounce, especially if central banks around the world continue to aggressively expand their money supply, as has been happening early on in the new century. However, along the way, gold will have severe price corrections as it works its way to $2,000 or more. This bullish secular move could last as long as the long secular bullish move in the Dow Jones Industrial Average (DJIA) from 1982 to 2008. There are just too many powerful tailwinds for gold, with central banks worldwide acting as "engines of inflation." At some point you'll need to get on board and ride this bull market freight train of gains. *As the inflation engines continue to rev up, with central banks around the world printing new money, the "gold bull train" will speed along like the "technology freight train" did in the 1990s.*

The next big speculative Internet frenzy in the market quite possibly could come in gold stocks, which will then mark the euphoric end of the gold bull market move. It will likely happen simultaneously with a U.S. dollar crisis or some kind of currency dislocation in the world. Hopefully, the United States will not experience the Latin American–type inflation that many of the most voracious bears predict. The United States could experience runaway inflation if the Fed doesn't slow the pace of new money creation and the U.S. government doesn't get its debts and deficits under control. It comes down to the Economics 101 message of supply and demand.

The fundamental backdrop is that "Helicopter Ben" will drop bales of dollar bills from government helicopters to avoid his current fear of a 1929 deflationary crash. If the dollar continues to fall, then Bernanke's printing presses will only magnify the supply problem of too many dollars floating around the world. The bears predict that as the U.S. twin deficits worsen, the demand for the dollar will deteriorate rapidly and the U.S. economy will go up in a puff of smoke. One weakness to this argument is that all that sloshing liquidity has to go somewhere. As the Fed chairman correctly stated in his November 2007 congressional testimony, "The U.S. markets are the deepest and most liquid and offer the widest range of investment opportunities." If he is also correct that the U.S. dollar is "the standard of value around the world," then look for the hottest economic and U.S. stock market boom in world history as liquidity flees China's bubble economy and the money finds a new home in the United States. In this scenario, who knows how high gold can go?

It truly appears that regardless of which side the economic coin lands on, gold investors and speculators win. If the coin lands on "heads" for the bears, then the fear of loss will push money to the safe haven of gold. If the coin lands on "tails" for a worldwide economic super boom for the bulls, then the inflationary wildfires will light up the biggest boom of all, and that's in the price of gold and the respective gold stocks.

The U.S. Dollar

The U.S. dollar has been falling for the first several years of the twenty-first century, and it appears to be threatening a potential U.S. currency collapse. In 2008, the U.S. dollar hit new all-time lows on the U.S. Dollar Index; it also hit all-time lows against a new competing currency, the euro. This means the United States came close to a dollar crisis. If the dollar continues a constant and persistent form of attrition like it has in the first several years of the new century, then the apocalyptic bears will have their way. Foreign central banks and investors on a global scale will flee U.S. assets for foreign assets, as well as move into gold and gold stocks. The bears have it half right, as money will flock to gold as a safe haven.

To avoid a catastrophe, foreign central banks found a level in 2008 at which they had to support the dollar because our weak dollar hurts export-dependent countries. However, as the dollar strengthens and rallies, it most likely will be a bear market rally until the trade deficit improves significantly from the weak dollar. The dollar bulls point out that this has in fact already happened in 2008 as the weak dollar has significantly helped U.S. exports. However, the weak dollar has also significantly increased the dollar cost of U.S. imports.

The apocalyptic dollar bears are confident of a coming currency crisis. They say with absolute certainty that the United States is heading in that direction because of the twin deficits (trade and budget). Certainly, the national debt is not going to improve anytime soon, as it exceeded $10 trillion in 2008. It is true that the negative compounding of interest on U.S. national debt risks getting completely out of control. The majority of U.S. debt is held by foreign central banks, so we can no longer say that the debt is not a problem because "we owe it to ourselves."

There are many in government who think that trillions of dollars in debts and deficits are just numbers on paper. Untold zeroes that represent the total sum of our nation's liabilities are numbers certainly to be feared. Hopefully, the Obama administration will think differently about the enormity of those astronomical figures of debt and deficits and take serious actions to do something about it.

Protect and Profit

The proliferation of the Fed's paper money creation combined with reduced confidence in dollars by foreign holders is a lethal mix. The eventual hyperinflation will lead to severe economic hardship if our nation is caught in that toxic combination. If this happens in China or the United States, there are only two ways to protect and profit. One is to short stocks and to profit as stocks and markets fall from an economy mired in stagflation. The second is the subject of this chapter—gold. Gold has so many specific catalysts that could come into play, a book would be needed to cover them all. Here are just a few:

- The United States or Israel makes a surprise military strike on potentially nuclear Iran. Oil and inflation will rise, stocks will fall, and gold will soar.

- Another terrorist strike, like a nuclear suitcase bomb or a biological attack, will send stocks tanking and gold stocks soaring as an investment safe haven. At his 2002 Berkshire Hathaway shareholder meeting, Warren Buffett said that a nuclear attack on U.S. soil is a "virtual certainty."
- As the U.S. dollar plunges, central banks worldwide that have been hoarding dollars and selling gold will reverse course and buy gold as they sell dollars, sending gold prices skyrocketing.
- Weak stock, bond, and real estate markets leave few attractive investment options, sending gold prices higher as investors flee to the perceived safety of this age-old store of value to protect their wealth.
- If the U.S. stock market and economy boom as the liquidity train leaves China for its next stop back in the United States, then demand for gold will rise for pure inflation protection.
- If China and India continue to experience rapid growth because of their artificially rigged currencies, their demand for gold will soar. They are already the world's largest consumers of the yellow metal. If the Chinese stock market bubble completely blows up, scared investors around the globe will run to gold. Chinese investors will hoard their gold to protect themselves, as their economic and stock market bubble bursts.
- As long as the world central banks continue to print their respective currencies (as is ever the case), gold has a long way to go on the upside because of the inevitable resulting global inflation. If deflation takes hold after central banks see the results of their folly, gold will be a safe haven for investors as asset prices in stocks and real estate worldwide deflate. Massive inflation will eventually force central banks worldwide to turn off the liquidity spigot, effectively cutting off the oxygen supply, the very lifeline of real estate speculation. I am referring to all the air being exhaled from the lungs of central bankers into the stock and real estate markets, creating huge asset bubbles.

Any investor looking for an inflation hedge should consider both the physical metal and gold stocks. If you are a more conservative investor looking to buy gold stocks, it is best that you focus mostly on the senior gold producers with the bulk of your money you allocate to the gold sector. If you are allocating 20 percent of your total portfolio to gold stocks, I would put 60 percent of that 20 percent total allocation in the largest and biggest producers. The largest producers are companies like Barrick Gold Corporation (ABX), Newmont Mining (NEM), and Goldcorp (GG). Agnico Eagle Mines (AEM) and Anglo Gold Ashanti (AU) are also senior producers, and all of these stocks trade on the New York Stock Exchange (NYSE). I would consider buying these names only on severe corrections because that's the best way to buy gold stocks. Be careful because gold stocks are very volatile and have violent corrections and crashes, even in the context of a long-term bull market.

My guess is that the major producers will consolidate the junior producers, and then consolidate within themselves. Because of this, many of the symbols I give you may no longer exist by the time you read this book. By the way, this expected continual consolidation is another long-term bullish catalyst for the gold stocks.

For those who can stomach extreme volatility, look to the intermediate and junior gold producer stocks. Investors with a higher risk tolerance should consider putting the other 40 percent into a basket of the junior miners. They will spice up the portfolio and be the future hall-of-fame winning stocks throughout the secular gold bull market. Here are some intermediate producers: Royal Gold, Inc. (RGLD), Kinross Gold Corporation (KGC), Gold Fields Ltd. (GFI), Golden Star Resources Ltd. (GSS), Yamana Gold Inc. (AUY), and Northgate Minerals Corporation (NXG). For silver stocks (poor man's gold), check out Silver Wheaton Corporation (SLW), Silver Standard Resources, Inc. (SSRI), Pan American Silver Corporation (PAAS), Hecla Mining Company (HL), Minefinders Corporation Ltd. (MFN), Mag Silver Corporation (MVG), and Endeavour Silver Corporation (EXK). For more aggressive investors and speculators, there are some very exciting, but much riskier, micro-cap stocks in the gold sector that trade in Canada and other countries as well.

Much of the success in investing in these smaller resource stocks results from fortunate market timing, disciplined buying, and lots of luck. An interesting phenomenon has occurred since mid-2007. Prior to this, gold and gold stocks were tightly correlated. Gold went up, stocks went up; gold went down, stocks went down. But we are now experiencing a radical divergence, which may represent a rare and potentially profitable high-risk opportunity. Since mid-2007, the price of gold raced up and then corrected down from its highs, but over that same period of time, gold stocks lagged on the way up and then imploded on the way down, with many juniors falling as much as 75 to 90 percent. There are some good reasons for this situation, but the bottom line is that the stocks have a lot of potential upside, especially as gold launches on its next up leg and credit becomes available again.

Most junior mining stock prices were devastated in 2008. A successful gold bug investor and good friend of mine whom I refer to as "research Bob" tells me that these stocks are down to "irrational extremes," and are "screaming values." Some junior miners that he says "have significant, undervalued, proven resources" are Kirkland Lake Gold Inc. (KGI.TO), Nevsun Resources (NSU), Orezone Resources Inc. (OZN), and two copper miners, Baja Mining Corporation (BAJ.V) and Bell Copper Corporation (BCU.V). Others with "excellent exploration potential, selling for dimes or even pennies on the dollar" are Almaden Minerals Ltd. (AAU), Benton Resources Corporation (BTC.V), Cadan Resources Corporation (CDN.V), Eagle Plains Resources Ltd. (EPL.V), Geocom Resources Inc. (GOCM), Golden Arrow Resources Corporation (GRG.V), and Riverstone Resources Inc. (RVS.V). Remember that these stocks are incredibly speculative and more will disappear to zero than will become big winners, so you've got to own a basket of them, assuming you even have the risk tolerance to go there. For sources of good ideas and likely updates on these junior miners, you might consider the *International Speculator* newsletter by Doug Casey.

Why bother with such tiny companies when they have so much downside risk? Consider the story of Aurelian Resources (ARU.TO). The company was formed in 2001 to explore a large tract of prospective land in southern Ecuador called the Condor Project. It went public in 2003 and by the fall of 2005, the stock had dropped to 40 cents, despite a fair bit of encouraging exploration success. All that changed in the spring of 2006, as Aurelian announced a spectacular drill hole at Fruta del Norte. Since then, they have drilled off a minimum of 14 million ounces of gold, with the stock rising as high as $40 (pre-split), a spectacular 100-to-1 move up.

Such potential rewards don't come without incredible risk, however. In April 2008, the government of Ecuador announced it was suspending all exploration while finalizing new mining laws. As a result, Aurelian's share price was cut in half overnight.

The truth is that once the next stage of the bull market in gold stocks is unleashed, they should all rise and fall together, so diversify into a basket of names to smooth out the volatile ride. The smaller stocks will rise substantially above the majors, but they get crushed much more on the natural crashes and corrections the gold bull market will experience along the way. Again, these names are suggestions, not current buy recommendations. The stock charts must line up with the fundamentals before any stock is to be considered, and gold stocks are very volatile, which means they are very high risk.

Gold and gold stocks are a negatively correlated asset class and will give your portfolio the diversification, as well as purchasing power protection, in the next secular synchronistic bear market in stocks around the globe. Just as stocks have had a long secular bull market, so will the price of gold. The gold secular bull has just started, so it's still in the early to middle innings. Like the secular bull market in stocks, the gold bull market will go into extra innings as well.

To get an idea of what future global stock markets and the current U.S. real estate bear market will look like when the final secular bottom sets in, we only need to look to gold. When I started in the brokerage business in 1988, I was introduced to two gold bug stockbrokers. They both were outright bears on U.S. stocks and bulls on gold. As you can imagine, these gold bugs got squashed as gold did nothing but go down while U.S. stocks basically went straight up, with only a few cyclical corrections. By the time gold was finally forming secular bottoms in 1999 through 2001, most were calling it a near worthless relic of the past as far as an investment choice was concerned. The talking heads on TV would say, "Gold doesn't pay a dividend," and "Endless central bank selling will keep gold prices down forever."

All Asset Classes Are Hated at the Bottom

I can remember gold trading at $253 and the bull channel, CNBC, mocking gold investors at the bottom, while praising technology speculators at the top in 1999. At the bottom, even the gold bulls were embarrassed to say they were bullish. The reason was that this admission meant they had been wrong, and who wants to admit that? Many gold investors had given up because gold and gold stocks had treated them so poorly for so long. Almost no one had much good to say about gold at the bottom, even the worn-out bulls. This will be precisely how stock and real estate investors will be at the next secular bottom in those asset classes.

The headlines will be negative, and investors will be apathetic toward the market. At the next significant bottom in stocks, investors will be depressed and hating both stocks and real estate. More importantly, stocks will be low and cheap, but few will be willing or in a position to even buy them. Gold will be like large-cap stocks today—at the top after a long secular move. Investors will be lining up to buy gold, as Chinese investors reportedly did in 2007 to buy Chinese stocks right at the top before a 60 percent market crash.

Here is an example of there being very few bulls at the bottom as the imploded asset in question is hated. On September 30, 2003, I spoke to a prominent gold analyst on Wall Street. His job was to be bullish on gold so clients would buy gold stocks through his firm, increasing the brokerage firm's commissions. He had plenty of incentive to be bullish on gold and gold stocks so gold companies would do banking deals with his firm, resulting in performance bonuses. Nevertheless, the atmosphere was so bearish for gold back then that even he couldn't say anything positive about the yellow metal.

This gold analyst and I talked about gold often. On a research call I made to him at the start of the bull market, he told me that there was "900 weeks of inventory, so $389 per ounce is a highly unfavorable risk-reward scenario for gold prices." He went on to say, "If gold drops below $350, then 300 tons' worth of speculators will sell and 500 tons of buying from the miners will go away and prices will collapse again." He continued with, "Ron, if inflation does rise, then gold prices will get killed." This was a new one for me. He speculated that the United States might sell its gold that was "collecting dust" at Fort Knox to pay off its debts, and that would devastate prices. He concluded his very bearish view with, "We don't need gold like we need corn."

This negative sentiment expressed by an intelligent and respected gold analyst at a "bulge bracket firm" was exactly how most felt at the bottom as gold was despised. The point is that at the bottom, investors hate the asset that has treated them so poorly. In this case, it was gold after decades of bear market decline. One newspaper article read, "Gold Lost Its Luster" and stated, "Central bank selling has pushed the price of gold to levels not seen since 1979." "Central banks have only sold 5% of their holdings and there are 11 billion ounces of gold on the world market." The article went on with, "The European Central Bank has said it will hold very little gold in reserve. The Swiss central bank plans to sell at least half of its gold reserve. Australia's central bank sold two-thirds of its reserve. Central banks are replacing gold with U.S. government bonds that pay interest." Gold had nothing but downside according to Wall Street and the media. This attitude is worth noting because, no matter what the asset class, the psychology at the bottom is always the same—gloomy and despondent. At the bottom, investors see nothing but downside.

Gold has traditionally traded inversely to the value of the dollar, so we need to look at this reserve currency once again. The U.S. dollar is fiat money. It is money because the U.S. government says it is money, and investors around the world historically had confidence in the stability of our dollar, even though it has no intrinsic value and nothing but government promises backing the paper. When President Nixon made the decision to abandon the gold standard in 1971, he repudiated U.S. government promises to redeem dollars for gold. This gave the Fed a free pass to print as much money as it wanted, effectively creating a bottomless checkbook.

Prior to Nixon's move, each dollar was theoretically backed by a percentage of the country's gold reserves. This limited the amount of money that could be printed by the Federal Reserve and kept the system honest and under control. As Greenspan got his taste of the forbidden fruit of unrestricted money growth, he freely exploded the money supply and committed the ultimate economic sin. As a result, stocks in the late 1990s and real estate early in the new century went wild to the upside due to excessive liquidity. As long as these markets were strong and investors were making more and more of those dollars in rising asset values, why would anyone care? If real estate crashes to a violent death, everyone in America and around the globe will surely care.

An excess supply of newly created dollars under Greenspan's watch found its way into stocks and real estate. Now that the secular bear's spectre has appeared in the new century, U.S. homeowners and stockholders are faced with diminishing asset values stacked against a mountain of debt. If the stock and real estate markets have a severe reversal of fortune rather than a correction, the falling value of the U.S. dollar will be widely recognized as a major global problem. At that point, investors could lose confidence in the dollar, here and abroad, and flock to a more true form of value and real money—gold. Central banks can't create gold out of thin air like they can dollars, so gold will continue to hold its value, just as it has for the past 5,000 years.

Another deep, dark "secret" is that the U.S. and Western European central banks have been "managing" the price of gold (and silver) overtly and covertly for decades, especially for the past dozen years. An excellent catalog of statements by public officials, major studies by well-known companies, and other evidence confirming this is found in an April 2008 speech by Chris Powell at www.gata.org/node/6242. In a nutshell, gold is a monetary "canary in the coal mine." By suppressing the gold price, the central banks have produced the illusion of monetary stability and low inflation. The gold price "management" has been done by swapping and/or leasing and subsequently selling metal into the physical market in order to meet a 1,000 to 1,500 ton (and growing) yearly supply shortfall. Meanwhile, the central banks continue to count this swapped and leased gold as still in their vaults.

The problem is that their limited supply of gold is running low, and to conserve what is left, the gold price is being "managed" at higher and higher prices. In fact, as mine production is falling and global demand is rising, they may very soon lose control all together. In the same way that the late 1960s' "London Gold Pool" gold price "management" failed and led to the gold bull market of the 1970s, so will the even more drastic "management" of our day lead to a generational gold bull market. Price "management" schemes may work for a while, but they always fail. The most basic economic law of supply and demand always wins.

If the U.S. Fed continues its policy of "short-term gain for long-term pain," we will remain on an inflationary path leading to exploding gold values as well as the creation of new asset bubbles. If excess liquidity isn't contained, then asset prices and the smoldering coals of inflation will ignite. The Fed will be forced to follow its late 1970's policy of choking the money supply. This will explode interest rates, and then the New Great Depression of the Twenty-first Century will unfold for reasons similar to the last Great Depression. How could this happen? If an unhealthy boom in unproductive assets collapses, then assets need to be liquidated to reduce the debt burden.

The question is: When this will happen? In late 2007, the DJIA made a gigantic head-and-shoulder top. In early 2008, the DJIA's inflated head at 14,195 got decapitated. These market melt-ups only led to even more new debt creation and uncontrolled excess speculation. If speculators believe the business cycle is dead and the downside is limited because of never-ending liquidity, then new debt for speculative purposes is continually created. This in turn generates new asset bubbles. Eventually, a final melt-up in the market happens and a mighty crash follows.

We saw this kind of speculative feverish melt-up in China in 2007 right before the China CSI 300 Stock Index cratered in 2008. We saw it happen in Japan in the 1980s, and an extensive stagnation followed for Japan's economy. We saw it happen in Nasdaq 1999, but the economy was spared by the new rising real estate market bubble that repaired investors' net worth. We saw the speculative high fever spread from the U.S.

real estate market in 2004 that led to the 2008 subprime mortgage sickness. And, we saw it in 2007 as the DJIA hit all-time highs on a head-and-shoulder top right in front of significant economic weakness and a price decapitation.

In uncertain times, gold is sought as a safe haven for investors to retain value. As the United States has gone through two major asset bubble bursts already in the new century, gold prices have ignited to the upside. In an economy with rapidly rising inflation, all investors must protect themselves from an abracadabra money-creating Fed, by owning gold. Hold on to your gold as a storehouse of value to preserve your purchasing power against inflationary government policies, both in the United States and abroad.

In this book I often refer to the flip side of every coin in every market. There are bullish and bearish viewpoints on every asset class, and they all need to be considered and analyzed carefully. There also needs to be a clear understanding and separation of short-term cyclical moves within a longer-term secular move. From a cyclical point of view, I do need to caution everyone about the price volatility of gold and the U.S. dollar as well. For example, in the first three months of 2008, gold powered on to new high after all-time new high. As it did so, hoards of new hot-money momentum investors began to sit up and take notice of gold for the first time in years, if ever. Some even began to buy gold and gold stocks. Sure enough, in late March 2008, gold experienced a major correction, dropping a stunning $124 (12 percent) in just 9 trading days. It was a very rude awakening to the world of precious metals momentum chasers, who were blown out and burned at the top as stop loss after stop loss was triggered.

By midsummer, gold had licked its wounds, consolidated, and was threatening $1,000 once again as the euro came within a whisker of $1.60. Here's how my friend "research Bob," who has studied the gold market for two decades, describes what happened next:

> A "funny thing happened on the way to the forum"—on July 15th, to be exact. One might speculate that Hank Paulson's secretive meetings with European leaders resulted in coordinated intervention. Suddenly the U.S.

dollar began to go straight up. The Dow rallied from a very ugly low. Simultaneously, commodities of every kind were bombed. Oil and gas were pounded. Central Bank gold from somewhere was marshaled and dumped day after day on the physical market in London (a new pattern). The COMEX paper gold players soon joined in the fun. According to official "Bank Participation in Futures Markets" data, by August 5th "three U.S. banks" added 78,611 short gold contracts (a 1,000 percent increase of 7.8 million oz. or 10 percent of annual world production), while "two U.S. banks" added 27,606 short silver contracts (a 445 percent increase of 138 million oz. or 20 percent of annual world production). Is it any wonder gold dropped $150 and silver $7 (38%) in a few short weeks?

John Embry, veteran gold fund manager with Sprott Asset Management, described this recently as "violent intervention by the paper players." They got the ball rolling in the direction they wanted, and then, as we all know, "an object in motion tends to stay in motion." Long, leveraged commodity funds, facing huge losses and redemptions, were forced to liquidate, resulting in further downward pressure, culminating with the recent, much-publicized blowup of commodity fund Ospraie Management, which knocked commodities down yet another notch.

By mid-September 2008, gold lost 27 percent and silver a shocking 50 percent from their March highs. It's instructive to remember that the same thing happened leading up to another election—of Jimmy Carter in 1976—when gold lost an amazing 43 percent, before rising 800 percent by 1980. Meanwhile, investors have been abandoning gold stocks in droves, with the resulting carnage described by John Embry as "the most depressed prices since this cycle began in 2000."

Lessons to be learned from this debacle are simple, but especially important for precious metals investors. Buy low. Sell high. Never, ever use excessive margin. And always have a short-side strategy to protect your core long position.

Where is the gold market headed now? Well, the artificially induced low prices have created an unprecedented

> feeding frenzy in the huge gold and silver markets of India, Asia, and the Middle East. Even in the United States and Canada, supplies of physical bullion (coins and bars) have all but disappeared. Meanwhile, new mines are not being funded at these low prices, even as older mines are shutting down. Soon, the law of supply and demand will cause the physical markets to trump the paper markets, and the coiled spring will release. Déjà vu, 1976?

The lesson here is simple. Buy gold and gold stocks only on price corrections to their respective long-term uptrend lines. When extreme speculative price spikes occur, maintain a core position, but trim back your exposure on a case-by-case basis and rebuy as the next base forms. This is the best way to maintain exposure to gold as this generational, secular bull market takes a "pause to refresh" before it starts the next leg up.

During this same time period, "everybody and their mother" were also shorting the U.S. dollar through exchange-traded funds (ETFs) and currency markets, driving gold to all-time new lows. For example, I received an e-mail from someone I wouldn't classify as a sophisticated investor by any means, as the U.S. dollar hit new all-time lows: "Hi Ron, I am interested in shorting the dollar; China may start selling them soon. What would be some good vehicles for doing this on E*TRADE?"

Odds were that the U.S. dollar was ready for a significant cyclical upside correction, which also meant that gold would have a price correction. This is because gold, as the alternative currency to all fiat money, is inversely correlated to the U.S. dollar. As the dollar has occasional yet powerful countertrend rallies, then gold, at least initially, will go down. So as the G-8 countries intervene to steady the falling dollar, gold stocks crash and then set up for a good entry point for long-term investors.

The person who sent me the e-mail should have considered shorting E*TRADE's stock (ETFC) instead of looking to short the dollar several years into a decline on the E*TRADE system. E*TRADE's stock had fallen from $26 to $2.84 on the announcement of gargantuan losses from their exposure in the subprime crisis. That 89 percent fall in E*TRADE's stock in three months was much more exciting and safer than shorting the U.S. dollar after it has already fallen 40 percent over the last several years.

Shorting ahead of a crisis can offer profit opportunity and hedge protection for your portfolio.

The Chinese express the concept of crisis using two symbols. The first, by itself, means danger. The second means opportunity. By putting the two symbols together, you get "crisis." My short-side strategy message is all about that, crisis and opportunity.

An e-mail I recently received from another friend summarizes my message in this chapter. This friend is one of the smartest, most successful, and balanced investors I have ever known.

> Ron, maybe all the currencies are going to become worthless, as there really is nothing tangible backing any paper money now. The Fed and Larry Kudlow may talk about little-to-no inflation, but that is not the way I see it. In 1959, I could stay in a hotel in Germany for one dollar and eat a filet mignon dinner on the Kufurstendam in Berlin at a swanky restaurant served by a waiter, not just in a tux but a tux with tails, for $1.25. My wife and I made a one-week ski trip to Austria for $21, which included room and two excellent meals. We made a trip to Stockholm for less than $100. Now these same activities would cost a small fortune. Even a room at a nice hotel in the bush in South Africa costs almost $500! The U.S. dollar is almost kaput. I have a long-term perspective. I can remember when gasoline in the U.S. cost about 20 cents a gallon, and it was difficult to find a person to save $1 a day when I started in the life insurance business in 1962. How does one invest today to protect his purchasing power? Are stocks, municipal bonds, money market funds or real estate the answer? I don't think so, and the government has them all rigged against us with taxes, which the Democrats will make even worse. The Fed and Treasury constantly create more fiat money. If the U.S. collapses, won't the world go with it? They are making our monster debt worthless because the debt is measured in dollars. Not a one of the politicians,

> Republican or Democrat, can be trusted nor can anyone of them wave a magic wand and correct the deteriorating situation. Where does one go to protect one's self? Maybe we should buy canned food, but even canned soup now can cost $2.50 a can.

My friend is no "perma-bear." He is no loudmouth, self-proclaimed genius, one-trick-pony bear always calling for a collapse, so you should seriously reflect on his comments. He started loading up on gold and silver at the bottom in 2001, and is adding to his position on the 2008 commodity crash. He knows that gold will continue to be the best hedge against the inflationary policies of central banks around the globe. In answering his question on where to go for downside protection, I reminded him that shorting stocks is one of the better ways to profit as stocks enter a new secular down phase in U.S. and global markets. It appears that shorting stocks at all-time market highs in 2008 was an opportunity equivalent to buying gold in 2001 at the bottom.

CHAPTER 6

NOTHING BUT DOWNSIDE: THE ROAD AHEAD FOR STOCKS, BONDS, AND REAL ESTATE?

Every prudent investor needs to be aware of the potential dangers that can permanently damage his or her portfolio. *Knowing how to protect and profit from these unknown dangers is the key to being a well-rounded investor.* I believe stocks, bonds, and real estate have nothing but downside coming if any of my predicted catalysts send the economic snowball rolling down the mountainside. *I see it as unavoidable that, at the very minimum, we will continue to experience many frightening periods of extreme downside volatility in these three main asset classes for a very long period of time. As I mentioned earlier, the question is when to short high as well as when to buy low, and therein lies the challenge.*

What if all the newly created money by the Federal Reserve is plowed back into real estate and stocks by foreign investors who continue to find our assets attractive? The result is that our economy will start another false boom built on a foundation of debt. This is entirely possible, as having too many dollars chase too few stocks, bonds, and real estate (asset inflation) is largely responsible for the worldwide boom we have experienced. We have also learned from the dot-com bubble that you never can tell how high is high really. Certainly, the Dow Jones Industrial Average (DJIA) of just 30 stocks can go a lot higher if the U.S. economy avoids a catastrophic meltdown and these newly created dollars by central banks around the globe just keep flowing toward stocks for asset inflation protection. This is why stop losses and a flexibility strategy are crucial in case your bear market assumptions turn into a bull market super-boom.

With the weak U.S. dollar, investors from around the globe may view the United States with a giant for-sale sign on it. Foreign investors may take advantage of their strong currencies and buy U.S. stocks and real estate that appear to be on sale because of the currency conversion advantage these countries would have. However, my contention is that even if the inflationary global asset boom reasserts itself, it will only lead to a much larger *ka-boom* later. Why? Because the attitude of today's worldwide investor is that the U.S. Federal Reserve is the global savior, and will come to the rescue and bail out real estate and stock market speculators whenever their chips get low. *The moral hazard policy the Fed has created and blueprinted for world central banks will not change until a major crisis cleans the system out. In other words, we'll need the Wall Street casino to burn down before the real estate and stock market speculators change their reckless, debt-induced ways.*

Where do I find truths for these bold statements? The United States is clearly experiencing the most significant financial credit crisis since the Great Depression from the "subprime mortgage crisis." As the real estate market has slowed, the pain from the fallout of all those exotic mortgages that were created has come home to roost as evidenced by the Fannie Mae (FNMA) government bailout. We could debate all day long whether the Fed will, or even should, save the day. Under the recent past Fed policy, that won't be necessary because, as I said before, we already know what will happen in any future crisis: The Fed will be there to come to the rescue. "Helicopter Ben" told us this several years ago.

Bernanke demonstrated this to the world with his first discount rate cut on Friday, August 17, 2007, and his continued cuts through 2008. He did this to save the hedge fund speculators and investment banks loaded with mortgage-backed loans, which, in effect, were creating a liquidity crunch. Bernanke came to the rescue of leveraged hedge funds and the reckless mortgage companies that went on a financial high-wire act with creative, exotic mortgages. He bailed out Bear Stearns as it imploded from this leveraged mess in 2008. The Fed has once again provided the safety net for the speculative side of the marketplace, cementing this "moral hazard" mind-set of speculators and investors alike. Then the Fed followed with additional aggressive Federal Funds cuts to provide support to falling stocks. Somehow, the Federal Reserve made it their mandate to eliminate the business cycle from downturns of any magnitude. The Fed believes that recessions are bad and that U.S. and global markets must continue to trend steadily higher. Here's the question I have with overpriced homes and stocks around the globe: What is wrong with more reasonably priced homes, stocks, and less unproductive debt? Why is that so bad? It's bad because we have multiple asset bubbles that the Fed cannot afford to let deflate. This would be contrary to its long-term pain for short-term gain monetary policy.

Just like Greenspan before him, Bernanke is pumping money and preventing necessary economic cleansing. *At this point, I can't imagine anyone ever worrying about future financial high-wire acts with such a wide permanent safety net thrown below by the Fed.* The end result of all this added liquidity will be the eventual spreading of an inflationary wildfire. "Hey, let's go borrow every nickel the banks and credit card companies will loan us so we can go speculate wildly," thinks the naïve speculator. Stocks and the economy could someday hyperinflate with the explosive combination of this moral hazard philosophy and the freely flowing river of liquidity. Look to China's inflating economy and crashing stock market in 2008 for a preview of what I am talking about.

Real Estate Bubble Alive and Well

Let me give you a real-life example of the dangerous psychology created by the reckless Federal Reserve loose money policies. In mid-2007, I went to a real estate seminar to see if the roaring real estate bulls had lost any of their zeal. At this three-day conference, I learned an immense amount about both the mind-set of real estate bulls and their specific strategies. This conference, held in Portland, Oregon, confirmed what I suspected. The gentleman running this conference said he has "never been more bullish on real estate" and this may be the "last great time to buy," as the subprime crisis has created such "great deals" in real estate.

Real estate speculators saw huge possibilities to steal homes from the people who are experiencing foreclosure by the droves. At this real estate conference, we were told to appear right before the courthouse auctions off the family's house and to give the homeowner, or soon-to-be former homeowner, a lowball offer as an alternative to the "nothing" they'll get once the auction takes place. This is just one of the big strategies I learned at this real estate conference, and one I plan on never using for speculative purposes. He also made it sound like they were doing a humanitarian service for these poor folks. If you want to be the generous humanitarian, then tell them that if you flip the house for a big profit, you will give him 10 percent to 20 percent of the profits. Now that would truly be humanitarian to the guy who's going through foreclosure and losing everything.

Here's the part that I found incredible at the conference. The featured speaker said that their goal at this three-day real estate conference was to "get everyone in attendance as far into debt as is humanly possible." They had a whole series on how to get $50,000 to $100,000 from credit cards and use that money to speculate in the real estate market. First, inventories of unsold homes around the nation were rapidly rising, hitting a 16-year high. Second, demand was sinking and banks were evaluating their lending standards. This made the real estate bulls that much more excited. I always thought that rising supply and falling demand was a recipe for lower prices ahead. Maybe we have a new form of "voodoo economics" here that doesn't make sense in the long run, but makes everyone feel great in the short run.

So there you have it—bullishness and debt creation alive and well, even in a severely correcting real estate market. If the Fed does save the market with its rate cuts and bailouts, then can you imagine how much more confident investors and speculators will get on the next correction? *This lack of fear is evidence of the moral hazard the Fed has created.* Whenever this house of cards comes crumbling down, you will want to have a short-side strategy in place as this all unfolds. As I said earlier, there will be only a few ways for the average investor to make money as the tide goes out in the stock and real estate markets. One way is gold and gold stocks on severe price corrections and shake-outs to hedge your portfolio from the inevitable inflation and "worth less" or "worthless" dollars. The other way is shorting overvalued stocks. This is the right combination for this new era of stagflation.

The Most Important Side: The Short Side

The best way to profit from the downside in any market is by shorting or selling short. Selling short is a very simple concept. Nevertheless, you'll hear people say silly things like "You have unlimited risk shorting stocks because stocks can rise to infinity." In theory or in textbooks this is true, but not in reality. Here's my standard response to that statement. *The number one rule in investing or trading is always to limit your losses, whether you go long or short, with predetermined stop loss orders.* If you buy or short a stock for a trade, never ride losses greater than 10 to 12 percent.

When buying a stock, you buy first and sell later, hopefully at a higher price for a profit. Shorting is simply the opposite. In shorting stocks, we sell the stock first, then buy the stock back later—hopefully at a lower price—for a profit. How do we sell something we don't own? We simply borrow the shares from the brokerage firm that has the shares gathering dust in its vaults somewhere. This is a very standard and acceptable practice. Shorting is the only sure way to make money when stocks, oil, China, or any other asset or market is ready to collapse. Understanding this simple concept will provide you with protection and profits in a downside market.

Some of you are thinking, why not short the market with exchange-traded funds (ETFs) like SDS (NYSE) and QID (NYSE) or buy puts and sell calls? Yes, you can do that, but it could be a much more risky strategy—one I would leave to the professionals. The reason is that you've got to be right on the timing of the market drop. With a short-side strategy, you can short stocks that can even fall in a bull market. Let's take a most recent example. As the Dow Jones exploded to new all-time highs, breaking records by the day in 2006 and 2007, many stocks were getting clobbered. The home builders are a great example.

As the DJIA and the Standard & Poor's (S&P) 500 were racing higher and CNBC was highlighting the excitement of new all-time highs and praising our majestic Fed, the home-builder stocks were crashing. These stocks had climbed to such terrific heights that when the real estate market showed just a small sign of slowdown, the stocks were sold with abandon. Of course, it just makes sense that as the industry slowed down, so did the earnings prospects of these home builders. Even though most kept saying, and still do, how cheap these stocks are, they just kept getting cheaper by the day.

In December 2004, Bank of America raised estimates and target prices on Toll Brothers, Inc. (TOL), Ryland Group, Inc. (RYL), Lennar Corporation (LEN), Hovnanian Enterprises, Inc. (HOV), and Centex Corporation (CTX), saying they had "attractive earnings at just 7.6 × 2005 E.P.S." and "continued strength in the fundamentals." They went on to say right at the top of the real estate market, "Margins are likely to increase in 2005 due to continued strength in home prices." The "raise your ratings at the top" and "cut them at the bottom" type of thinking is very prevalent with most analysts on Wall Street. The Bank of America analyst raised the target price on TOL to $65 right as it started its descent to $16. HOV was raised to a $52 target price right before it started heading south to $5. RYL was upped to a $59 target price right before it crashed to $20 and CTX to a $61 target before it imploded to $15. Nice work, guys. When these stocks are down 90 percent and the fundamentals absolutely stink, most of the Wall Street analysts that cover these stocks will finally cut their ratings to a sell. Then you will know these stocks are at, or near, a trading bottom and ready for a rally. Analysts have a buy-high (increase rating and target prices), sell-low mentality (cut rating to sell) that you can use to your advantage.

In 2007, brokerage, bank, and real estate stocks all fell from grace even as the DJIA hit 14,000. Seeing the bank, broker, and builder stocks implode is proof that stocks in weak groups fall in bull and bear markets. The only time I would not recommend shorting stocks is in the beginning of a bull move after stocks have already crashed. Cash is a better hedge if you are nervous and just want to preserve gains versus shorting. Obviously, the best time to be short is in a bear market decline. In this 2007 example, we have evidence that stocks can plunge even as the DJIA and S&P 500 print new cyclical and secular all-time highs. This is contrary to what most investors and market prognosticators think and say on the subject of shorting. *Shorting is the Rodney Dangerfield in the investment world. It is time for shorting to get the respect of a profit protection strategy. You not only can hedge your downside with short positions, but also have the opportunity to make money in down markets.*

The Black Cross

There's one fairly dependable way to effectively short stocks, and all you have to do is go to the Internet and find a site that will give you charts on stocks that include two moving averages, the 50-day moving average (DMA) line and the 200 DMA line. There's a pattern called the "Black Cross" that occurs when the 50 DMA crosses down through the 200 DMA and signals that a stock is ready to severely correct or even collapse. When a stock or market index does this, it means that it is in a clear downtrend and prices are heading south. This works for stocks, bonds, commodities, or any market that's charted. If you are going to buy puts, or an ETF that plays the downside of the major market averages, then look for this pattern to emerge before you do, and use stop losses for protection. When a stock you short goes up against you, so does your short market value in your margin account. This is why you must not let losses go very far or they will get out of control and wipe you out. Trust me—I have had to learn that lesson the hard way. Keep your trading losses to a minimum on all stocks, long or short.

I have one final comment about using the SDS or the QID to get short exposure on the markets. In retirement accounts you cannot short stocks, so an ETF like the SDS that trades on the NYSE is a tool for you to get short exposure on the S&P 500 in an individual retirement account. So as the S&P 500 falls, the SDS will rise, but again, market timing is very difficult and risky so use it for hedging versus speculative purposes.

When we discuss the long side of the market and stocks, we will address the Golden Cross. This is just the opposite of the Black Cross. Find stocks that are doing the Black Cross and do some fundamental homework on the company and its industry. Short the stocks in the industry groups that are falling out of favor and you have the perfect combination of winning shorts in boom or bust, bull or bear markets.

Your Edge Is on the Short Side

Whether you are a professional or an individual investor, the best side of the market to gain an edge on Wall Street is the short side. This is because there is so much tainted research on the street that most analysts are barely on top of the companies that they recommend. Most analysts are very aware that it's the investment banking side of the business where the money is made. So research analysts must keep their employer's top-paying customers happy, and those customers are the investment banking clients, the very stocks the research analyst covers.

If an analyst is covering a company he has lost confidence in, chances are very high he will have to look the other way and keep a buy rating on the stock even if he feels it should be a sell rating. Analysts have learned from negative reinforcement that they better keep positive on the stocks they cover or face a backlash from those companies, or from the investment banking arm of their employer.

Analysts will also get cut off from needed access to management once they turn bearish on a company they cover and say anything negative about the stock. The brokerage firm that this analyst works for will lose any possibility of investment banking fees from his employer's top-paying customers. Any analyst expressing negative comments on the stocks he covers effectively hurts his boss, who signs his paychecks. His boss will also decide on the size of the year-end bonus the analyst receives, and again this is mostly based on the amount of investment banking fees that the firm earns throughout the year. This is an unspoken understanding from a regulatory standpoint. This is the main reason why brokerage firms have 90 percent of their recommendations as buy versus sell.

Unless you have access to the analyst directly, the research reports by Wall Street analysts are practically worthless because you don't know what they really believe. They are indirectly paid to be optimistic and to keep their investment banking clients happy. The best way to do that is to put out glowing reports that say "buy" or, worse yet, "strong buy." The reason behind this is that commissions have imploded on Wall Street to the advantage of institutions and individual investors, but to the disadvantage of the brokerage houses. When institutions can trade for under one penny per share in commissions, it's tough for a hedge fund manager to pay a broker multiple times above that unless the broker provides you great ideas and access to initial public offering (IPO) deals. This is especially true as Wall Street research has become so distrusted since the dot-com bubble burst, where analysts had strong buy recommendations on stocks all the way down to the bottom.

In 2000, many dot-coms had buy ratings from analysts even though they were ridiculously overvalued and soon-to-be permanent residents of the bankrupt Internet stock graveyard. When the technology stocks eventually crashed and there were no more opportunities for investment banking fees, many analysts dropped their ratings to hold or sell, right at the bottom. On Wall Street, "hold" means "sell" and "buy" means little more than keeping their investment banking clients happy. Since the investment banking fees are one of the few remaining high-margin areas for brokerage firms to make money today, they'll do whatever they have to in order to protect this last remaining area of high margins.

The good news for any institutional investor, like a mutual fund or hedge fund manager, is that they have direct access to any analyst with whom they want to discuss the covered stock idea. These analysts do not want their most prized clients reading a glowing report they wrote on a stock they really don't like and have the manager go buy the stock. They risk having the covered stock blow up in the manager's face. The backlash would then be harsh for the analyst, as the hedge fund manager puts the analyst and the brokerage firm that caused him this pain in the "penalty box." That basically means that the brokerage firm will lose trading commissions and the analyst will be blacklisted, at least temporarily, for making a bad research call on the stock.

Personally, I can't see how anyone could work under such a lose–lose situation. The client loses with poor research, the analyst loses with a bad reputation, the brokerage firm loses with ticked-off clients, and obviously the covered company who ultimately disappoints loses, so no one looks good.

The advantage fund managers have on Wall Street is that because most institutions understand this situation, they call the analyst directly to find out if the analyst truly likes the stock before they even read the report. I can remember, as a hedge fund manager, reading a glowing report on a stock that I wanted to load up on for our fund after I read the report. I called the analyst, who worked for Hambrecht & Quist (H&Q) at the time, to ask a few questions, and he said, "Ron, throw that research report in the garbage." I said, "Why? It reads like a table-pounding buy." He laughed and said, "Ron, throw that report away. The company is an important investment banking client. Need I say more?" Between institutions and analysts, this is all well understood.

Essentially, this means that individual investors who don't have access to Wall Street analysts get shafted as they read these tainted research reports, buy the stock, watch it fall, and never know they've been had. This is where you, as an intelligent investor, can get an edge with some independent homework because most of the Wall Street research is compromised and geared so positively. Ultimately, this leads to the stocks trading above true value with such positive coverage on the street, increasing the odds that at some point these stocks will fall hard, as they are very high and overvalued. Having so many overhyped investment banking buy reports on Wall Street has created plenty of great short candidates.

The question is: How do you know which of these stocks are the tainted stocks you should sell short? The truth is that the majority of Wall Street research is published with little attention paid to market timing. Have you ever noticed how a Wall Street analyst will have a "strong buy" on a stock at $50, then the stock blows up on a bad earnings report and goes to $20? What does the analyst do? He cuts it to a "hold" and, in rare cases, a "sell" after the stock has already gone down. This buy-high, sell-low pattern creates huge opportunities for everyone because, ultimately, Wall Street analysts put in tops and bottoms in stocks. They are by nature most optimistic when the news is great and most pessimistic when news is bad.

Later, when the news turns good, they usually have to wait before they change their mind and their negative rating. Typically, they wait until the news is so great they are almost forced to go from a "sell" or "hold" to a "buy" rating right near the top, or at the very least, after the stock has long advanced. *Buy high, sell low on Wall Street is your short-side strategy of short high and buy low, hence the opportunity.* You'll also know that when an analyst downgrades the stock and investors are selling, it is likely the stock is now on the lower end of its price range and will eventually put in a bottom. Here is where you watch for a base to develop. This is the buy-low, sell-high part of the short-side strategy. As a general rule, it is far better to be a buyer when an analyst downgrades a stock to a hold rating, and a scale-out seller when an analyst raises a stock to a buy or a strong buy.

I don't want to paint all analysts in a bad light because some of my best friends on Wall Street are analysts and they are great at what they do. A good analyst is worth his weight in gold, and you can ask any money manager to verify that statement as truth. The fact of the matter is that predicting where prices of stocks are going is one of the most difficult jobs. Making money trading those price moves is an even harder job, so finding a manager who can do that consistently is better than gold.

Another way to spot your short stock picks is to do your own fundamental and technical work on interesting stock candidates. Most hedge fund managers have their own in-house research to do just that. In fact, hedge fund managers hire the best analysts on the street to work for them. This phenomenon also leads to poor Wall Street research as the best analysts join the hedge fund world. As an individual investor, there is easy access to information from independent research and company web sites that are full of all the information you could ever want. As an investor, you can call competitors or visit their web sites, or sometimes it's easy to do your own fieldwork to get an edge. Here's a real-life example of what I mean.

Commonsense Research

In 1992, Snapple Beverage was a high-flying stock after its IPO. Most of the analysts covering the stock had buy ratings with thoughts that Snapple would be the next big brand name like Coke or Pepsi. I could see that insiders were selling and the stock appeared to be overvalued. The stock chart also looked like it was at the top and ready to fall. I decided to do some fieldwork, and I went to various shopping centers and convenience stores and checked their iced teas. I noticed, week after week, that competition was intensifying as more and more new brands of teas were crowding Snapple for shelf space. I tried these competitive teas for myself, and found them to be as good as, if not better than, Snapple.

This was a couple of years after Snapple's very successful 1992 IPO, so their tremendous success quickly attracted competition. When I called many of the bullish analysts about this detective work, they laughed and seemed unconcerned because they had so much confidence in the brand name. Again, for the analyst, it's better to look the other way or risk not getting the investment banking fees from a secondary stock offering or some of the insider stock sales on their trading desk.

Then I called some beverage distributors and asked questions. I discovered that wholesalers were getting overstocked because of the intense competition. This meant that Snapple was likely to face an inventory problem. These simple store checks I did on this one-product company in a new-era industry were invaluable. It gave me the confidence and conviction I needed to go against Wall Street bullishness, even as conditions were obviously worsening. This stock was a great short going into what I refer to as a Stage 4 Decline chart pattern. In a short period of time, the stock tanked from near $30 to about $10 per share on excess inventory issues.

After the stock got pummeled, Quaker Oats came in and bought Snapple Beverage for $14 in 1994. Interestingly enough, you could have then covered Snapple and gone short Quaker Oats stock because this problem didn't go away soon. This acquisition ultimately became a major drain on Quaker Oats from the intense competition and inventory problems in the iced tea category. In fact, on March 28, 1997, Quaker Oats agreed to sell its Snapple juice and iced-tea business to Triarc for $300 million. This was $1.3 billion less than what Quaker Oats paid for it in 1994. That's what I call capitulation or giving up. This capitulation from Quaker on Main Street is no different than the capitulation of investors on Wall Street. Small investors typically sell at the bottom and "give up" as they capitulate.

From the Hottest IPO to Bankruptcy

Boston Chicken's IPO shot up 143 percent on the first day of trading in late 1993. When BOST went public, it had a trailing price-to-earnings ratio (P/E) of 344 and traded 45.2 times book value. Even with these obviously absurd valuations, analysts loved the story. The research I read on the stock was very bullish, and many believed that BOST was going to be the next Kentucky Fried Chicken success story. The only real research anyone needed to do on Boston Chicken was to get some of their takeout food. I did and vowed never to return. This lack of repeat customers is exactly what caused Boston Chicken to go bankrupt in November 1998.

The competitive pressures and the drop in repeat customers left the company unable to meet its debt obligations. The franchisees couldn't make the interest and fee payments on the debt. BOST dropped from $40 in 1996 all the way to $0.31 per share, and they eventually filed Chapter 11 bankruptcy in 1998. This is a classic example of one of the many commonsense short picks that still litter Wall Street, presenting opportunities for the savvy investor.

A Little Homework Can Go a Long Way

There are many reasons, apart from investment banking conflicts, why the research you read from a brokerage firm, in which short opportunities can be found, may be tainted. In 1994, a friend called me about a stock he thought might be a great short idea. He said he had heard this particular short idea candidate had been advised by a consulting firm that its main product was "worthless." A company with a worthless product is obviously a very exciting short idea, but one that's not easy to find. This stock was called Pacific Animated Inc., the stock symbol was PAID, and it traded around $10 per share.

When I heard this, I was excited because these kinds of short ideas are what I call "titanic stocks." When the bad news gets out on these stocks, they sink to oblivion, never to rise again. I called the brokerage firm that covered the stock and the analyst I spoke to had very little worthwhile information to share. I then called the chief financial officer (CFO) of PAID directly. With small companies like PAID, the CFO usually takes on the investor relations role as part of his job, and even the smallest of investors usually have access to upper-level management. Simply tell the CFO you are an active private investor and that you are researching the stock and have just a few questions.

When I spoke to the CFO, I referred to the buy recommendation I had in hand. He asked me politely if I could send the report back to him, a request I had never heard before. When I asked why, he said that "the report was written by some tiny brokerage house back east and it was a bogus report, mostly for their clients who owned all the stock." He told me he didn't want anyone seeing this report because the "claims were false" and that the hot product they were referencing had not even been fully developed. He went on to say, "We don't even know if there is a market for it once development for the product is completed." He continued, "Those earnings projections are ridiculous and unrealistic" and that the company "won't earn a penny and is years from a developed product." I couldn't help but laugh and wondered why in the world this company was public in the first place. I told the CFO I would toss the report in the garbage and suggested he and all the insiders dump all their stock before it collapsed.

This is an extreme case, and with the new Sarbanes-Oxley laws, corporate insiders are extremely cautious about what they say because of so-called Fair Disclosure rules. The point here is that much of what you read is garbage, and that's where most Wall Street research belongs.

Many investors are able to take a more proactive approach to their investments. In today's world, you can trade your own stocks cheaply at discount brokerage firms, especially with information so accessible on the Internet. Some of the research you read can contain valuable information, but don't always trust the recommendation or the opinions. Just stick to the facts.

Most investors still use an adviser or broker. Stockbrokers at the large houses earn either commissions from selling or fees from gathering assets. They are not responsible for doing their own research, so you can't depend totally on their advice. To place trust in their recommendation is placing total trust in someone else you don't know, perhaps regarding a company about which you know even less. The research that most brokers get from their firm may be tainted or biased, so go with a broker or an adviser who does an intense amount of independent research work on his client's behalf. The right professional with well-researched timely stock picks is worth every dollar you pay him.

Since the stock boom of the 1990s, the preferred investment choice is mutual funds. Since most mutual funds underperform the S&P 500, you can't depend on picking the 20 percent that do beat the market. Another option that has become very popular is to use hedge funds. They are much more flexible than mutual funds and are often quite secretive. Hedge funds can't advertise, so you mostly hear about the ones that get publicity after a blowup. You are likely not to go there assuming you even had the required net worth to invest with Wall Street's cream of the crop. So where does that leave you to make outsized returns in bull and bear markets? *It leaves you with the smart decision to take responsibility for your own portfolio and to work with advisers who manage money with stocks, long and short.*

Remember, there are two sides to your portfolio—the long side and the short side. Both sides need to be full of well-researched stocks with defined stop losses for protection. You must have a short-side to your portfolio as the market goes south into a protracted bear market decline. This is why I am such a proponent of hedge funds because they trade and invest on both sides of the tape. This shorting of stocks and markets provides a floor to the market as short players are future ready and willing buyers when the market corrects or crashes.

The other reason to have a short-side focus is that your short side can perform in bull or bear markets, whereas the long side will perform only in bull markets. In a bull market you can still short stocks because many stocks have their own private bear markets. There are, however, more bull market periods than bear markets, and bull markets tend to last much longer. In addition, bear markets have such fantastic bear rallies that you must always prepare to have a long side with a short side. Lastly, the short side will be the best way to profit as the market repeats either the deflationary 1930s or the inflationary 1970s, one of which appears to be a certainty if radical fiscal and monetary policy changes aren't made soon. Always be hedged for protection, and that primarily means to always have short ideas for bull and bear markets or have your money with a professional manager who goes long and short.

My Personal Stint as a Research Analyst

At Viewpoint Securities (VPS), I started to write research reports for institutional clients with my institutional tag team partner, Emile Lemoigne. I would do the research and write up the target prices, stops, the story, and the catalyst, as well as the risk. We would then time-stamp the report and send it out to our database of hedge fund clients and prospects. Then Emile would call the hedge funds to pitch the story and solicit the trades. We were written up in the August 2003 *Oregon Business* magazine with a picture of Emile and me in our trading pit. There were days Emile and I got so beat up by the market it felt as though we had just done a stage dive into a violent "mosh pit" of punk rockers.

My picks helped us open doors to new institutional clients. I formally initiated over 100 stocks (long and short), and I had predetermined stop losses and target prices on every report on all of my picks. The *Oregon Business* article on August 23, 2003, said, "VPS likes Microsemi Corp. (MSCC) and began coverage in February when the stock was worth $7.99. The stock was hovering at $14.89 in mid June and closed at $16.92 on July 11." The interesting thing is that we found Microsemi completely by accident.

We were researching a local company that had Microsemi as their biggest client. During our initial visit, management told us that Microsemi's business was "on fire." I went to research MSCC and found a completely undiscovered stock and initiated coverage. The magazine went on to say, "Shortly after VPS chose this cheap stock as a buy recommendation, CIBC World Markets and Adams, Harkness & Hill followed suit." We laughed when we read this line, because the editor made it sound like they initiated after they saw us do so first. The truth is that the Adams, Harkness brokerage firm didn't know us from Adam, and neither did many others for that matter.

We also recommended many shorts and did quite well on some of those picks even though the market was at the bottom. The same magazine also highlighted our worst short pick, which was Harley-Davidson (HOG). We got stopped out on the stock with a small predetermined loss, but my thesis was overall correct, just three years too soon. I learned a valuable lesson shorting Harley-Davidson. Rarely, if ever, short a stock where the company's corporate name is tattooed all over the bodies of the investors who use the product of the stock you are shorting. Investors buy and hold tattoo stocks until death, just like their tattoos.

We had one pick where Emile went out to do a road show with the management team to present the stock to institutional investors. He sat down with a hedge fund manager who was from Russia to pitch one particular micro-cap stock. In the first five minutes, the manager said to Emile in a thick Russian accent, "We need small-cap stocks like bullet in brain." To this day when Emile tells me this story of "bullet in brain" in the heavy Russian accent, I crack up into tears. Emile said that meeting with the analyst ended quickly, as no one on the street wanted small-cap stocks in 2003. Many were calling them "small crap" stocks because of how crappy portfolio managers had been treated by them in 2000 through 2002. This, of course, was a great opportunity to buy them, as most small stocks were all at the bottom. In 2008, small and micro-cap stocks have been smashed and have valuations comparable to 2002, 1994, 1990, and 1987. Patient and farsighted investors might begin to look in the small- and micro-cap sector for undervalued stocks to own.

In 2002, Emile and I were very bullish on the gold and silver stocks. We recommended Pan American Silver (PAAS) and Silver Standard Resources (SSRI) when they were single-digit stocks. Those stocks traded into the $40s at their highs in 2008 before they finally collapsed. Emile and I couldn't get one manager to buy a gold or silver stock. They thought we were absolutely nuts to look at gold stocks. The charts were great and our thesis was simple. We wrote that the Fed was "exploding the money supply" and that "future inflation fears" would drive these stocks higher. We also wrote that the stocks were "hated by everyone" so they had to be at the bottom. Finally, and most importantly, we featured the charts, which all looked fantastic heading into a Stage 2 Advance. In 2008, these stocks all went into Stage 4 Declines.

In 2007, gold stocks exploded to new highs as investors and hedge fund managers finally took those stocks seriously. Wild speculators also jumped on board for a ride. Unfortunately for the hot-money speculators, hedge fund managers, and the gold bugs, gold and silver stocks put in blow-off tops in early 2008. As the gold stocks crashed, the gold bugs got squashed. The good news is that gold stocks will have severe corrections and crashes even in the context of a long-term secular bull market.

We got involved with another micro-cap stock named Metron Technology (MTCH) that had fallen from $10 per share to $0.50 a share. We couldn't believe it, as the stock's collapse was due to a careless comment during an institutional conference call by the soon-to-be-ousted CFO of MTCH. I had an analyst friend over at Merrill Lynch who covered the stock. I called him and asked him his thoughts, and he said, "Ron, at 57 cents per share, this stock is trading like a bankruptcy candidate, and that just isn't likely to happen." Emile and I reinitiated coverage on this stock and bought it for our clients. I say reinitiated because we had originally recommended the stock long before it collapsed and we were fortunately out of this name after it hit our target price. We watched it crater all the way from $10 to $0.50, sitting on the sidelines, that is, with none of our monies invested.

I asked an investment adviser friend to look at MTCH. He took all of my information and read it very carefully. The next day he came back to me and said, "Ron, I wouldn't touch this stock with a 10-foot pole; you're nuts buying this piece of garbage stock!" He was a Certified Financial Analyst (CFA), so who was I to argue with him. I said, "These guys are a great takeout play because they have good technology, a solid reputation, and it's a dirt-cheap stock." He didn't bite. Three days later, MTCH wound up getting bought out at $5.50 per share (+100 percent) by Applied Materials. We cleaned out our entire position on the news. I guess this is an example of one man's garbage being another man's treasure.

In 2003, Emile and I were recommending the oil stocks, saying we thought that the main objective of President Bush was Iran and not Iraq. Our thesis was, and still is, that Bush had always had his finger on the trigger and he was itching to pull it right up until the day he left office. We figured that whether he pulled the trigger or not was not important—either way, oil stocks could go up on just the fear of such an event. This was a good call, and oil stocks rallied into early 2008. The oil stocks have performed fabulously, but it wasn't until 2007 that our Iran fear thesis really started to surface in the news. I think Bush had his eye on Iran from day one, but he never anticipated the blood-bath civil war that would ensue in Iraq.

As a result of the regulatory overhaul after the Nasdaq crash, the rules changed to such an extent that I stopped formally covering stocks all together. It was a good run while it lasted, and some of the calls Emile and I made were epic, but we had some big blunders as well. Some calls were embarrassing, or just too early, but we had stop loss protection on every pick we had in print.

If I were an analyst today looking out to the future winners, I would be recommending selected longs in Nasdaq that look to be putting in bottoms. I would continue to look for selected overvalued short picks in China. In addition, be alert for opportunities in gold stocks on violent shake-outs because central banks around the globe will continue to print money excessively. I would never recommend chasing gold stocks up because their nature is to have periodic crashes like we saw in the third quarter of 2008.

Oil stocks saw the top in 2008 and will continue to be some of the great short opportunities for the next few years as they likely repeat past down cycle moves. As an analyst today, I would have a more global perspective and look to cover stocks from all around the globe and cover multiple asset classes that are noncorrelated as well. Remember, the charts and the fundamentals must line up, and predetermined stops must be placed before any long or short positions are initiated.

If It Sounds Too Good to Be True, Then It Is

Hedge funds are an unregulated pool of assets in which only high-net-worth investors can participate. I am a big believer in hedge funds because they will be the only funds standing if the coming raging inflation leads to a cut in the money supply, crashing bonds, and then into an extended period of stagflation. However, hedge funds are very aggressive, and when you are going for outsized returns, blowups inevitably happen. Also, there are a rare few that are just outright frauds.

In May 1997, a client of mine told me he was ready to "put a big pile of money" with a hedge fund manager in Portland, Oregon, who had unbelievable returns. He sent me a fax showing the guy's performance numbers and I was amazed. This commodity fund manager showed a 422 percent return in 1995 and a 171 percent in 1996, and was apparently averaging 15 percent per month in 1997. I told my client that I was very skeptical and that he needed to be careful. He told me that he trusted this young guy because he had gone to college with his father. He was insistent that I go meet this guy on his behalf before he put his money in. I was thinking at the time either this hedge fund manager was the next Jesse Livermore or he was a fraud. My other thought was that if he was that good, then maybe I would put some money with this manager, too.

I called the fund manager and explained the situation. I told him I was going to be in Portland and asked if I could spend 30 to 45 minutes with him. Surprisingly, he agreed. My analyst, Rodrigo, and I took a drive from Bend, Oregon, to his office in Beaverton, Oregon. He had a secretary out front to greet us. I thought it was strange that his office door had no windows to see inside his command center. We were shown into his big, secluded, oval-shaped office that had computer and TV monitors everywhere. Quite frankly, it was a very impressive sight to behold. I asked him how he was getting such fantastic returns. As we asked him more specific questions about how he got these returns, he started to act very nervous. He could instantly tell I knew some things about the very high-risk strategies he was employing and that I wasn't buying what he was telling me. After about 20 minutes, we were both uncomfortable, and Rodrigo and I left.

On my way home, I told my client that I wouldn't put any money in that money manager's hedge fund and was unconvinced about the high-risk strategies he was employing. His stellar and consistent performance seemed just too good to be true. My client went ahead and gave this manager a third of what he was originally going to invest because 15 percent per month was "just too good" for him to completely pass up. Less than two weeks later, on June 3, the *Oregonian* newspaper headline read, "Court Order Shuts Down Beaverton Firm" and, "The Commodity Futures Trading Commission files a complaint accusing investment fund of losing more than 75% of the assets in the fund." It appears that this bit of homework saved my client some serious money by doing a little due diligence. *The moral of the story is: Do your own homework, and if it sounds too good to be true, it probably is.*

How about a stock that has "risen 8200 percent", and whose prospects "have never looked better"? The May 15, 2000, issue of *Fortune* magazine had Cisco Systems' (CSCO) CEO John Chambers's face plastered all over the front cover. The 13-page piece on Cisco asked the question: "What if you were stranded on a deserted island and could own just one single stock, what would it be?" The answer: "CSCO rose 8,200 percent and that would be the stock." The piece went on to say, "No matter how you cut it, you have got to own Cisco's stock." The piece made you think a repeat performance was coming. This was obviously way too good to be true.

At the time, Cisco was the most valuable company on earth with a $555 billion market valuation. Cisco was trading at the sky-high P/E of 193 times earnings. By July 2001, only one year after the *Fortune* cover, Cisco's stock had plunged 84 percent. The Nasdaq and Internet bubble in 1999 was way too good to be true.

A Nasdaq 2000 kind of froth happened in China in 2007, and Petrochina Inc. (PTR) reached a market valuation almost twice the size of CSCO at the top in 2000. Chinese stocks built one of the biggest bubbles in the history of mankind. Petrochina was two bubbles for the price of one to short, China and oil, so the stock got cut in half in 2008 as a result. We witnessed Chinese IPOs skyrocketing as "1.3 billion Chinese came on-line to dominate the world in growth." This sounded even better than the technology revolution talk right before the dot-com bubble burst that took those stocks down 90 percent to 100 percent.

The worldwide consensus is still that China ultimately has nowhere to go but up. I believe Chinese stocks have nothing but downside pressure, as these stocks had their final blow-off in early 2008 as speculators rushed in to buy them ahead of the 2008 Olympics. That speculative rush was a signal of the top in Chinese stocks. Chinese stocks greeted the Olympics with a crash similar to the beginning of the Nasdaq 2000–2003 crash. If China had a face, then *Fortune* magazine would likely have put it on their front cover right at the top in early 2008.

From Fame to 60 Minutes *in Shame*

A broker friend of mine introduced me to a fund manager, whom I will refer to as Burton. Burton and I became acquaintances, and we shared ideas several times a week. He was making money with some of my technology stock picks at the time. He was so happy with me that he introduced me to his wife. Burton mentioned that he wanted to put me in his will in case "something happened to him." I would then become executor of his "multimillion-dollar estate," as well as part of his will. The more I got to know Burton, the more nervous I got.

He started to send me all these astrological predictions on how the moon and the stars were lining up for a market crash. He sent me multiple candlestick charts on how the crash was going to happen any day. He then went out and bought tens of thousands of dollars of IBM puts with several brokers on the street, expecting this stock to crash along with the market. I was bullish at the time and told him I didn't think this was a great idea. Soon after he bought those put options, IBM came out with a record-breaking better-than-expected earnings report. The stock then rocketed higher, and his options immediately were nearly worthless.

Later, I found out that Burton was threatening to sue my broker friend who bought some of the puts for him. He alleged that his put-option plays were "unsolicited," and that he actually wanted to buy calls rather than puts. I had proof from all the charts he sent me by fax, with his notes, that this was not the case. I sent Burton a return fax saying not to contact me ever again.

My broker friend said that a few weeks later he received a notice that Burton apparently died in a terrible car crash, and that the death was being disputed by the insurance company. Several months later, Burton was featured on *60 Minutes.* It turned out that he was running organized crime money and when he lost, he faked his death. He dug up a dead body out of a graveyard and put the body in his car and pushed it over a huge cliff. The problem for Burton was that the teeth of the dead body didn't match up to his. He was hoping to scam the insurance company to pay off the mob from his disastrous astrological market call. They later found and arrested Burton.

The good news for my friend was that he didn't have to defend his lawsuit any longer. The moral of the story is to know who you are talking to, and don't trust the moon and the stars to make market calls. His astrological market call was like an asteroid from outer space smashing into his portfolio.

The Other "Trader Vic"

I have another too-good-to-be-true story, which relates to a well-known trader named Victor Niederhoffer. I bought Victor's book, *The Education of a Speculator* (John Wiley & Sons, 1996) in 1997. The title of this book was fitting because Victor himself was ready for the market education of a lifetime shortly after the book was published. My assistant portfolio manager at the time saw this book lying on my desk and asked for my thoughts. I told him I was enjoying the book but that, based on what I was reading, Victor was a "blowup waiting to happen."

Victor claimed to be the "best commodity trader in the United States" and managed $130 million in his hedge fund. When the Asian crisis happened in October 1997, excessive speculation in Thailand trounced him. Victor then saw a great opportunity to make a bullish short-term bet for a U.S. stock market rebound. Victor's hunch here was correct, but his bet was crazy. He was so confident that he took most of the remaining assets in the fund and sold puts short, betting on a market rebound. His put-option play was too early and, according to Victor, "the entire equity position in the fund" apparently "has been wiped out."

Victor's market call for a U.S. rebound was correct, and he may have cleaned up if the market had rebounded more quickly. If you are correct on your call, but wrong on your timing, then you risk a wipeout when you are using leverage like puts and margin.

Apparently, Victor has made a comeback, but not the unlucky investors who lost $130 million on Victor's hedge fund blowup. Many hedge funds target outsized market returns. To get those kinds of returns, managers have to take on greater risk, and often that involves the excessive use of leverage.

There are some great hedge fund managers, so I don't want these examples to scare you away from hedge funds. Take, for example, the true "Trader Vic." Victor Sperandeo is the author of *Trader Vic—Methods of a Wall Street Master* (John Wiley & Sons, 1993). He also wrote *Trader Vic II—Principles of Professional Speculation* (John Wiley & Sons, 1994). The true Trader Vic is one of the all-time great money managers, and his books are excellent. His number one rule is "preservation of capital." His philosophy comes down to disciplined risk management and having the patience to "put the odds heavily in your favor" before putting on any trades.

Another Wall Street legend is Julian Robertson, probably the best hedge fund manger in the world in his time with the Tiger Fund. My money management style is very similar to Robertson's philosophy of a traditional long/short manager. He has stocks on both sides of the market like I preach throughout this book. These are some of the best hedge funds to invest in, and they are typically called market-neutral funds. They rely on their stock-picking abilities rather than pure market timing.

If you are not comfortable with hedge funds, you can invest with mutual funds that go short as well. Mutual funds that also go short didn't start to sprout up until the bottom of the market in 2002, which was bad timing. The performance numbers of the funds that short look similar to a long-only mutual fund that started at the top in early 2000. This was another sign that the market was making a bottom as mutual funds that go short started popping up to take advantage of all the market bearishness in 2002. The important fact is that you must have some short exposure or hedge protection in your portfolio, a short-side strategy. If the market comes crashing down and you are long only, you risk a wipeout. You should have stocks or funds that win in case we enter a new long-term secular bear market. In essence, you need to become your own hedge fund manager, even if you are not doing the investments directly. This means thinking like a hedge fund manager who looks at the downside risks and for short opportunities in the marketplace.

In my opinion, the greatest money managers are hedge fund managers, and the greatest hedge fund managers initially address the catastrophic downside risks, making preservation of capital their highest investment objective. If the DJIA, the S&P 500, and the real estate market replicate the Nasdaq 2000 crash, then you must approach every investment this way.

I have one more story to end this chapter. There was a small brokerage firm in the early 1990s. Let's call them STO Securities (STO). They were known to be a firm run by organized crime. They did IPO deals that required the IPO buyer to buy more shares in the aftermarket, but did not allow them to sell their allotment of IPO shares. STO kept their IPO deals to themselves so they could control the supply and demand for their stocks. The Securities and Exchange Commission (SEC) wanted to shut them down and tried to force STO to make some changes. One change was that they had to syndicate at least 30 percent of the IPO to outside brokerage firms. Cleverly, they had some of their brokers leave and form a second brokerage firm that took most of the other 30 percent. In order to make it look like they were complying with the SEC, they gave a few thousand shares to several outside firms as well. STO gave some stock to a Denver brokerage firm that did a lot of IPO deals. An older broker in his 50s from the brokerage firm called STO and convinced them he would be a good partner. He got an allocation of 5,000 shares of the IPO with the understanding that he would keep the shares and buy 10,000 more in the aftermarket. This helped push the IPO stock shares artificially high.

One particular IPO deal came out and went up threefold in price on the first day. A couple of months later, STO was holding a due diligence meeting in New York City with a new IPO company, and was simultaneously having a closing party for IPO deal number one. They invited the Denver broker who was allocated the 5,000 shares of the first deal to attend. Thinking he was getting into the next hot deal, the Denver broker readily hopped on a plane and went to the New York City meeting. Partway through this extremely rowdy meeting, the head of STO got up and started making some introductions. He introduced the Denver broker, who rose and went onto the big stage. As the broker stood there, the STO guy changed the story and said, "This is the guy we gave stock to on our recent IPO deal." The crowd all applauded and chanted approvingly. Then the STO guy says angrily, "He told us that he would hold the stock, but he lied to us and he sold it!" He then asked the crowd of rowdy mob brokers, "What should we do to this lying "piece of s**t broker?" (This scene could have been in the movie *The Godfather*). The crowd then turned violent and chanted "Beat him, beat him up!" The head STO guy agreed and, with several fellow mobsters, started to physically kick the shaken broker around, right on the stage. As this was happening, the crowd continued chanting, "Beat him."

This poor broker was apparently the only seller away from the two sister firms, so they knew for certain that he sold the 5,000 shares of stock he was allocated. This illegal practice went on for years, until the SEC closed STO and put many of those STO guys in jail. The broker wasn't seriously hurt, but his recurring dreams were not pleasant. The crazy shenanigans that take place on Wall Street never cease to amaze me.

CHAPTER 7

THE SHORT SIDE: THE ONLY SIDE TO MAKE MONEY IN A BEAR MARKET

As the legendary investor Bernard Baruch once said, "Bears make money only if the bulls push up stocks to where they are overpriced and unsound." I will add to this statement: there is only one way to profit when overpriced stocks fall back to earth: Sell them short when they are up on stilts, and buy them back when they fall. Stocks crash all the time in all kinds of markets, bullish or bearish. Long-only investors who are not shorting stocks are missing out. *By not having a short side to your portfolio, you are totally dependent on the market rising in order to make money.* You are also exposing yourself to the risks and pain of market corrections and meltdowns. *Shorting can reduce risk, and significantly increase your profit potential.*

Many in the media attack short-side traders and investors. They think of the short side as the dark side and all the folks who go short as part of some evil empire. On the contrary, shorting can help put a floor on the market when stocks are crashing. Shorts are ready and eager buyers on corrections or crashes, so short-side traders provide added liquidity to the market. This added liquidity actually lowers the downside risk in the market and makes the market that much more efficient. There's something very exciting about selling a stock short, watching it fall to earth, and then buying the stock back for a profit. The best part is that declining stocks tend to fall on their own weight, so they fall faster than they rise. By incorporating short selling into your investment strategy, you become a more balanced and sophisticated investor and you can make money doing what most will not even attempt. Shorting is no more difficult than going long, yet the majority of investors see it as a losing strategy. Many hedge fund managers today, who are expected to short stocks, have pursued long-only strategies because of their experience in the recent long secular boom in the stock market. The process of shorting a stock is easy—you just hit the short button versus the buy button on a stock you think will fall. The hard part is making money shorting, but it's not any harder than trying to make money on the long side. Both are hard to do.

The problem for all investors is that when the bullish tide goes out and you are only long stocks, you are fully exposed to the downside risk of the marketplace. Institutional investors call this "swimming naked." Shorting not only reduces your downside, but also the volatility of your portfolio. The secret is to do it safely and properly, and this book will map that course. The biggest benefit of shorting is that it hedges your downside from a complete wipeout in future bear market environments. For proof, look at past wipeouts that happened in 1929–1932, 1973–1974, 1987, 1990, 1994, 2000–2003, and 2008.

Creating a short side to your portfolio also allows you to sleep better. You won't worry about tomorrow's headlines: "Stocks on Wall Street Had a Severe Sell-Off on Friday" and "Traders Fear What Monday Morning Will Bring." CNBC's description of the market won't bother you. You certainly will not be one of the angst-driven traders who are frantically selling. Even if you are a buy-and-hold mutual fund investor, an aggressive day trader, or a hedge fund manager, you must pay as much attention to the short side of the market as you do the long side. *Remember, the long side is the wrong side in a bear market.*

It's certainly possible that an unexpected downside event could take stocks down 50 percent to 70 percent. Watching Nasdaq stocks, which the new-era bulls were in love with in 2000, going from triple-digit prices down to single-digit prices should convince you that shorting is practical and profitable. In 2000, I was shorting Sun Microsystems (JAVA) as it raced to over $100 per share. Today, I find it astounding that eight years later, the stock is still in single digits. My favorite is JDS Uniphase (JDSU), which went from $150 all the way down to single digits. JDSU and many other technology stocks got back to double digits simply because the stock prices sank so low the management teams of these companies decided to reverse split their stock to get the price back above $10 per share.

The New Bubbles: "China.com" and "Oil.com"

Do you think that what we saw happen in Nasdaq 2000 was a once-in-a-lifetime experience and that a short opportunity like this will never occur again? It is partially true. Yes, we may never see the kind of speculative fever we saw in dot-com stocks. However, look at the spectacular rise in China and oil stocks and the shorting opportunities they presented in 2008. They both go hand in hand. I say this because $50 from $145 came out of oil partly due to slowing demand from China, so as China's market and economy implodes, oil and oil stocks will continue to follow.

"China.com" saw a speculative fever similar to what we saw at the height of Nasdaq in 2000. Stock trading accounts exploded in China right at the top. A record new-account-opening day was set on May 28, 2007, when 455,000 new accounts went live, boosting the total to over 100 million. China's day-trading culture took the Nasdaq 1999 playbook and ran with it. Fortunately, there are plenty of Chinese stocks traded on U.S. exchanges to go both long and short. The China Fund (CHN) on the New York Stock Exchange (NYSE) rose from $3.50 in 1998 to $52 in early 2008 (unadjusted for splits and cash distributions) and then it got cut in half later in 2008. On the Nasdaq, BIDU, a Chinese Internet play, went from $45 to $420. BIDU then went back down to $200, and then up near the old highs again before crashing another 125 points in 2008. If you can time these upside and downside moves, you can take full advantage of both sides of the market in China. This way, you can take full advantage of these volatile moves, long and short, versus being a long-only investor riding these stocks way up and then all the way back down.

In 2005, the Chinese chairman for Citigroup Global Markets Asia observed at the Wharton China Business forum that "the four major state-owned banks in China are technically insolvent from the staggering levels of non-performing loans." In two short years after that statement, the largest of those "insolvent banks" launched the largest initial public offering (IPO) in history ($22 billion) and wound up with a larger market capitalization than Citibank. Chinese banks make loans to money-losing state-owned factories to cover the losses of selling below cost to America. They also make loans to build office buildings that sit unoccupied in many parts of China.

China doesn't play fair. They rigged their money by devaluing it by 40 percent in 1994. This gave China an unfair advantage over their Asian neighbors, the United States, and Europe. It appears that China followed the Enron playbook. When China's questionable accounting and economic practices are exposed, the Chinese economy will follow their stock market and start to implode.

China set up technically to short in 2008. Now that China's bubble is bursting, look for it to repeat Nasdaq 2000–2003. I suggest you get prepared to get short Chinese stocks on big bear market rallies, as the charts have now aligned with the questionable fundamentals. Investors will have an even greater opportunity to make money on the short side once Wall Street stops funding "China.com" through the IPO market and hot money turns tail and heads home. The red-hot China IPO market in 2007 and 2008 should be a movie you have seen before in the 1999 dot-com stocks. In "China.com," investors are buying minority positions in grossly overpriced Chinese companies. The movie I call "China.com" will have the same ending as its sister dot-com bubble show in Nasdaq 2000 before it hits the absolute bottom.

China has experienced unrest and riots that they call "mass incidents." According to a commentator on CNBC, there have been 87,000 riots forcing China to raise workers' pay. This erodes China's price advantage with their low-wage workers, and it will only get worse. With access to the outside world via cell phones and the Internet, workers' demands for higher wages and benefits have increased. The deflation story on Chinese exports have quickly turned into an inflation story as prices have risen across the board in China. As their comparative advantage in low-cost labor declines, China's economy is suffering and ultimately will implode. Recent disclosures of health and safety shortfalls in imports from China have already caused a dramatic effect on trade.

The United States has built state-of-the-art factories to cut costs and increase productivity, closing the gap on China's predatory pricing practices. However, American CEOs of giant U.S. companies continue to move production and jobs to China, eliminating jobs in the United States. This is shortsighted and self-serving (bonuses, options, etc.). They have also used the savings to announce stock buy-backs, which drive up the value of their personal shares. Will U.S. workers revolt? Who could blame them? Imagine being laid off when the CEO makes tens of millions of dollars at your expense. This short-term gain strategy will cause long-term pain as the air quickly comes out of the China bubble. China will be forced to eventually let their currency float freely. When that happens, the currency revaluation will take their artificially depreciated currency advantage away from them completely.

On May 23, 2007, even Alan Greenspan recognized a bubble in China as he noted, "There is going to be a dramatic contraction at some point in China." As Fed chairman, Greenspan had claimed he couldn't recognize the Nasdaq and real estate bubbles he created in the United States, but he was mysteriously able to recognize the China bubble before the air started coming out. With so much created liquidity and so many resulting bubbles, why do people still call Alan Greenspan the greatest Fed chairman of all time? I just don't get it. As China's runaway speculation stops, investors will continue to pull out, Chinese stock prices will drop even further and crash, and perhaps lead to a depression. Stock markets worldwide will be rocketed in the process, but the U.S. economy might benefit in the long run as many manufacturing jobs return to America.

China's pollution is a growing problem affecting the entire world. Many athletes worried about breathing the dirty air at the 2008 Olympics, and some pulled out before the games even started. Over time, the world will be exposed to the breadth of the problems in China. China's one-child policy is also creating a future demographic problem. The air has already started coming out of this puffed-up, overhyped, and heavily polluted nation that many still think is the new economic superpower.

A Heavyweight Past His Prime

China is like Mike Tyson when he was in his prime. There was so much power and excitement, China's economy appeared invincible to most. As Chinese stocks get knocked out like Mike Tyson did by Buster Douglas, everyone can now see the true weakness, and the prospects for "China.com" will change drastically. Like Mike Tyson after his fall, China will never be the same again.

The Dow Jones Industrial Average (DJIA) and the Standard & Poor's (S&P) 500, however, are like aging prizefighters past their prime. They are viewed with great respect, but their legs are weak and wobbly. One good hit like they took in 2008 and both could fall like a column of loose bricks. The S&P 500 and the DJIA sprinted to all-time highs in 2007, ending the secular bull market run. The steroid injections of the tax and rate cuts wore off and the apparent strength started to weaken in 2008. Now the new records have been all but forgotten. So many stocks are at such high valuations appearing as short opportunities that it's impossible to keep track of them all. There will always be stocks bid up to insane values, ready to come crashing back down to earth. Look to the oil stocks on bear market rallies as that bubble bursts after an insane and speculative rise.

The Nasdaq market is more like Rocky Balboa. In the movie *Rocky,* Sylvester Stallone plays the role of a boxer who can take incredible hits but manages to get back up off the canvas. *Rocky* would be Nasdaq early in its life cycle, always overshadowed by the champions DJIA and the S&P 500. *Rocky II* is Nasdaq in the mid- to late 1990s, where it took the crown from the champion DJIA (Apollo Creed). At the top in 2000, Nasdaq went down on the canvas, similar to Rocky in the first bout in *Rocky III* against Clubber Lang. Rocky went down hard, as did Nasdaq in 2000–2003, but was set to make a big comeback in the next fight. Nasdaq, after getting bloodied up in its worst beating in its short history, is set to make a comeback. Nasdaq is still down nearly 80 percent from when it got hit hard in 2000 and 2001. Nasdaq technically looks like a potential double bottom, and, at the very least, appears to be setting up to outperform those aging prizefighters, the DJIA and S&P 500.

In Nasdaq you'll find the most exciting growth companies in medical, computer, biotechnology, Internet, telecom, and the future new exciting industry groups and companies. Nasdaq is also full of the best short ideas as well. Many of the young, exciting companies face new competition, and they stumble hard. Like a lumberjack yelling "TIM-BERRRR," these stocks crash like a falling giant redwood.

There are exchange-traded funds (ETFs) that move inverse to markets like Nasdaq, which can make money and hedge your portfolio as the market goes down. The point is you must protect your downside by having a short-side strategy to your stock market investing or trading mind-set.

If you have a short-side strategy to your portfolio and we have a Nasdaq 2000 repeat, or if Israel strikes Iran and stocks tumble, the short side in your portfolio will provide you with the protection and opportunity for profit lacking in the portfolio of most long-only investors. *Good years or bad, bull markets or bear, boom or bust economies, you can make money because you are on both sides of the market, LONG as well as SHORT.*

A Brief Look at the Past to Remind Us Why

Just think back to the pain when stocks in all markets plunged in the Nasdaq 2000 crash, followed by the additional fear after 9/11 struck, causing stocks to plunge even more deeply. With short-side stocks, your pain at the very least would have been lessened compared to a long-only investor. The other benefit of having a short-side strategy is that at the bottom you will have additional cash to add to the long side of your portfolio. But, more importantly, you will be less likely to panic and sell at the bottom.

One of the important investment and trading disciplines highlighted in this book is risk control, where stop losses will prevent you from riding stocks down more than 10 to 12 percent and never down 50 to 80 percent. This 10 to 12 percent can be as low as 3 percent if stocks are bought or shorted close to the ideal pivot point, or the best place to put on the trade. This means buying stocks in the price support area of a base, or where a stock has held its price. On the short side, this will be selling in the price resistance area of a top, or where the stock hits an upside ceiling. This way you will be closer to the point where you should stop out of a loss. If the price you bought falls below the price support of the base, then you are out. If the price of your short rises above resistance of the top, then you are out. The closer you are to these pivotal price points, when entering buys or shorts, the less of a percentage loss will be taken on the stop if you are wrong. Let's discuss why we need short-side exposure based on past market environments.

In 1994, interest rates were rapidly rising and stocks and bonds were sinking, generating rampant fear. Those who had short-side stocks were less impacted and more profitable than 95 percent of all investors that year. Merrill Lynch did a study in late 1994 that showed 50 percent of Nasdaq stocks were down 40 percent or more that year. That means you could have shorted half the Nasdaq market in 1994 for huge profits. That most certainly would have lessened the pain from the long stocks that were down in your portfolio.

How about 1990–1991? When Iraq invaded Kuwait, investors sold stocks in the fear that the world's fourth-largest army was set to take over the Middle East, causing frenetic rises in oil prices. Long-only investors, mutual fund holders, and anyone else without shorts got crushed during that sell-off. Investors heavily on margin that year were completely wiped out as the correction in stocks was so fast and violent that new margin calls were issued daily. The pain that investors experienced was totally unnecessary because a short-side strategy would have minimized their losses and resulted in nice gains instead.

During this time, a client named Sven walked into my office as his account was up big. He wanted to double up on his gains by going on margin. I had very few margin accounts at that time and told him that leverage can work both ways. He signed the margin papers and instructed me to "double up" on all his stock positions. It was a few days later that Iraq invaded

Kuwait. His portfolio got crushed. He had one stock called Lattice Semiconductor (LSCC) that he doubled up at $18 per share. The stock fell to $5 so fast in the market sell-off that he couldn't believe it. At $5 he was forced to sell to meet his margin calls created by all his crashing stocks. LSCC had $4 per share net in cash, and the company was a leader in their field. Knowing the stock was dirt cheap, he was still forced to sell to meet his margin calls. When a large percentage of investors are forced to sell like this, you have what I call a "hock-the-house buying opportunity."

When stocks reverse course, they sell off hard and fast. You can see the advantage of shorting in times like these, as it can result in fast and furious profits. You are also lowering the risk against long stocks you don't want to sell, by shorting weak and falling stocks. This achieves excellent risk-adjusted returns, delivering above-market-average returns with lower risk. Most hedge funds are focused on risk-adjusted returns by going long and short.

Let's go back to 1987 and relive the sudden slide that created the fear and loss that investors went through. I was a margin clerk for Merrill Lynch. By the time the year was over, many margin investors had to send money into the accounts just to bring their accounts back to zero, their losses accelerated so fast. Investors who were only long stocks or mutual funds saw their portfolio drop between 40 percent and 60 percent in just a few short days. The news that was coming from the floor of the exchange in October 1987 was that stocks were having the worst crash since 1929, causing investors to panic and prepare for a New Great Depression that never happened.

These past examples show the benefit of having exposure to the short side of the market. Can you see how you could sleep better at night knowing that you (or your investment adviser) have safely and conservatively hedged your downside for protection? Just as having insurance on your home is important in case there is a fire, *short-side stocks are the CRASH INSURANCE for your portfolio, and the most important side when the market severely corrects or crashes.*

During the 1973–1974 bear market, actual losses to common stocks were even greater than they appeared. Inflation was accelerating through this period, so real losses were greater than the nominal loss of 58 percent. Owing to inflation, investors suffered a real inflation-adjusted loss of 71 percent through the 1970s, not much less than investors experienced during the Great Depression. As inflation rears its ugly head, you need exposure to gold, which is the ultimate hedge against inflation. You must have a short-side strategy as stocks entered a new secular bear market in 2008. Cash reserves on the sidelines will just lose value when dollars become worth less as prices rise. Can this happen again? The market must have feared this possibility when commodities of all kinds hit all-time highs and the dollar hit all-time lows before reversing course in 2008.

In 1929, as prices began to fall sharply, companies all across the country were forced to cut wages. Disappearing wages from lost jobs and a crumbling economy caused widespread repossessions of automobiles and a wave of foreclosures on homes. The economy imploded as stocks crashed and investors were wiped out. Suicides also became common for men who lost everything and couldn't face their families and deal with the despair and the shame they felt from their losses. The Fed confronts a similar fear in 2008 as it desperately attempts to keep the financial system liquid.

Now let's fast forward from 1929 to 2007. An economics reporter for the BBC stated on November 5, 2007, "A wave of foreclosures and evictions is about to sweep the United States in the wake of the subprime mortgage lending crisis." I have no idea when the real estate market will finally bottom or begin a recovery, but the point is valid regardless of what happens. Stocks in 1929 were bought with 10 percent down on margin. Today, homes have been widely bought for speculation with little or nothing down. It is entirely feasible that a 1929-type event could happen again due to overleveraged real estate. The Fed is fighting this possibility fiercely to prevent such an occurrence. Even if the Fed does hold off such a calamitous event, it is possible it could happen sometime down the road as debt continues to pile up against further inflated assets. If that were to happen, wouldn't you be glad to have damage control to your portfolio ahead of any such calamity? Of course you would, and that's at the heart of this book and my short-side strategy.

Why Worry? All Dips Are Buying Opportunities

Prior to the 2008 market collapse, there was less fear than there should have been. Investors had been conditioned by a long-running booming stock market with minor bumps and bruises along the way. Most investors believed that if they just held on long enough, bought the dips, and didn't panic, they would come out fine in the long run. The year 2008 has shown you why now it is more important than ever to have a short side to your portfolio, as well as to your mind-set.

It is now clear that no matter how you analyze it, stocks' long-term secular bull market that began in 1982 is more than likely over. If real estate values were to go from weakness to an outright crash, then the mortgage debt is large enough to create the New Great Depression of the Twenty-First Century.

We have had several cyclical sell-offs and mini-bear markets over the recent secular boom years in the DJIA and the S&P 500, as were mentioned earlier. Those were cyclical bearish moves within the context of a long-running secular bull market. That means we may be at, or close to, a new secular move where prices have a long protracted downside in stocks. That would be very bad news for long-only investors.

The good news is that just like the secular up-move we have had since 1982, we will also have mini-bull and mini-bear markets during the new secular bear market that could last 10 to 20 years if history is any guide. I say good news because with a short-side strategy you will navigate more smoothly through all of this just like buy-and-hold investors have ridden through the secular bull market over the past 25 years. This no-brainer buy-and-hold approach will leave you feeling brainless if you do not recognize that the stock market does not just rise.

For evidence of this, let's look at the peak in 1929. Twenty years after 1929, stocks were still down 58 percent, in what must have felt like a lifetime of misery. It took until 1954 to return to former highs on the DJIA. Then we had a new secular up-move until it climaxed in 1968, and it took until the early 1980s to finally bottom. Once again you would have felt like that was a lifetime ago, as you lived through the oil and the dollar crisis of the 1970s with the pain a bear market brings with it.

When Ronald Reagan became president, he cut taxes sharply, invested heavily in the military, and invested money to stimulate stocks and the economy in a new secular uptrend. Ronald Reagan, like FDR before him, had the good timing to come into office as both the economy and the market had approached natural secular bottoms that economic busts create. This is how stock markets find a bottom; an economic bust wrings out all the excess the previous boom brought on, and a new healthy uptrend begins.

That bull market was longer than we have seen in the past due largely to the Greenspan money supply explosion, which caused asset inflation in both stocks and real estate. This should open your eyes wide to why having a short side today may be more important than at any time in your investment life. Understanding how stocks and real estate reached such incredibly high levels of valuation should be an "aha" moment for you once you study the situation more closely. Extremes beget extremes, so the long down cycle ahead could get ugly.

With this understanding, you should never look at stocks, the dollar, and real estate the same way again. You will stay safe and profitable in the coming secular bear market if you deploy a successful short-side strategy. *As the sun sets on the 1982–2008 secular market and moves into a prolonged bearish trend, you will want to have an intelligent strategy to see it rise again. The potential economic darkness is not something to be feared, only something to prepare for, because the sun will shine once again when the dark times end. It always does.*

The Other Side of Your Short

To better understand why there is so much opportunity for you on the short side, let's look at the psychology of the other side of a market call, the other side of your short-side trade. This involves a person's buying what you are selling, who believes the exact opposite of you. They believe that the stock is going up and they will make money owning the stock you have shorted.

I will give you an example of the other side of a market call. After a very big year in 1995, I was still bullish and predominantly buying stocks. The market was great that year in an environment of extreme bearishness on the part of the investing public. The

Federal Reserve was raising interest rates in 1994 and early in 1995 to squelch inflationary pressures. When my hedge fund started in January 1995, I could see the light at the end of the rising interest rate tunnel. There were so many cheap stocks in 1995, and sentiment was so bearish, that you almost couldn't go wrong being long. All great bull market bottoms start to lift off when investors are scared and stocks are cheap, which was how most felt at the end of 1994 right before the bull market launched in 1995.

I did business with Lehman Brothers, whose chief investment strategist was Elaine Garzarelli. She was one of the few vocal bulls I was aware of at the time. Lehman Brothers fired Elaine at the bottom of the market and hired Katherine Hensel to replace her. The reason was that Elaine was just too bullish and obviously wrong and Katherine was very bearish and obviously correct (bull vs. bear). Katherine was featured in the investor's corner of the *Investors Business Daily* newspaper that year explaining her bearishness. She, like most investors at the time, was looking in the rearview mirror for her forecast. She was concerned with inflation and feared "some skids or accidents" in the market. The only accident I recall that year was her recommended portfolio allocation of only 40 percent stocks at the bottom, in front of a huge bullish move starting in early 1995. Market timing is difficult, but here it was evident. Katherine, the bear, had her clients selling stocks as bulls like Elaine were on the other side of those trades buying.

The market bears see risk to the downside, and the bulls see blue skies ahead. Another point with Elaine versus Katherine is that pure market timing can be deadly to your portfolio and career. This is why every investor needs to look at both sides of their portfolio, long and short, and have a short-side strategy. *By being short as well as long and addressing the downside, an investor can minimize the need for perfect timing to consistently make money.*

Vista 2000

I am going to give you an example where I was on the wrong side of the trade. In this story I was on the long side of a stock idea with the symbol VIST.

Let's get back to the psychology of the long-side buyer in a stock that is going down. In February 1996, two brokers I did business with were recommending I buy a stock called Vista 2000 (VIST) which had been a big winner in 1995. VIST had risen from $2.50 per share to $10, and the financial forecasts were so explosive that $20 per share seemed like a slam dunk. Vista 2000 designed, developed, manufactured, and marketed consumer products in home safety, housewares, and convenience, as well as for the travel and outdoors markets. My brokers both told me that very smart money was buying this stock, and I listened. I called the chief financial officer (CFO) of Vista 2000, and he confirmed all the wonderful current earnings momentum and the bright future outlook. So I enthusiastically bought the stock around $10. The stock rose and, as my style dictates, I bought more stock, averaging up my position.

My psychology was that smart money guys were buying and the CFO was very positive on Vista 2000's current and future prospects. I was only taking the word of the CFO and my two brokers and I didn't do further research. I was buying on the assumption that the information I had heard was correct.

After a few weeks of watching the stock work to $15 per share, something very unusual started to happen. Dan, my partner at the time, noticed huge blocks of selling hitting the bids on the stock, like someone had just learned something awful and wanted out at any price. I immediately called the CFO and he sounded cautious, even nervous, directly opposite of his enthusiasm a few weeks earlier. So Dan started to sell as fast as he could as I was giving him the thumbs-down sign while I was on the call with the CFO. The stock was gapping down all the way to $11 as we were aggressively selling. Then our worst nightmare happened: The stock was halted from trading and we were stuck with the shares we were not able to sell—over half our large position. I called around the street to get a handle on what was happening; all kinds of rumors were flying around.

Vista 2000 had a decent short position in its stock. Sometimes the shorts will spread rumors to scare the longs out of their stock and force the stock down. One rumor was that Vista 2000 was cooking their books and the company's profits were actually huge losses. Another rumor was that the management team had gone down in an airplane crash. Unethical short traders spread false rumors when they are ready to do a "bear raid" on a stock to drive the price down. I knew we were in big trouble—this stock may never open again. If you are short, this is a dream come true. If you are long like I was, you are looking at a potential 100 percent loss.

Two days later, news hit the tape that management was holding a conference call preopen, and then the stock would reopen for trading. Relieved, I hoped the fear and rumors would be extinguished by that call. Then maybe the stock would not gap down 50 to 70 percent at the market open like I feared. The next day I got up really early to get onto the conference call held by the CEO of the company. To my surprise, he enthusiastically told everyone on the call how terrific things were at the company. He even mentioned that a new buy recommendation might be coming out shortly from a very large brokerage house on Wall Street, creating even more hope for the bulls on this stock. The call was over and the stock opened at $9.75, down from $11 where the stock was halted.

We immediately started to sell as the stock, to our surprise, rose to $11 again. At that price we sold our very last shares and were slapping each other high fives because we averted a total disaster. After we finished selling, the same two brokers called me and told me they were buying with both fists. I realized that we had sold all our stock to these two brokers. I asked why they were buying and they both mentioned that the buy report to which the CEO alluded would send the shorts who spread the false rumors running for cover. I told them I was out of the stock and that being able to sell was an early Christmas present.

One of those brokers called me back a few days later when the stock sank to $8 per share, wanting me to buy back the stock I sold, as he was averaging down. I told him I thought Vista 2000 was going lower and that we should be shorting the stock. A few days later he called me back and told me that the stock at $5 was a "no-brainer" and he was "doubling up his position" for his clients. One week or so later he called me, as VIST was now at $3 and said that he had "no choice but to hold on and buy more." He told me it should bounce back to $6 and his averaging down would get his clients to break even.

He said, "Ron, the stock can't get much lower than this," and he was averaging down again. The guys who were short this stock were selling short VIST to those investors and brokers riding this "slippery slope of hope."

A few days later the stock got an "E" attached to it, so now VIST was facing the prospect of being delisted from Nasdaq and going to the pink sheets to trade. On May 13, 1996, the Securities and Exchange Commission (SEC) launched an informal investigation of Vista 2000 and the stock was at $2.75 per share on that day. Not long after, the stock went to $0.50 per share, where it was temporarily halted yet again, and this time fell all the way to $0.09 per share before it bottomed out.

The psychology on a falling stock is that at $8, $5, and $3 per share it must be a great buy if it was $15 only a few weeks earlier. The psychology of the short investor is that the stock is falling like a knife so they pile on and short even more. The shorts are thinking about riding the momentum down for huge profits as long-only investors ride their losses and, worse yet, average down.

In hindsight, I am embarrassed that I ever bought a stock like Vista 2000, but at least I had enough sense to cut my losses and move on to the next idea. This stock turned out to be a great fundamental short, as well as a technical one on the charts. Yet I was on the long side of the trade. In this case, the long side was the wrong side.

When I received Vista 2000's "Hot Product Catalog," it was full of flashlights, canteens, travel cups, and squeeze bottles. Had I waited for my investor's kit before I bought this stock, I would have wondered how Vista 2000 was putting up huge earnings numbers when they were selling such low-margin, highly competitive "hot products." They should have been more imaginative with their products. I laughed as I glanced at their glow-in-the-dark catalog of squeeze bottles and "solar-powered radio sun visors." I half expected to see something like a beer-filled hat with a long straw for drinking Budweiser at ball games. My favorite product was the "tropical colored glow-in-the-dark fly swatter." Imagine that!

Remember, this was an example of a short stock idea in the heart of a rip-roaring bull market. *Short ideas that can fall in bull or bear markets not only boost your profit potential, they also cut your risk dramatically if the market falls apart. Having stocks long and short for bull or bear markets is at the heart of my short-side strategy.*

Run for Cover: The Dreaded Short Squeeze

As a hedge fund manager, I am expected to short stocks, and I enjoy doing just that, except in the blow-off stage of a bull market, like what happened in 1999. However, shorting can be very risky, and there are times when you can get caught in a "crowded short." A crowded short occurs when a stock that has a very large short position is in a stock relative to the company's outstanding float. These stocks can be hard to borrow to even be able to put a short position on. The reason you get into a crowded short is that the stock seems to be obviously heading toward a crash. These "no-brainer" stocks can leave you feeling brainless (but not painless) if you get caught in a short-squeeze play.

A short squeeze occurs when a heavily shorted stock, for whatever reason, is bought by the shorts scrambling for cover. Typically, it's when the stock starts to take off and the shorts panic and run for cover. The pain of the rising stock is just too much to bear, and the shorts climb all over each other trying to get flat on their short. Then the word gets out that the shorts are being squeezed, and the long players jump on board to buy, only increasing the pain of the traders who are short. All this buying pressure sends the stock screaming higher until the price gets to a point that the longs start to sell and the more savvy short players add to their position.

Here's an example of a short squeeze I found myself in. On May 10, 1996, I started to short a company called Copytele (COPY), a stock many short-side speculators knew well. The stock had a $500 million market valuation with no sales and big losses, trading at $12.50 per share. The insiders were also selling their stock, hand over fist, so I followed these smart money insiders. As I researched the stock, I knew it was a future single-digit stock, or even a future bankruptcy candidate. What I didn't know was that everyone else saw this and they were expecting the same result.

Just after the short position had been established, the stock decided to shoot up. This painful event happened on May 5, 1996. I immediately put in my buy to cover stop loss orders from $13 on up, and the stock just kept rising. I was finally able to cover at around $15 per share for a quick but painful loss. The stock wound up going to $18.50, up $3 on the very next day. The stock continued to go higher still and I was relieved I was out. However, by the end of the year it was down to new yearly lows and I kicked myself for getting into this squeeze in the first place. This happened because many of the shorts got spooked as it was rising and covered the stock to cut the loss and the pain.

After getting caught in a short squeeze, many short players are afraid to go back in and try again later, and this is what happened to me. This filters out the weak shorts and keeps the strong short players in. In this case I was the "weak hand" who got stopped out for a loss. The longs who were squeezing the stock higher knew the stock was overvalued, so they wound up selling to the covering shorts for a profit. The smart money longs usually don't come back to the stock because they know it's not one to own, except for a short-squeeze trading opportunity. Eventually, the stronger shorts get control of the stock as the longs stay away, and down the mountainside it goes. To my amazement, COPY was still trading 11 years later. Its market value was still high, at $100 million, even as it traded below $1 per share.

The Dreaded Buy-In

Remember that when you go short, you must find the stock to borrow to build your position. In April 1996, a friend of mine named Mark was a semiconductor analyst for a major Wall Street firm. He was about the best analyst I knew at the time. He was so good that I would immediately research any stock idea that he gave me. After a series of visits with some technology companies he clued me into Integrated Pack STK (IPAC). This stock was very thinly traded, and it was very difficult to find stock to borrow and get short. Mark explained that this company had a product that he felt would become effectively worthless because of some competing technologies. My ears perked up. He was calling me from outside of the IPAC headquarters. I asked him if he had just visited the company. He said, "Ron, they won't let me in the building." I asked him why, and he said, "I think they are hiding from me." He even told them he was interested in initiating analyst coverage on the stock and they still would not let him in. Obviously, something was dreadfully wrong at IPAC. The stock was $10 per share, and it appeared to be putting in a double-top stock pattern after rallying from $5.50 just a few weeks earlier.

This looked like a gift and my lucky day. I borrowed all I could and shorted the stock. Unfortunately, the word got out somehow to the guys who were long on this stock and they decided to run me in. Immediately after I put out the last shares short, the stock started to rise. I realized I was the only seller, so when my final sell order was completed, the stock started to lift. I was now getting sweaty palms because I was thinking the stock was about to collapse. Then I got a call from the prime broker of my hedge fund telling me the stock is on a buy-in. This meant that I had to buy the stock back in the market and deliver the shares back to the firm I borrowed them from. This buy-in situation is a catastrophe for shorts in stocks that are illiquid like IPAC.

I went in to start buying back the shares, which was mandatory to meet the buy-in. There were no sellers for me to cover—none! The stock continued to rise until it hit $12 and I was down 20 percent on day one. I knew that if they had cornered the stock, they could take the stock up 20 or 30 points in my face. That kind of a loss was a frightening thought as I had no ability to cover my short position.

The next day I woke up early and waited for a seller. There still wasn't one. I started buying and the stock started climbing again. I was feeling sick at this point. Finally, around noon that day, I found some sellers around $14 and was able to get flat on my short. It was a sizeable loss, but all I could feel was the relief of getting out. At my very last purchase of the IPAC shares, I put in the absolute top on the stock. The worst part is that initially I had to cover against my own will. I basically created my own stop loss when I was forced to buy the shares in the open market, moving it higher as the long guys ran me in. The message is clear—never short thinly traded stocks.

Liquidity is king, so when shorting, stay with stocks that trade a good deal of volume, and stay away from those that don't.

Meanwhile, I had Mark telling me that the stock (IPAC) was going to $1 per share and that this was a "buy-and-hold short idea." The stock literally never looked back from where I covered as it proceeded to drop to Mark's $1 target price in January 1998. It was a helpless feeling as I watched the stock go all the way down and there was nothing I could do. If there are very few shares to borrow on a thin stock, you worry about the buy-in, or you can't find any stock to borrow and short. This story is a great illustration of some of the perils of shorting. Forced buy-in is one of them. Inexperienced investors need to be very cautious about short selling, so go very slowly or employ the services of a professional. I recommend letting the experts do it for you in a professionally managed portfolio.

The bottom line is to be careful shorting thin, illiquid stocks, as well as heavily shorted stocks. The pain of a buy-in, or a short squeeze, is why initially you want to go slowly into any short-sale position. If you charge in headfirst as I did, you risk finding your head in a noose. That's where I found myself as those longs on the other side hung me out to dry. Knowing these perils ahead of time will make shorting that much less hazardous a strategy for you. Regardless of these perils, shorting stocks intelligently remains an effective way to hedge your downside for protection.

CHAPTER 8

THE LONG SIDE OF YOUR PORTFOLIO AND THE FOUR STAGES ALL STOCKS TRAVEL

My concept of a short-side strategy, of course, also includes the long side of your portfolio. The market obviously has two sides, the upside (long) and the downside (short), so both sides of your portfolio must be positioned properly. Since the market has an upside long-term bias to it, every investor needs to have long positions. Even if you are the most bearish investor in the world, bear market rallies are more powerful and exciting than real bull market moves. Let's take a look at the rallies that took place during the Great Depression to show you why you can be trading longs even in the worst of economic times.

After the first market smash in 1929, stocks were setting up for a "dead cat bounce." It's referred to in this way because the market can bounce just like a dead cat, which if thrown down hard enough will bounce. So if you bought the oversold extreme on November 13, 1929, and then sold the bounce around the peak April 17, 1930, the Dow gained 48 percent. From February 2, 1932, to September 9, 1932, the market almost doubled. From July 26, 1934, to March 10, 1938, the Dow Jones Industrial Average (DJIA) rallied 127 percent. Remember that all these bear market rallies happened in the midst of the Great Depression. We had very similar rallies through the Nasdaq 2000–2003 crash and recoveries as well.

The bull market in the 1920s was great, but these bear market rallies can be better than the real thing. This is because bear market rallies go up much faster and are more powerful. Since there are more cyclical bull market periods than bearish ones and the fact that they last much longer are reasons to take the long side seriously.

From the top in November of 1929 through September 1939 there were six powerful bear market rallies. Yet, on April 28, 1942, the DJIA was still at 92.92 or 76 percent below its September 3, 1928 high of 381.17. If you lasted through that 14-year period, you were basically wiped out and this is precisely why a stop loss discipline as well as a short side exposure is critical to investing success. An investor with $100,000 at the top of the 1929 market had only $24,000 13 years later, if he was lucky. Most stocks were down 95 percent and many just went bankrupt, so $100,000 likely turned into $5,000 or zero. Odds are you would have given up at the bottom or would have needed the money elsewhere, thus making a recovery impossible. For those investors, like my trading hero Jesse Livermore, shorting stocks was the best game in town. That will also be the case in the next major market correction, crash, or long sideways-trading market. *Long-only investors in a bear market are wrong-only investors.*

Here's how you need to look at the downside potential and why you must have shorts to hedge your downside at all times. If the DJIA drops 89 percent like it did in 1929, that would be 12,460 points or to the floor of 1,520 on the DJIA from the 2007 highs of 14,000. However, with so many newly created dollars chasing too few stocks, the DJIA could repeat Nasdaq in 1999 and we could go to 20,000 or even higher. Who knows, with enough inflation and liquidity the DJIA could repeat Japan and go to 39,000 before it collapses. In this case, the crash will be much greater in both pain and percentage terms. Pure short players with no stop loss disciplines would get killed without longs on the way up to 20,000 or 39,000 on the DJIA.

Since the market might recover and go higher before its ultimate peak, we must have stocks with long-side exposure. This is especially true because the Fed has continued to balloon the money supply beginning in the summer of 2007 to the present. Since no one can see the future, let's start to focus on some great ways to get the lowest-risk, highest-reward exposure on the long side in case we enter a new inflationary super-boom.

How to "Beat the Street" in the New Century

My favorite way to make great profits on the long side is to find and own a nice profitable company that is riding a bullish industry trend and is soon to be discovered by Wall Street. This is called growth stock investing, where you buy stocks that are growing faster than the economy as a whole. In August 1996, the hedge fund I was managing started to buy a company called Benchmark Micro Inc. (BMRQ). I was looking for additional plays on the booming laptop computer market. After coming off a huge move in a company called Trident Microsystems (TRID), I discovered BMRQ was the de facto standard in power management for notebooks.

I called the president of BMRQ and he confirmed that both the notebook computer industry and BMRQ itself were enjoying exploding profits. I aggressively bought this stock around $10 per share. The amazing thing was that there was no analyst coverage on BMRQ by any large brokerage firms, so I knew that once the stock was discovered it would go through the roof. I also felt very confident that since laptop sales were exploding, and BMRQ was the power management systems supplier, they would have a great quarter as well.

Suddenly, the stock started to rise, so I bought more. My business partner at the time and I went to a Hambrecht & Quist technology conference and BMRQ ran to $15 per share right before they reported earnings after the bell. There was one small brokerage firm in Texas that had a $.19 estimate for the quarter. They blew away the quarter and came in at $0.29 per share instead. As we were slapping each other high fives, we thought the stock would immediately gap up to $20-plus the next morning. What happened then is a perfect example of "buy on mystery and sell on history" as the stock opened $1 higher to $16, then immediately crashed back to $12. I was completely shell-shocked. I owned a concentrated position of about 20 percent of the total assets in the hedge fund. I had several people call me asking what happened, and my comment was, "I don't know why the stock is falling, but hold on or buy more."

This is a prime example of where homework or research can be critical in keeping your head when everyone else is losing theirs. I knew the BMRQ management was planning on attending the famous annual American Electronics Association (AEA) conference shortly after the stock fell. As a hedge fund manager, I was friends with numerous analysts on the street. I called about 15 technology analysts to look at BMRQ at AEA and to tell their best clients to do the same. The stock immediately started to work its way back toward the highs as many of these analysts started to make the calls and even buy BMRQ for their own accounts. Then I mistakenly decided to sell a big chunk of the stock when it returned to the high teens.

The very next morning, *Investor's Business Daily* featured BMRQ in an article titled "How One Manager Exploits Conferences." This manager said that after seeing the BMRQ booth so busy at the conference, he immediately phoned his trader and bought a huge position in the stock. This exposure exploded BMRQ higher, to the tune of $25 per share in just a few short days. The good news was that I was the primary reason for that excitement at both shows as well as BMRQ being featured in *Investor's Business Daily*, so I looked like a hero to many. The bad news was that I had just sold my BMRQ, leaving a considerable amount of money on the table. This is why scaling out of a position slowly as it rises is a good trading discipline. This practice reduces the pain of selling too soon. I made big money on the trade, but my early exit from the stock cost me and my investors even greater profits.

Feeling foolish, I started to buy the stock back as it dipped back again to the low $20s. The stock then wound up shooting up to the mid $30s as several Wall Street analysts started covering BMRQ, right near the top, of course. When any analyst initiates coverage on an undiscovered stock, institutions bid the price up in a feeding frenzy. That's the best time to sell and "feed the ducks while they are quacking," as many Wall Street traders say. *Buying great companies in the midst of a powerful fundamental trend, undiscovered by Wall Street, is a great way to get long big-winning stocks.*

Both Fundamental *and* Technical Analysis Is the Key

Doing your homework to get some kind of edge is critical to good stock selection on both sides of the market. The other equally important variable is the technical read of the stock charts. BMRQ had a breakout run up to $15 from $8 from April 1996 to May 1996. Then it proceeded to drop all the way back to $8. This is where I would have ultimately liked to start buying BMRQ, on this testing of $8 the second time. This double test of $8 per share made the chart put in a "double-bottom" pattern. The first bottom was $8 in April, and the second bottom was the retest at $8. Once it successfully moved off $8 the second time, a technical formation called the W emerged. They call it a W pattern because the double bottom looks like the letter W, with the bottom of the letter W being $8 in this example.

A completed W pattern presents a low-risk entry point to start buying a stock. You can put a 5 to 7 percent stop loss in below this price, and that's your likely downside. Sometimes the second bottom slightly undercuts the first bottom to shake out weak holders (weak hands), but it is basically just a retest of the previous bottom. BMRQ was trading between $8 and $10 before it launched to $15 the first time. When it bounced off $8 the second time, the double bottom was successfully completed. When it broke out above $10 again on big volume, the stock was ready to explode.

There's no rocket science to using technical analysis, but it's more of an art than a science really. *Technical analysis can help you know when to buy and short stocks at the best time.* Buying stocks using only fundamental or only technical analysis is like driving your car at high speed in an ice storm without snow tires. You may eventually get to where you are going, but the risk of crashing is dramatically increased without combining both technical and fundamental analysis. Everything is clearer and much safer using both. To avoid driving blindly in the stock market, make sure you apply both forms of analysis. Later in the book I will discuss a pattern recognition indicator using technical analysis for timing, execution, and identifying bullish and bearish trends.

The same basic pattern works in reverse to spot tops, except in this case it's called a double top. If you look at the chart on Nasdaq in 2000, you will see that Nasdaq launched to 5,048 and then sold off to the 4,500 level. On the next rally it got back near the high and failed on light volume. This light volume was a clue that demand was waning. Then the Nasdaq sold off violently on heavy volume and it had nothing but downside from there (see Figure 8.1).

Sometimes the double top is slightly above, but usually slightly below, the first high price point, as shown in Figure 8.2.

These are very easy, but effective, patterns to identify.

If you look at the two closed-end China funds CHN (NYSE) and the Greater China fund (GCH/NYSE), you will see what I mean in Figure 8.3.

In October 2007, both of these funds put in double tops and abruptly sold off. Sometimes these sell-offs will recover and put in a triple top or a right shoulder. Once that right shoulder is formed and the market fails, look out below. If a rally breaks out above that resistance, you take your lumps, and

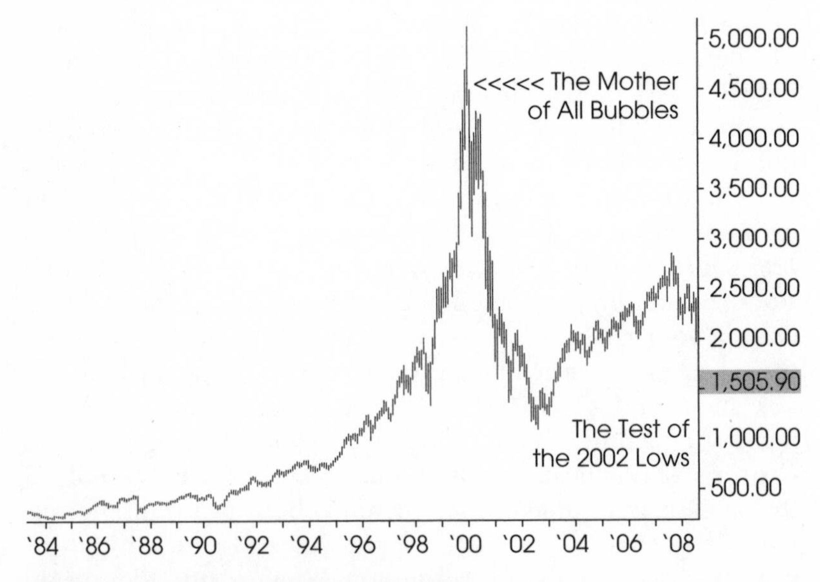

Figure 8.1 Nasdaq Index 1983-2008
Created with TradeStation

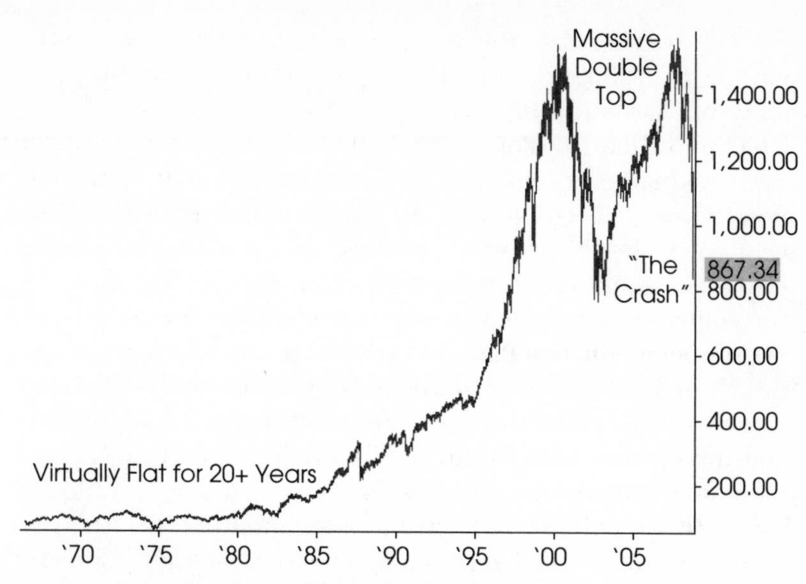

Figure 8.2 S&P 500 Index 1966-Present
Created with TradeStation

Figure 8.3 Greater China Fund 2007-2008 Black Cross
Created with TradeStation

wait for a better day. But keep trying this strategy in bubble markets like China because these markets are a giant house of cards in a hard-blowing wind.

The Standard & Poor's (S&P) 500 and the DJIA had both completed large head and shoulder tops in late 2007. That was soon followed by the Black Cross pattern. This was a lethal combination in early 2008, which resulted in a severe stock market sell-off. Sometimes these patterns reverse and fail. This is why a risk-control strategy deploying stop loss disciplines is critical.

The next pattern that works for tops and bottoms is the "head-and-shoulders" pattern and the "inverse head-and-shoulders" pattern. Like the W pattern, the head-and-shoulder pattern looks exactly like a head with two shoulders. The head's price point obviously is in the middle slightly above the two shoulders. The last price point is the right shoulder and will form near the first price point of the left shoulder and then the right shoulder will head down to complete the pattern. Many times, this right shoulder sets up the Black Cross where the 50-day moving average (DMA) crosses below the 200 DMA. Again, once that happens, stocks or markets are usually ready for a big fall. This is exactly what happened to the markets in late 2007 before they tanked into the worst January on record.

The opposite of the Black Cross is a pattern called a Golden Cross. This is where the 50 DMA crosses up through the 200 DMA. This typically happens as a new bull run in a market or a stock is about to happen.

The inverse head-and-shoulder pattern is exactly the opposite. This pattern is what helped me advise all my clients in March 2003 that the nasty bear market was likely over. Here, the head part of the pattern is the absolute low, the opposite of the head-and-shoulders top where the head is the top. Again, these patterns repeat themselves over and over again, and they work most of the time.

Remember that for all stocks bought, and especially ones sold short, you should enter mental stops. A mental stop is a price point at which you will "say uncle," acknowledging that you may be wrong. Accept your small loss and move on. You should identify your mental stop before any stocks are bought or shorted. A stop loss should be no more than 10 to 12 percent and ideally no more than 5 to 7 percent from the point you entered your buy or short.

Here are a few additional trading tips. First, whenever you enter a position, do half of the position initially. So if you are going to buy 10,000 shares of a stock, buy 5,000 and see what happens. If the stock goes in your favor and is acting well, you then put on the other half of your position. If the stock goes against you and acts poorly, then don't add the other half of your position. Instead, stay true to your stop loss and see what happens. If the stock reverses and goes to a profitable position and again acts and feels better, then put on the other half of the position.

This scaling discipline will help you to do three very important things:

1. It will limit your losses by only averaging up on your winners.
2. It gives you the discipline of getting a feel for the stock you just bought or shorted, telling you if it's acting right. This will get you more comfortable in buying more, or less comfortable with the position giving you a blinking yellow light of caution.
3. It gets you in the discipline of not averaging down and only averaging up and pyramiding your winners. Pyramiding involves increasing the size of a profitable position by declining increments when the stock you are trading is rising. This is a practice that all the great traders and money managers employ when entering long or short positions.

Whenever you are looking to take profits by selling a long or covering a short, always average in or out of your position slowly. As a reminder, one of the best practices is to see if you are right or wrong on the covering buy or the sell of the long position. If the stock continues lower after you are partially covered, let it continue to fall before you buy in the other half of the short position. If the stock you are taking profits on keeps going up, let it go for a while before you sell the other half of your long position to average up your sale price. If the first half of the buy on the long sale is correct, immediately close out the other half position before it drops any further.

Averaging in and out of positions will get you in the habit of riding your winners and maximizing your profits. In the old days of high commissions, this practice would have been too costly. Today, commission costs have compressed so much that this practice is worth the extra small cost of an additional trade because of the increase in your trading profits. The other benefit to doing this is that it lowers your frustration of selling too soon, like I did with BMRQ. When you work your way out of the position, you will greatly reduce that frustration. Whether you are a long-time professional or a novice investor, these rules apply and are simple to do.

High-Conviction Stock Positions

My friend Wally is a genius when it comes to finding undervalued and undiscovered stocks. He even had the ear of the world's greatest investor, the late John Templeton, who was a client of his. When my friend finds a stock, he does an incredible amount of homework, which gives him confidence in each stock he purchases. This helps him to take on larger positions and to stay with those positions for a long period of time. Intense levels of homework lead to high-conviction positions and more peace of mind on the stocks you buy or sell short.

This high-conviction principle applies for technical analysis as well as fundamental analysis. The formula is this:

- The more homework you do, the more confidence you will have in each stock pick.
- The more confidence you have, the more shares you will comfortably buy.
- The increased confidence from the homework will increase the success rate.
- These high-conviction positions will lead to higher profits and greater success.

If your analysis is based on wrong assumptions or information, then you have your stops for protection.

For example, Wally did a sales training program for the firm I was working for at the time. During the course, he mentioned a small oil and gas stock that he was buying called Basic Petroleum (BPILF), which was trading at $4 per share. The next year when it hit $8, I paid more attention and put the stock on my monitor to watch. It traded between $6 and $14 for a few years up until 1994.

Wally showed up at my house at 7:00 on a Saturday morning in early 1995 with a bunch of large maps under his arm. He said to me, "Ron, do you want to get rich? If you do, I have something to show you." We went to my home office and Wally proceeded to lay out all these maps on the floor. They were giant maps showing all of Basic Petroleum's oil fields in the jungles of Guatemala. He showed me why BPILF stock was going to go from the current price of $10 to his target of $100 per share. He thought some other oil company may discover Basic Petroleum and buy it out before it got to $100, but it was going to make a fortune nonetheless.

He described the incredible research he had done to come up with his strong convictions, including going into the jungles of Guatemala to see the company's management team and the oil fields. Guatemala was in a civil war and there were reported multiple guerilla attacks on the workers at the oil fields, as well as reported assaults and kidnappings. After interviewing several candidates, Wally took his 64 son David with him on the trip to act as his personal bodyguard. The president of Basic Petroleum was part of a very influential family in Guatemala and arranged for military protection for Wally and his son. Wally then made arrangements with management and was even willing to be escorted by machine-gun–toting soldiers into the jungles of Guatemala to inspect Basic's oil fields and refinery. After this trip, he was absolutely convinced that BPILF had huge reserves of oil, and they had the ability to transport and sell the oil for huge profits. Wally advised me to buy big before the stock took off, so I did, to my gain.

BPILF wound up having a three-for-one stock split along the way, and by the end of the year in 1995, BPILF exploded to the $30s. Later, it was bought out for $40 per share, as Wally anticipated. On a split-adjusted basis, Wally's $100 per share target price call was conservative, as the stock finished at $120 per share when factoring in the three-for-one stock split. Now, I am not advising anyone to risk his life for a stock idea, but I suggest that you put your money with an investment adviser or money manager who does this kind of homework. Wally and his clients rode BPILF all the way to $120 and made millions.

A Big Red "F"

Here's another example of Wally's successes: He told me to buy Flir Systems (FLIR) in 2000 just as the stock was collapsing, right along with Nasdaq stocks in general, at $3 per share. He was absolute in his conviction that this stock was a "table-pounding buy" at the very same time Wall Street was downgrading the stock to a sell. I gave this idea to Eric, my junior analyst at the time. He called the company's chief financial officer (CFO) and wrote up a report giving me the "10 reasons not to buy the stock." I sent a fax of that report over to Wally and he graded that report by putting a giant red "F" at the top of it and mailed it back me. After I stopped laughing hysterically at the graded report card, I gave it to Eric to learn from it. Wally went on to make 50 times his money on that stock, and it never looked back from the lows where he was buying.

Wally and I are still good friends and he shares his picks with me whenever he finds them. Recently, another one of his table-pounding stock ideas, that he bought around $1 per share (CULS), got bought out in 2007 at $11.75 per share. Cost-U-Less Inc. operated 11 club-style stores in the Caribbean. I am sure going there on a due diligence trip was much more enjoyable than going to the jungles of Guatemala, but much less memorable.

All-time great investors like Wally are the ones who go to great lengths developing deep convictions on their stock positions. Wally also studied the chart on BPILF and knew when to add to his position all the way up. Whenever you find a great idea, you'll want to get the most out of it like Wally seems to do on the majority of his picks. In 2008, Wally thinks that the future risks to the stock market are as high as any time he has seen in his long and distinguished career. He too thinks that Chinese and U.S. stocks, U.S. bonds, and global real estate are in for a long period of contraction.

Four Stages Every Stock and Market Travel

There are four stages that every stock or market travel. The first stage is a Stage 1 Base stage. During this phase, a stock or market has been going sideways for quite some time and is building the foundation from which it will launch to the second stage, the Stage 2 Advance.

During a Stage 2 Advance, the stock rises rapidly and the objective is to ride the winning stock until it climbs to a point at which it runs out of gas and starts to go sideways again. This sets up the third stage, which is the topping-out phase. Here the stock may go sideways or parabolic, as large sellers are distributing or selling their stock to the investing public.

A Stage 3 Top typically sets up the final phase of a stock's cycle, a Stage 4 Decline. Ideally, this is when you are shorting the stock as it is falls until it gets back to a support area and starts a new Stage 1 Base again.

If you are wrong on buying or shorting any of these stages, you will be protected with your buy or sell stops, which you should always have in place. Sometimes a Stage 1 Base will break down and continue its Stage 4 Decline, but you will have stops in place. A Stage 3 Top can sometimes be a new base being built versus a top, but again you will have a buy stop in place if you have misjudged this. What appears to be a Stage 3 Top might be a new base, but you will be able to recognize the double top/bottom, head-and-shoulder top/bottom, and the Black Cross patterns to confirm the correct stage. Classifying the stocks you buy, sell, or short in this manner gives you a visual of which direction you believe your stock or the market is traveling.

In a Stage 1 Base, the stock is basing and you are slowly accumulating a position, waiting patiently for the stock to go into a Stage 2 Advance. In a Stage 2 Advance, you will add to the position you initially took in the Stage 1 Base. This is where you will average up your winners, as they are advancing. As the stock rises, you will increase your stop price all the way up to ensure the gain never turns into a loss. At a Stage 3 Top, the stock will stop advancing and may go sideways for quite some time. This is where you begin to take action.

At a Stage 3 Top, you will sell the stock if it acts poorly or if the chart patterns we discussed confirm the top in the stock. After the stock stalls and completes a Stage 3 Top, you can initiate a small short position. As the stock breaks down and goes into a Stage 4 Decline, you can add to the short position, again averaging in your winners. Typically, it takes months for a stock to complete its top before it enters a Stage 4 Decline. At a Stage 4 Decline, you add the other half of your short position and ride the stock down until it sticks and starts to base. As it goes sideways for a few days or weeks, you will look to cover the short position. Remember, as the stock is falling, you will lower your buy stop once again to ensure that profits don't turn into losses.

Once the stock bases, it will take several months of a Stage 1 Base before it's ready to go into a new Stage 2 Advance stage. A Stage 2 Advance is the breakout stage where a stock launches off a well-formed Stage 1 Base on strong volume. The stock in a Stage 2 Advance is making a new cyclical or all-time high on big volume as institutional investors bid the stock up. The most profitable and timeliest point to buy a stock is when it breaks out from a Stage 1 Base.

Volume is another key technical tool to use when buying or shorting a stock. The generally stated rule is that "volume precedes price." The more volume a stock has on the breakout or the breakdown, the better. If a Stage 3 Top turns out to be a base, then the stock will start a new breakout. At that point, it will enter a new Stage 2 Advance. All these patterns and stages are very simple and extremely effective. What's not so simple is making money trading and investing, as the easiest thing to do in the stock market is lose money. This is why it is so important to have a sensible investment strategy and the necessary tools to determine when to buy and short stocks or anything else that trades for that matter.

Let's review the stages and the emotional state of investors at each one. At a Stage 1 Base, you are buying at or near the bottom. This is the place that many value buyers accumulate a stock. Investors are usually depressed or disinterested at the Stage 1 Base bottom. At the Stage 1 Base, most investors are sick and tired of the stock and basically have had enough. A perfect example of this was Newmont mining in 2007. NEM came out with a terrible quarter, and the stock was down the next day. The stock had been building a terrific base and had already discounted the bad news.

A well-known perma-bear had mentioned he had given up on Newmont mining (NEM: NYSE) and on his web site said he sold the stock the day after the bad quarter. The stock then immediately went into liftoff from $42 to $56 in a few short weeks. In all fairness to this well-known bear, NEM has been a huge disappointment to the gold bugs for a very long time. When a lead gold bug gives up on a former leader in a hot group, you know it's got to be at or near a bottom. The Stage 1 Base pattern gave you the final confirmation that the stock was going to rise regardless of a good or bad quarter.

In a Stage 2 Advance, investors get hopeful and then excited. At the end of a Stage 2 Advance, investors will be in a state of euphoria and will act in a "get me in at any price" mode. Slowly, the euphoria and excitement fade, and distribution begins signaling a Stage 3 Top. As the stock or the market enters into a Stage 4 Decline, investors will first experience anxiety, then denial, as prices fall. As the stock or the market accelerates down, investors start to experience a high degree of pain. Then, at the bottom, they will panic and capitulate with a "get me out at any price" mentality and sell. Then unsophisticated, fearful investors will be depressed, and the stock or the market will begin to repair. A new base will form, and the whole process starts all over again. I don't want this process to sound easy, because it is not. I simply want to help you understand investor emotions at each phase in a market cycle.

One great tool to find timely stock ideas, both long and short, is *Investor's Business Daily* (IBD). IBD is a great financial newspaper, as it features strong stocks that are in a Stage 2 Advance in specific strong industry groups every single day. IBD monitors about 197 different industry groups. The Stage 2 Advancing stocks with the strongest momentum can be found in the highest-ranked groups. The reason these strong stocks perform together is that there is something fundamentally positive taking place in that industry. Whenever something positive is happening in a particular industry, you will find that "a rising tide will lift all boats" in that particular hot market sector. Gold stocks benefited from gold's new bull market that initially exploded the earnings of the senior gold producers. These stocks steadily rose as a group for several years and also crashed as a group in 2008.

We can find great short ideas that are in a Stage 4 Decline in IBD's lowest-performing groups. The home builders have been one of the poorest performers since their peak in 2005.

This low-ranked sector has simply imploded taking most of these stocks down as much as 80 percent. One day soon they will start a long period of basing. When the real estate market is ready to have a mild recovery, the home-builder stocks will head into a Stage 2 Advance pattern. When that does happen, the home-builder stocks will absolutely explode to the upside as the large amount of short sellers will be aggressive buyers scrambling to buy back their shares.

IBD gives you the company's accumulation-distribution ratings (Acc.-Dist.). The ratings go from A through E. The Acc.-Dist. rating of "A" or "B" is ideal for stocks to be long because these stocks are being accumulated. The rating of "D" and "E" are the stocks to be short because these stocks are under distribution. The IBD ratings are critical because they tell you the supply and demand of a stock and of the market as well. An accumulation rating of "A" usually precedes and then accompanies an advance, and a distribution rating of "D" coincides with a decline. The distribution ranking of "D" or "E" will go to an accumulation ranking of an "A" or "B" right before the Stage 2 Advance pattern. I need to warn you, however, though these stocks are strong and under accumulation, but they can quickly change. I have seen and experienced firsthand a strongly accumulated stock have bad news and gap down 30 to 50 percent overnight. This is why exchange-traded funds (ETFs) can be advantageous over an individual stock. An ETF can give you exposure to a group or a country without taking on risk of bad news from one particular stock that might be down big while the group may still be hot. You still have the systemic risk of a complete meltdown with both an ETF and a stock.

IBD also has its own earnings-per-share (EPS) ranking as well as a relative strength (RS) number. The rankings are from 1 through 99. A 99 EPS ranking means that the company's EPS growth over the previous 12 months outperformed 99 percent of all other stocks. A 99 RS ranking means the stock price has outperformed 99 percent of all stocks. I am not as concerned with the EPS ranking, but typically you'll want a ranking of 87 or higher on both the EPS and the RS for longs in a Stage 2 Advance. On shorts you'll want anything under 60 and falling on both counts. Here again, I must warn you that you could have a weak EPS-ranked stock that out of the blue reverses. There is nothing more painful than being short a stock that gaps up on news that's unique to that stock versus the group it trades in.

Make the Necessary Adjustments

Remember what the late, great trader Jesse Livermore said, "There's the bull side, the bear side, and then there's the right side." That's the side you want to be most weighted toward—the right side of the market. Things change quickly, so be aware and prepared. *The key is to be in sync with the market and to make tactical asset allocation adjustments to your portfolio along the way.* There's a time and a season for every market to be bullish or bearish. Tactical asset allocation is a portfolio management strategy to maximize profits while simultaneously reducing risk.

Gold has been in a long-term uptrend, but it will continue to have violent corrections along the bullish path until it enters a final blow-off Stage 3 Top, like the oil market in 2008. Domestic and foreign stocks may head back up on mass money creation, but they, too, will have severe corrections and crashes along the way. Oil may again explode on some sort of disturbance in the Middle East and then suddenly reverse and enter a new bear phase on recession or depression fears. As demand from the United States and China wanes from an economic and stock market contraction, oil stocks will crash like the DJIA in 1929.

The only way to stay on the right side of various markets is to let the market tell you what to do by the trading activity as reflected in the charts. Don't argue with the charts. They are always correct—win or lose, up or down. And don't forget, you must always be hedged for protection with your short positions. *Being a long-side investor in a bear market is synonymous to being a wrong-side investor.*

If you can recognize what stage the market and the stocks you own are in, then you can be weighted more short or long at the right times. If you recognize a Stage 4 Decline, then increase your short side to be more heavily weighted on the right side of the tape. If the market is in a Stage 2 Advance, then we can cut back some on the shorts and increase your long-side exposure to be more heavily weighted on the right side of that move as well. *The market may not "ring a bell at the top," but it certainly gives off some very important clues.* Remember, you must always address the downside of the market and be willing to position your portfolio for protection and profits on the short side. Finally, you must always use stops and be patient to put the odds heavily in your favor with high-conviction stock positions.

In summary, the more homework you do, the deeper conviction you will have, the bigger position you will take, and the more profits you will make. This last sentence is important, as it is critical to have the courage of your convictions in your stock picks, long and short.

Remember, you can easily get your edge over Wall Street by doing your homework as well as having great tools like an IBD newspaper and stock charts to find and confirm great picks long and short. If you have stocks ideas on both sides of the market, you are lowering your risk and doubling your profit potential. Your ideal investment portfolio is one designed with favorable risk/reward parameters. It should be based on your investment objectives and risk tolerance. All stocks bought or sold short should have their parameters (stops and targets) preset for risk control.

Foreign Stocks

In this global economy, investors must also go long (and short) foreign stocks for diversification. The most famous global investor, the late John Templeton, had "16 Rules for Successful Investing." Rule number 7 on the list: "Diversify." In John's own words, "No matter how much research you do, you can't predict or control the future. You must diversify by company, by industry, by risk, and by country." Investors can get foreign diversification in three ways:

1. Buy shares in a wide selection of global companies that that trade on U.S. exchanges in the form of American Depositary Receipts (ADRs). These include: Turkey (TKC), Switzerland (ABB, SYT), Finland (NOK), Spain (TEF), Brazil (GGB, GFA, TMB, ITU, PBR),

Canada(CP), South Africa (SSL), the United Kingdom (VOD), India (HDB, SLT, TTM), Russia (MBT, ROS, VIP, WBD), Luxembourg (TS), Mexico (TMX, CX), China (CTRP, STP) Israel (FNDT, AIP), Germany (AIXG, DT), Argentina (TEO, IRS), Japan (TM), France (TOT) and many, many more. There is no shortage of foreign stocks to choose from on U.S. exchanges, from the deepest and most liquid in the world. These I've listed are just a few from the new 52-week low list and are only observations. In no way should you consider these to be my suggested buy or short recommendations.

2. Buy foreign stocks directly on foreign exchanges. Few investors do this and not many firms provide direct global access to stocks on foreign markets. The benefit of going directly to foreign markets is the access to high-dividend-paying foreign stocks not available on U.S. exchanges. As a rule, you can get much higher dividend-paying stocks in foreign countries, but you must buy directly on foreign exchanges. By buying foreign stocks, you are diversifying out of the dollar and securing a future income stream to be paid in the foreign currency diversifying your portfolio globally.

   Very few high dividend-paying stocks are listed on U.S. exchanges because most U.S. investors are more interested in price appreciation than dividend yields. U.S. stocks have boomed since 1982, with only a few interruptions along the way, so this has seemed reasonable. At or near a secular market top, investors look at only appreciation and market gains. At secular market bottoms, they are fearful and limit stock purchases to those with stable cash flows and income streams.

   At the top, the investor's motto is, "Who needs dividends when I know stocks will rise!" At the bottom, the investors reverse the strategy to, "Who wants stocks when all they seem to do is go down!" As the stock market moves into a severe bearish phase or to a long sideways market, desire for dividends will rise once again. Higher-dividend-paying stocks will replace momentum stocks as market momentum slows and reverses as it always does.

Investors can best look for income in the foreign markets—countries like Australia, where you can find many depressed stocks yielding 7 to 10 percent. High-dividend stocks can be purchased in Canada, Finland, France, Great Britain, the Netherlands, Norway, Singapore, Sweden, Switzerland, and literally all over the world. These high-dividend-paying stocks are utilities, telecom, real estate investment trusts, refineries, and various infrastructure plays. Many are very high quality and relatively safe. You must be very careful here to make sure that you are not buying a high-dividend-paying foreign stock loaded with debt. You don't want to let the dividend convince you to average down because you think the stock is safe or cheap. Remember Enron? The fact of the matter is that all stocks, big and small, have the risk of going to zero. There's no such thing as "crash proof" stocks because any stock can crash.

3. Get foreign exposure through ETFs or closed-end funds that trade on the New York Stock Exchange. This is a safer way to get foreign equity diversification and avoid individual stock risk. If you buy the wrong stock in a performing country you want exposure to, you lose. If you buy an ETF, you eliminate the risk of buying the wrong stock in the right country. There are other risks, like systemic risk, to be aware of as well. Personally, I think this is the best way to get foreign stock exposure and take advantage of the proliferation of ETFs for broad diversification among foreign markets.

Regardless of what you are told, when the U.S. market and economy goes into a severe recession or depression, global stock markets and economies will follow. We are not isolated from the world economy, since the United States accounts for 28 percent of global gross domestic product (GDP). The emerging BRIC countries (Brazil, Russia, India, and China) have collectively surpassed the United States, accounting for 30 percent of the global GDP. That's 58 percent of global GDP in five countries, and most of that is in the United States and China. The old saying, "If the United States sneezes, the rest of the world catch a cold" should change to, "If the United States or China sneezes, the rest of the world will catch a cold."

Some experts are advising their investors to get all their assets out of the United States because the rest of the world is "decoupling" from the U.S. economy and will continue on a boom. Their logic is that as the U.S. dollar implodes, other countries will be richer and much better off without the United States as a global partner. The U.S. dollar is 65 percent of the world's reserve assets, so if the United States truly crashes, world economies will suffer right along with it. This has happened with every severe market crash in the last 100 years. One only needs to look to 2008 as a most recent example for evidence of what I am saying. The majority of foreign stocks and markets were clobbered right along with U.S. markets—so much for decoupling theories.

Here are some ETF shares and their respective countries: Brazil (EWZ), China (FXI), Canada (EWC), emerging markets (EEM), France (EWQ), Mexico (EWW), Singapore (EWS), and Taiwan (EWT). There are some great opportunities on the short side in foreign stocks. Investors today are enamored with stocks in the BRIC countries, especially China, because investors from around the globe have bid these stocks to extremely high and risky levels. Because investors have become overly enamored with stocks in the BRIC countries, it is there that you will find some of the best future places for short ideas.

In summary, foreign stock exposure is an intelligent way to diversify one's holdings and lower risk. Every investor has different objectives and risk tolerances, so each investment must be considered carefully before going long or short. This is especially true in volatile foreign and emerging markets. In the next chapter, you will read about what goes on behind the scenes in the private placement world, as well as read about some of my "wild adventures" in venture capital.

CHAPTER 9

ADVENTURE CAPITAL: OPPORTUNITIES AND RISKS IN PRIVATE PLACEMENTS

Venture capital presents some very high risk/high return investment opportunities. This is where speculators are trying to get on the ground floor of a private company hoping to find the "next Microsoft." My experience with venture deals has been decidedly mixed, however. I have very little confidence in most private placements, but a small allocation in the portfolio is fine. Be very selective and deploy no more than 10 percent of your total assets in this high-risk area. I'll give you some real-life success and horror stories. Based on my experience in the venture capital game, I'll refer to it as *adventure capital.*

Adventure Capital

The first private venture that I want to discuss was in a company I will call Air Freight Transpo (AFTPO). AFPTO was a private financing wherein I got in on the "founders' round." The founders' round is the best place to get in on these private venture raises because you come in at the same initial investment level per share as the founders or insiders of the company. AFTPO provided various transportation services, mostly in the air freight industry. The company started with only a few dollars out of the founder's apartment. The CEO had some experience and past success in this industry that he applied to his new company.

AFTPO got off to a great start, and as they grew, of course, they needed more money. Fortunately for me, I was in at $0.10 per share on the founders' round, and the next raise was at $1 per share. The company continued to open offices around the nation and needed further financing. This is a big drawback with venture-stage companies, as they always need more money. This was in 1999 and the stock market was red hot, so AFTPO's management decided to go public. They chose a small brokerage firm from the East Coast to do the initial public offering (IPO) raise. By the time we were ready to launch, it was early 2000. I met the management team in Chicago because they were doing a presentation to the Regional Investment Bankers Association (RIBA). At RIBA, the goal is to make the pitch to a huge gathering of stockbrokers who hopefully like your story and place the IPO deal with their customers.

When I landed in Chicago, I met the CEO in the bar at the hotel where we were both staying the night before he was to give a formal presentation to the stockbrokers. To my astonishment, he said they were trying to do the IPO at $10 per share, 10 times above the last raise and 100 times above what we paid in the founders' round. He grabbed a napkin and a pen and started to draw all these lines indicating his "hub-and-spoke" strategy. He described how they were going to open up a number of strategic offices and become a huge dominant player in the industry.

I grabbed the pen and flipped the napkin over, drawing an arrow from the top of the napkin to the bottom. I said to the CEO, "Do you know what this line represents?" He said to me, "No, what?" I answered, "This is the future price direction of Nasdaq, and if you overprice this deal, you will not sell it and likely never get public. We're in a bubble, and when it pops, the IPO window will be shut down completely and for many years to come." He looked at me like I was some kind of a nut because we were seeing companies go public with insane valuations, companies like JDS Uniphase (JDSU) trading at market valuations of $33 billion with minimal revenues and huge losses. AFTPO actually had profits, but in 1999 that was a bad thing.

This RIBA meeting was kind of frightening to me. It seemed as if I were in the middle of hundreds of used car salesmen all trying to dump their damaged inventories on each other. I watched several presentations from companies that had zero sales and huge losses. Small companies with faulty business models were doing IPOs or secondary offerings at crazy valuations. I just sat through these presentations thinking, "This is going to end badly."

Sure enough, the reception we received was not great. Our transportation company looked boring in comparison to all the exciting dot-coms, and besides, we were profitable. We probably could have gotten $10 per share if we quickly renamed the company AirFreightTranspo.com. In early 2000, not many investors seemed to really care about profits. The focus was instead on the Internet and the "new era."

I tried to convince the management of AFTPO to lower the IPO price to $5.00 per share. I told them that if at that price the stock was cheap, then the stock would rise to its fair valuation in the marketplace once it was publicly traded. I also told them that if they got greedy, then we would all get trapped in an illiquid investment. I sent letters to the CEO and the board of AFTPO stating my case that we needed to sell the deal at a much lower price or the coming Nasdaq collapse would shut the door on us forever. They lowered the IPO price to $7, but that was not enough. The walls came crumbling down on Nasdaq just as the brokerage firm was ready to take us public. We missed that window, and nine years later it is still shut. Hopes of an IPO are no better in 2009 than they were right after the stock market was devastated in 2000.

I should have offered my shares at $3 to the insiders in front of that IPO, but that's hindsight. The fact is that the only remaining hope for AFTPO is that at some point they are bought out by another transportation company. Unfortunately, the margins of that business, with high fuel prices, have compressed right along with the value of the company shares.

Illiquidity is one of the biggest risks you take participating in private placements. Unless you have a leveraged control position in the company, you are at the mercy of the people who run it. Sometimes the interests of management just don't align with the private investors. When that happens, you are basically married to the company until a liquidity event takes place.

Another Private Adventure

In early 1997, I participated in a capital raise for a sports supply retailer. This company had private investors do a management buyout. I helped raise the money with my hedge fund. The plan was to do an IPO immediately after the transaction took place. A decent-sized brokerage firm in Oregon was chosen to do the IPO. The price was set at $9 per share, which would have been a huge profit for my investors from the private financing. The new issue deal was ready to go when the Asian currency crisis came across our shores like a tsunami. The markets tanked, so the IPO was delayed.

When the markets looked like they had recovered, they dusted off the prospectus to try again in October 1998. As luck would have it, the Long-Term Capital Management hedge fund debacle roiled the markets and the deal was delayed once again. Finally, in late 1999, at the height of the Nasdaq frenzy, they decided to dust off the prospectus one more time and try again in early 2000. The Dow Jones Industrial Average (DJIA) and Standard & Poor's (S&P) 500 started the year off on a very rocky note. By the time the company had plans to raise the money, Nasdaq started on its freefall decline, and the window for the IPO was slammed shut yet again.

A few months later, I recruited Merrill Lynch to consider being the banker for this company. Merrill Lynch was excited about the deal and still bullish on the stock market. They took us on with a plan to raise the company "$20 million" in a private round so the company could expand and go public once the market repaired. We had five investment banking people assigned to this deal after Merrill Lynch was retained. Soon after retaining them, Nasdaq was down 60 percent on its way to down 80 percent. All five of those people were laid off due to the market crash, and our hopes were shattered once again. The company CEO understandably had no interest in talking to bankers or brokers ever again, and my investors and I were trapped for sure.

I knew our only way out was a merger-and-acquisition transaction. I called the analyst at Bank of America who covered Gart Sports Inc. (GRTS). Gart Sports was also a sporting store retailer, and the fit seemed like it would be perfect; the analyst and bankers at Bank of America agreed. As we went down this path, things looked hopeful. Garts had agreed to a sit down with the company after Bank of America bankers told them this would be a great fit. Two days before the meeting, GRTS made a surprisingly large acquisition of another public sporting goods company. My merger deal was then DOA and so was I with my investment and my investors. At least that's what I thought at the time.

A few years later, the sports company's CEO made a formal offer to buy our convertible preferred stock for 20 cents on the dollar. I was shocked and dismayed. I called the CEO and asked if I could sit down with him as a representative of the shareholders to discuss all of this. He reluctantly agreed. Then I contacted my friend Tom, who also had his money and clients in the deal. He told me that angry investors had already gone to an attorney and were about to file a lawsuit against the company's management team. He and I both knew this would spell disaster for the company and our clients' investment. We quickly drew up a proposal to present to management.

When I sat down with the CEO and his attorney a couple of days later, I was pleasantly greeted. I politely reminded him that it was the original investors who were responsible for his becoming the CEO and largest company shareholder. I also reminded him of all that I had tried to do with Merrill Lynch and Gart Sports for both his and my shareholders' benefit. I told him there was a shareholder revolt brewing and lawsuits were in the works. I handed him and his attorney the new proposal. The company's attorney said, "Go ahead and sue us; we don't have any money for those angry investors to get anyway."

I said to the CEO, "Look, the shareholders have a loaded gun pointed at your head right now. The only thing stopping them from pulling the trigger and suing you is me and this proposal." I continued, "This will get very ugly for you. It's easy for your attorney to say go ahead and sue. He gets paid, but you will get humiliated in the press as the word gets out you offered us 20 cents on the dollar after eight years of holding the stock. Do the right thing and accept my deal." I told the attorney, "The angry shareholders at this point don't want corporate money; they want the CEO's stock and his hide." I looked back to the CEO and said, "I'll expect an answer in

24 hours before I tell the shareholders about the results of our meeting."

Within one hour after I left the boardroom, I received a call on my cell phone from the CEO, agreeing to my proposal, which was 100 cents on the dollar versus the 20 cents he had offered. This got my investors' principal back, plus we were able to keep our converted common stock. That was a big deal because the original offer was 20 cents for everything—the convertible note, which included the common stock. About two years after we got our original money back, the company received a $5.50 buyout offer. After 10 years and several failed attempts at liquidity, we finally got liquid. That was a long time for my investors to wait and too much disappointment to make it even close to a worthwhile investment. This is why I have guarded interest in private placements. Unless it's an amazing deal and you are willing to marry the deals with a time horizon of at least five years, I wouldn't advise you to put one penny in a private adventure transaction.

Dot-Coms to Dot-Bombs

I had two other private placement adventure capital deals go completely bust. Both were Internet plays I participated in at the top in 1999. The first one was a company that built web sites for youth sports clubs and various youth organizations. I'll call this company Youth Shorts.com because I took it in the shorts with this dot-com.

Last-Ditch Efforts

The company's business model was to pay up-front money to other strategic partners to get "eyeballs" to their site. I remember they gave a large nonprofit organization $500,000 to be designated their "chosen web site provider" for members of the club. This organization cashed the $500,000 check and laughed all the way to the bank. This adventure company's only accomplishment in this idiotic decision was to move up their date with destiny—bankruptcy.

As Youth Shorts.com was about to meet its maker, a savior came in to fund the company before an untimely death. This guy was a stockbroker, and he was completely out of his mind.

He apparently believed in the "eyeballs to web site" business model because he put about $2 million of his own money in the company to save it. Then he brought in his biggest client, who flushed an additional several million dollars down this dot-com drain.

The broker called me one night to say he was going to do a "dumb-down" investment round. He said that unless I put more money into the company, my investors and I were "screwed." A "dumb-down round" is where the adventure company, on their knees, begs for money to avoid bankruptcy. They are forced to do the raise at a heavily discounted price to the original investors' rounds. The original investors get screwed with massive dilution unless they participate in the new round. I was at least wise enough to say "thanks, but no thanks" to this raise. He went ahead and did the deal and took 98 percent control of the company, but of course 98 percent of nothing is still nothing.

After five years of fraud and embezzlement, the company finally went bankrupt. That broker called me up one more time, threatening to sue everyone on the board because he lost $2 million.

The other Internet private venture company I invested in tried to compete with eBay. They apparently had a reverse auction idea, putting the buyer in control versus the seller. I still don't understand why I invested in it, but the idea sounded good to me at the time. I hated dot-com stocks, but even I couldn't help tasting some of this forbidden fruit. This particular company was the ant and eBay was the elephant, and we got stomped on. I had very little money in each of these, but they both went with the Pet.coms of the world into the giant dot-com trash heap.

Other Private Plays

We had one private play that performed hugely because of the technology bubble. We invested money at $0.10 per share on a founders' round in a small telecom play. The company, U.S. Online (USOL), wound up getting public in the 1999 telecom bubble, and the stock exploded to $10. I sold as soon as my stock was released for sale and made several thousand percent return in a few short years. I initially felt stupid because I sold the stock around $5 and it immediately doubled. I felt much better later on as that huge winning stock wound up going very quickly to zero when the telecom bubble burst. I got lucky.

The last and the biggest private play I made is in a company I'll call Bluetooth Wireless (BTW). BTW was a company that I did several private money raises for. They are a Bluetooth short-distance wireless play. In the early years of the financings in which I was involved, most people I spoke to had never even heard of Bluetooth. I remember raising this company money with my investors saying, "Blue what?" I had told everyone that I thought Bluetooth was going to take the world by storm. Most thought I was nuts.

The good news is that BTW looked to be as well positioned in the short distance wireless segment as anyone. The bad news was that the Nasdaq bubble burst delayed the roll out of Bluetooth by several years. By the time it finally took hold, Broadcom bought our largest competitor, Widcom Inc., and they took the Bluetooth market by storm. Here is where you can be right on the theme and wrong on the company. As the Bluetooth rocket ship launched toward to Mars, our Bluetooth Company's CEO sat there waving as he ate dust in the Bluetooth wireless space.

We then hired a consulting group to give us advice on what to do. We all flew to Chicago for a board meeting to hear their suggestions and to discuss them. It was a very sobering meeting. These technology consultants told us that our value was dropping by the day and that we should sell the company immediately. Apparently, we partnered with the wrong chip company and our ship had already sailed. We were shocked because our two biggest competitors in the Bluetooth space were just acquired, so the CEO of BTW mistakenly thought our value skyrocketed right along with the competitors.

These consultants essentially said that the two chipmakers with the best silicon made their play and were dominating the space. This meant that we went from a potential industry leader to a small player relegated to the other small chip players left in the Bluetooth wireless space. After my chin hit the floor with this reality, the consultants gave us the valuation estimate for the potential sale of the company. Their projection would have given us a modest return, but not what we were looking for. Besides, the hired consultants couldn't guarantee a sale at their estimated sale price.

After seven hours of deliberating, the board came up with a new game plan. They decided to make a run at the next generation of short-distance wireless software, estimated to roll out in 2009. The thought among the board members was that if BTW could be the first to market a product, like our competitors in Bluetooth, we could be taken out just like they were. The board hoped that BTW could take all the failure and education from Bluetooth, then apply that knowledge toward a successful next-generation rollout. So off BTW went with Bluetooth behind and a next-generation software roadmap ahead.

The software engineers at BTW developed a potential "killer application" software product I'll call Y-connection. Y-connection is wireless connectivity software that allows any device to connect with any type of wireless device with a simple click of the mouse. For example, if you wanted to connect your pocket PC to your printer, all you would do is click on the Y-connection icon. It then asks you what two devices you want connected and what wireless radio connection you want. It then does all the wireless management functions automatically and your pocket PC is magically connected to your printer, using a Bluetooth radio connection. The software is fully developed, and it works for wireless area network (WAN), ultra-wideband (UWB), WiFi, and Zigbee as well as Bluetooth, and in all types of devices.

The good news is that the company is getting some early interest from the largest PC makers throughout the world who are doing mission-critical tests on the product. BTW also looks like they could become the de facto standard in the next generation of short distance wireless software. They have first-mover position in the space, so they at least accomplished that. They are designed in with many of the major chipmakers rolling out software in first-generation products. The bad news, as with every other small company, is that it takes a lot of equity capital to expand and grow and compete with the big boys. They are once again trying to raise their "last" few million dollars in 2008. If they fail in raising the needed capital, they will be forced to sell off assets to stay alive.

It has been eight very long years since our initial investment, but the company thinks they are on the 30-yard line in this long game. The only question is whether they will get sacked on the 30-yard line or successfully get over the goal line for a game-winning touchdown for my investors. It's entirely possible the company will be forced to kick a field goal for a much lesser score for my investors. I have personally helped raise the majority of the company's early financings with my clients, and I have a decent equity stake in this company. With the 2008 mortgage and credit crisis, stocks and real estate tanking, the dollar imploding, and fear levels skyrocketing, I can tell you I am as nervous as a cat.

Hopefully, it will end well and my investors and I will be celebrating in the end zone after BTW crosses the goal line. They are currently in discussions with several acquiring companies to get the shareholders liquid. If they get sacked and lose, it will hurt, but it's all part of the adventure capital game.

The True Value of a Private Investment

In summary, you can see that a lot goes on behind closed doors in the private and public investment world. I have respect for active venture capital investors and money managers because I know how much hard work goes into making a private investment liquid and successful. Be very careful and wary because the private placement world is a dangerous one indeed. If you are a hedge fund manager, my advice is to stay away from venture capital or limit your exposure to 10 percent of the fund in private deals. If you are a private investor looking at a hedge fund, I would advise staying away from any fund investing more than 20 percent of the portfolio in private companies. The reason is that you never really know if the manager has priced these private companies correctly. If they are overpriced, you risk getting in front of a mark-to-market markdown.

Hedge fund managers most likely will have their private investments priced at what they paid for them. This price could be substantially above or below what the private company is actually worth. When a private company is doing well, the manager will increase the value of the private investments in the fund simply by instructing his prime broker to mark the price up. The hedge fund manager only needs to sign off to the accountants and bookkeepers that this value is correct based on his best judgment. It may in fact be correct, but until the private investment is liquidated, no one really knows what the true value is. You could come into a fund with the private company valued significantly above its true value or below, with no one really knowing what it is worth without a public market for accurate pricing. It's important that you understand this if you are considering putting your money with a hedge fund manager that has exposure to private placements and adventure companies.

At the end of the day, the big money gets to see the best adventure deals: That's just how the game works. Everybody else is simply fighting for the scraps the big money lets fall from the table. I can tell you firsthand that I've tasted a lot of the scraps and that there are far safer ways to earn a good return with your aggressive money.

HOW TO IDENTIFY THE BOTTOM FROM THE TOP

Imagine the perils of driving if drivers did not understand and heed the warning signs along the road. These signs are very evident to an alert driver: yellow lights warning us to proceed with caution; signs that warn of congested areas, sharp curves, and railroad crossings; and red lights that tell the driver to stop. To ignore the warnings can be deadly.

The stock and financial markets present an abundance of warning signs to the alert and educated investor. These signs can be strong indicators of when to sell because of a weakening market, or when to buy as the market is preparing to rise. The smart investor employs a strategy that includes a portfolio of stocks long and short. That same investor has learned how to identify the bottoms and tops, and uses that knowledge to enhance his chances of success.

As I mentioned earlier, there are secular (longer-term moves) in all markets, with some longer than others. There are also cyclical (short-term) up-and-down moves within the context of long-term secular bull or bear markets. This is important because one needs to recognize both cyclical and secular moves to make the necessary adjustments to a portfolio. The Nasdaq top in March 2000 marked a secular or long-term top. It could easily take 10 to 15 years for the current secular bear market to run its full course before setting up for another long-term uptrend.

As Nasdaq was collapsing, there were significant bear market cyclical rallies when the market got oversold. The techs rallied until they encountered overhead resistance from sellers before resuming the downtrend. As an example, from the all-time peak of 5,048 on March 10, 2000, Nasdaq crashed to 3,164 on May 23. This sell-off created a great opportunity to cover short positions and go long stocks. Nasdaq then exploded 1,200 points, at which time savvy traders could book profits on their longs as the market peaked in July. The market had rallied into overhead resistance, and gave traders an opportunity to go short again as stocks resumed their downtrend. That May-to-July move up was a bear market cyclical rally in the context of the Nasdaq secular decline.

As a declining market sets up for a bear market rally, it presents an opportunity for traders to buy back their shorts and wait to reshort after the rally has played itself out. Traders can buy into these oversold markets for the inevitable countertrend rally. Secular short players in a bear market can choose to ignore these rallies and stay with the major trend until a final bottom is reached.

The real estate market will experience recoveries similar to bear market rallies in stocks. You may get a clue that a short-term recovery is coming by following several of the home builder stocks like D. R. Horton, Inc. (DHI), Toll Brothers, Inc. (TOL), KB Home (KBH), Beazer Homes USA, Inc. (BZH), and NVR, Inc. (NVR). These stocks will bottom on the charts as the corporate insiders step up and buy their stocks in anticipation of a recovery. You should use these temporary recoveries to reduce your exposure in this new long-term secular bear market that started in 2005. These stocks will have to develop Stage 1 Bases for a very long time before they launch off into a sustained Stage 2 Advance.

It is important to understand where we are today and where we are likely to go in the future. The best way to do that is by analyzing the charts of the market averages as well as individual stocks.

In a Base, you are slowly accumulating long positions.

In the Advancing Stage, you add to these positions.

In the Topping Stage, you are selling your longs and initiating shorts.

In the Declining Stage, you should be adding to your short positions.

In the Standard & Poor's (S&P) 500 and the Dow Jones Industrial Average (DJIA), we began a cyclical bear market move in 2000 that resumed its secular bull market in March 2003. This secular move started in 1982 for these averages and then shot up fantastically starting in 1995 with Greenspan's money supply experiment. In early 2008, we have completed the final stage of a huge secular bull market move in the S&P 500 and the DJIA that started in 1982. We saw evidence that the previous secular bear market trend was near its end in 1979 with *BusinessWeek*'s now infamous front cover, "The Death of Equities," on August 13, 1979. The market bottomed shortly after that bearish article. Then we saw evidence that this long secular bull market trend was near its end when Mr. Market himself (Jim Cramer) was featured on the front cover of the September 2005 issue *of BusinessWeek.*

If you are an unbelievably patient buy/hold investor and can ride secular down markets like the past ones, then be ready to hold 15 to 20 years or more just to break even. However, with the decline of the dollar's purchasing power, you may never recover your lost wealth by holding your longs through a full secular bear market. It can often take a full generation before the previous highs are reached again.

To prove the point, look at the high-flying Nasdaq stocks in 2000 that are either bankrupt or still down 80 percent to 90% from their highs. The so-called "nifty 50" stocks in the 1960s took until the 1980s before many of them, the ones that still exist, made a final bottom. If you examine the average length of the big bear markets of the last 100 years (1906–1921, 1929–1949, and 1966–1982) the average length was 191 months or almost 16 long and very volatile years. I will discuss the signs of a secular top, and contrast that to signs of a secular bottom. Later, I'll share a story to demonstrate how most investors feel at the top and how they will feel at the next bottom.

Signs of a Top

In order to better understand signs of a bottom, we first need to look at the signs of a top and contrast that with some specific signs of a bottom. *Historically, the first sign of a top forming is when the Federal Reserve begins to raise interest rates.* They do this to squelch inflationary pressures or excess market speculation. Either way, "Don't fight the Fed" has been the general rule on Wall Street, as propounded by the well-known mutual fund manager Marty Zweig. If the Federal Reserve raises interest rates, you should be selling stocks by cutting long positions and adding to short positions. This is still good advice that will keep you from wiping out in a bear market.

The Federal Reserve started raising interest rates in 1999 several months before Nasdaq made its final high. The widely acknowledged rule is "three steps and a stumble." The first hike provides an opportunity to lighten up on long positions. You want to slowly exit your positions—be a scale-out seller, as the strong stock market momentum could send stocks much higher as it did from mid-1999 to the early 2000 peak. The second hike gives you an opportunity to position for the inevitable fall by adding to your short positions as Wall Street starts to anticipate the next hike. Usually, the Fed makes several consecutive moves when they embark on a new cycle of tightening or loosening. Look to Bernanke's repeated emergency rate cuts in late 2007 and throughout 2008 as the Fed aggressively pursued a new cycle of loosening credit. The third step, or hike, will be your green light to add to short positions and continue to cut back on long positions.

Many investors have used the 6 percent rule that says if the Fed hikes the discount rate to 6 percent, the stock market heads down fast. This theory is backed by some very strong evidence that when the Federal Reserve eventually is forced to raise the discount rate to 6 percent, investors should get short or raise cash aggressively.

On the following days, the Fed hiked the discount rate to 6 percent. A major market correction or crash soon followed:

January 23, 1920: Led into the brief, but painful 1920–1921 Depression

August 9, 1929: Right before the crash and Great Depression
April 3, 1969: A terrible market followed
April 11, 1973: A nasty bear market followed
October 26, 1977: A vicious bear market followed
September 1987: Preceded a 36 percent frightening drop in the DJIA

At a speculative blow-off top, stocks are usually running wild to the upside, which often causes the board of directors of these companies to split their stocks after a big run-up in price. This happens quite often at the top of a market. Before the 1987 crash, there were 169 stock splits in the previous 30 days before the crash. In June 1996, there were 155, and the market corrected 19 percent from the interday high to the interday low. Most stocks sold off 30 percent to 50 percent in a period of three weeks. In 1997, we saw 170 stock splits in the previous 30 days before we experienced the Asian crisis that sent stocks tumbling. Stock splits exploded to over 200 in June 1998 as a prewarning of the 1998 "market smash" from the Long-Term Capital Management debacle and the Russian crisis.

Another sign of a top is when there is record low short interest reported in the market combined with record high new issue activity. The low short interest lowers future potential demand from short covering. A subsegment of short interest is odd-lot short selling, that is, shorting from unsophisticated small investors, which will be almost nonexistent at the top. "Dumb money" odd-lot short selling will explode at the bottom in record levels, 15 to 99 shares at a time. For example, on February 28, on the eve of the 2000 market smash, short interest hit a five-year low. This short capitulation is one of the most reliable signs of the top. Another indicator along these same lines is the put–call ratio. In general, depending on which put–call ratio you follow, a high number of puts purchased indicates excessive bearishness, and that is bullish. A low number of puts purchased is a sign of complacency, another sign of a top.

Record high new issue activity is another clear warning sign of an approaching top. *The record high new issue activity increases supply that eventually overwhelms the demand, sending the stock market down.* This was very evident in the 1999 Nasdaq market and again in 2007 with Chinese stocks before they got cut in half.

At a secular top, mutual funds will have very low levels of cash of 3 percent to 4 percent and be fully invested in stocks, defenseless against a crash. By the time the market is at the absolute bottom, mutual funds will have cash levels of 10 percent to 15 percent. Traditional stock market valuation measures are almost useless for timing tops, but they will be very useful at the bottom. At the top in 2007, we had record- or near-record-high levels when using traditional measures of valuation like book value, dividend yields, and price to earnings (P/E). By contrast, stocks will trade at single-digit P/Es, and below book value, at the next secular bottom. I am talking about *the* bottom before we see these low levels of valuation.

At the 1949 bottom, the S&P 500's P/E was 5.4×, the dividend yield was 7.6 percent, and the price-to-book value was 0.89× book. At the 1982 secular bear market bottom, the P/E was 7.9×, the dividend yield was 6.3 percent, and the price-to-book value was 0.97× book. At the 2007 top, most stocks traded at 6 to 10 times book value. Dividend yields have been nonexistent for many years and are near worthless at timing the top but will work well to spot the next secular bottom. Dividend yields on stocks will be in the high single digits at the next bottom to compete with the high yields offered by collapsing bonds in the rising inflationary environment that is surely coming. When you look at the National Bureau of Economic Research on dividend yields going back to 1870, you could make the argument that dividend yields will spike to 7 percent to 10 percent at the next secular bear market bottom. It will take a severe bear market to see valuations reach the equivalent of past major market bottoms.

At the next top, you will see record new stock highs in the neighborhood of 800 to 1,000 on the new daily high list on the Nasdaq and New York Stock Exchange (NYSE). At a bottom, you see between 800 and 1,000 new lows on the new daily low list. We hit 941 new lows on October 8, 2002, on the NYSE, right at the bottom. There were over 1,500 new lows in Nasdaq at the exact bottom in 2002. New lows are exploding in 2008 as the U.S. market tries to find "a bottom" but that is "a bottom" versus "the bottom" of a secular bear market.

At the top, you will read about record amounts of money in mutual funds and hedge funds. In February 2000, right at the top, investors poured a record $60 billion into stock mutual funds, up from the $39.98 billion the previous month. In 1929, mutual funds were called investment trusts. From 1921 to 1925 these trusts took in $75 million. That number jumped to $1 billion from 1925 to 1927. By 1928, total assets in those funds rose to $4.5 billion. After the great crash in 1929 that $4.5 billion dropped to $31 million in 1933. In 1990, when the Japanese Nikkei hit its 39,000 high, there was $250 billion in Japanese equity funds. By 1996, that $250 billion dropped to $30 billion. In the future, trillions of dollars in mutual and hedge funds will dwindle to hundreds of billions of dollars before we see *the* bottom.

In the 1990s, record amounts of money were being poured into mutual funds. Today, there are more mutual funds than stocks, and as deflation intensifies, trillions of dollars will be lost and only a fraction of today's funds will be left standing at the absolute bottom. In the new century, we are seeing record amounts of money flowing into hedge funds. Hedge funds are like mutual funds on steroids, so the downside destruction in stocks will be even worse as the momentum turns downward. The reason for this is that hedge funds reverse course and heavily short stocks, adding to the downside pressure.

Prior to 2007, hedge funds would have to wait for a stock to uptick before they could sell it short. With the uptick rule no longer in effect, hedge funds can just hit bids driving stocks relentlessly lower. Hedge funds have become powerful forces moving markets up or down, depending on the upward or downward trend. *This is why you will need an active portfolio management style for this new era of market volatility that is upon us.*

Near the top, you will hear the most amazing things from analysts and see stocks do even crazier things, like Amazon.com in 1998, which turned into "Amazon.bomb" in 2000. I am reminded of Henry Blodget's Amazon $400 target price call that went from $260 per share to $400 in four weeks after his target price increase. The bad news is that the reason

I remember that day so well is that I was on the wrong side of the trade and was short Amazon. The irony is that 18 months later AMZN went down 80 percent from that high.

At the next top, the news in the papers will be glorious, positive, and booming. In March 2000, newspapers across America reported that "a red-hot economy roared ahead with a 7.3 percent growth rate in Q4 1999." In 1999, when I was pitching my hedge fund to a group of high-net-worth investors at a Bank of America conference, I used my local newspaper's headlines to illustrate all the good news. I did this to make my case from a market top. At the next bottom, the news will be incredibly depressing on the economy and stocks, and outright scary in the New Great Depression of the Twenty-first Century.

Often at a top, the government will be hiking taxes, and at a bottom they will be cutting them to spur economic growth like we saw with the Bush tax cuts. This was also the case with the Reagan tax cuts. *Tax cuts are very bullish for the market, while tax hikes can often be bearish signals.*

At the top, insider selling is extreme and sets new records as in 1999 and 2000. At the bottom, insider buying explodes like it did in the aftermath of 1987 and the 1990 recession. There has been some active insider buying in the volatile 2008 stock market, which is a sign the bulls like to see when searching for a bottom. *At the top, you will read about record high prices paid for a seat on the NYSE.*

At the top, investors go on margin and buy twice as many shares for twice the gains. Margin debt explodes to crazy new highs, marking another reliable sign of an impending market top. In February 2000, margin debt increased 50 percent from September 1999 to $265 billion, right at the top. In a bull market, margin debt is expanding, and in a bear market, margin debt will be contracting. At the bottom, margin debt will be cut in half like the $130 billion drop in margin debt before we bottomed in 2003. In 2007, margin debt exploded past the 2000 highs right before the market tanked in 2008.

A technical tool that's effective in detecting crashes is the advance-decline (A-D) line. You can find this in *Investor's Business Daily* (IBD). If the A-D trend line is declining, then the bears have the upper hand in the market over the bulls. The A-D line is simply an index of advancing stocks minus declining stocks and the A-D figure is plotted so a trend can be identified. Those who went to cash or shorted on the A-D warning in 1987 avoided the plunge in October. Investors would have also avoided the 1973–1974 bear market that sent the DJIA tumbling from 1,036 to 578. The A-D line was hitting new lows in early 1999, giving advance warning of the top to come in 2000. Most stocks had already started a bear market before the top in 2000. The four horsemen of IBM, CSCO, SUNW, and MSFT led the selected few technology stocks (outside of pure Internet companies) to new highs in 1999 before the March 2000 top. The A-D lines in 2008 shows that the bears clearly have the upper hand.

At the bottom of the secular bear market, investor friends will threaten to smack you in the back of your head if you mention the market one more time to them. In other words, your friends will not want to talk about any financial market when the market is at the bottom.

Calling a Top

Trying to call the top of the market is not only difficult; it can be a regrettable act. Marty Zweig and Elaine Garzerelli became quite famous for predicting the 1987 crash, but that fame didn't last. Of course, Marty Zweig is one of the coolest money managers ever, so he'll always be famous to many fans like me. I remember James Stack was the "Number One Market Timer" for several years back in 1996 when he made a big call on TV. On March 15, 1996, he was quoted in the IBD as saying, "A good size correction is long overdue as breadth is too narrow. You'd be foolish to underestimate the risk in the market." In hindsight, of course, it was foolish to underestimate the strength of the market as it exploded for several more years. The famous "Sell All Stocks Now" call made by Elaine Garzerelli on January 20, 1996, was right before stocks soared higher. Then there was Michael Metz, the high-profile bear during the 1990s' roaring bull market until he finally quit shortly before the top. On April 24, 1995, he was chief investment strategist of Oppenheimer, Inc., when he was quoted in IBD saying, "The stock market has factored in all the good news and the risk vs. reward is not great." Of course, in hindsight, we know it was great. Michael kept his scowling bear face on for many years as the market rallied powerfully.

CNBC interviewed Michael Metz near the end of his career at Oppenheimer. I watched him go from a growling, confident bear to a timid pussycat as the commentator asked him, "Where do we go from here?" Michael knew exactly where he was going, but had no clue where the market was going. Michael looked up and said, "This market has humbled me once again and I'm looking for a new career." On June 22, 1998, *Fortune* magazine ran an article titled "Say Goodbye to the Last Bear." In the article, Metz was asked why he gave up after "screaming that the sky is falling since 1995." Michael Metz, the "last truly bearish big shot," replied, "I was tired of being wrong." That was a fast-blinking yellow light that the market was not too far from putting in its ultimate top. Surprisingly, Metz had made a return to Wall Street. In May 2007, I saw him once again on CNBC, and to my amazement, he was a roaring bull; about 10,000 Dow points higher than when he started screaming "sell" years earlier. All secular-trend-thinking bears should find that fact very comforting.

How High Is High?

After watching Nasdaq go to 5,048, you have to ask yourself, how high is high? I remember on May 3, 1996, Comparator Systems (IDID) was in the headlines. This was a fingerprint identification stock that exploded on huge volume from $0.03 per share to almost $2 per share. The company had no sales, enormous losses, and 600 million shares outstanding. How does a company go from near bankruptcy to a billion-dollar market valuation in a few short days? Again, how high is high? About a month later, IDID was halted near $2 and later opened with a zero bid. Here we have the answer to the question, how low is low? The answer to how high is high is, "Who knows?"

Once I talked with a guy I knew who was buying VA Linux (LNUX) in the aftermarket the day of the initial public offering (IPO). The IPO price was $30 per share; and it traded up 698 percent in its first day of trading; he was buying it after that big move. I remember asking him, "How much higher than 700 percent in one day can a stock really go?" In 1999 I got my answer as I watched JDSU climb 830 percent. At the top, I got a research report on JDSU from my Sutro & Co. stockbroker that stated, "We are initiating coverage of JDSU with a buy rating and we believe JDSU should trade at 100× earnings or a $260 billion market valuation." In 2008, JDSU trades with a $1.2 billon dollar market cap, which is a far cry from that $260 billion projection in 1999.

On December 29, 1999, my wife and I visited a married couple who were our friends. The husband was trading Qualcomm (QCOM) online. We watched QCOM climb 156 points that day to $659 per share. When I woke up for the next trading day, QCOM jumped another $81 points to $740 per share. Unless you traded through this crazy dot-com time period, you wouldn't believe stuff like this actually happened.

Why did this speculative nonsense happen? Look to Alan Greenspan for the answer. The so called "Maestro" created more money than all Federal Reserve chairmen combined since the creation of the Fed in 1913. I remember watching Aeriel Corporation's stock jump 1,000 percent in just one week of trading. On November 13, 1998, shares of AvTel (AVCO) rose 1,277.8 percent after simply announcing it was "launching high-speed Internet access." On this same day, the Internet mania saw Theglobe.com (TGLO) jump 500 percent on its market debut.

Only excessive amounts of liquidity and greed could create these astronomical short-term price gains. This is why I was amazed when in late 1999 Greenspan claimed he was unable to identify a bubble until after it has popped. Greenspan should have raised margin requirements and bank reserve requirements to squelch this speculative nonsense by recognizing these obvious bubbles earlier.

Another broker I used told me to buy Applied Micro Circuits (AMCC) at $200 per share. I pointed out to him that AMCC was trading 540 times earnings, 20 times book value, 271 times cash flow, and 115 times revenues. I also pointed out to him that there were 20 insider sales totaling 1.1 million shares and zero buys. Again, How high is high?

We must look at other bubble crazes to answer this question of how high is high. The 1634 tulip craze in Holland took prices of tulips up 5,900 percent before crashing 93 percent.

In the early 1700s, the Mississippi Scheme bubble rose 6,200 percent before crashing 99 percent and the South-Sea share bubble in England rose 1,000% before falling 84 percent. *It's so easy to be wrong trying to call the top of any market because we don't know how high bubble markets can go.* This is yet another reason why my short-side strategy of utilizing stocks long and short, with predetermined stops and price targets, can be so effective.

When I started in this industry, I met two gold bug brokers who were betting against the Japanese stock market, which had skyrocketed from 6,000 in 1980 to near 25,000 in 1989. Because of this huge run-up, these brokers were betting heavily against Japan, and why not? These were obvious stock and real estate bubbles. At the top in 1992, Japan's real estate market was valued at $16 trillion. Japan is smaller than Montana, yet it was valued more than all 50 U.S. states. Tokyo's Imperial Palace was reported to be worth more than all of California.

These two brokers were buying Japanese Nikkei put warrants that traded on Nasdaq. These guys were getting murdered, but they kept buying and even went on margin because at 30,000, the Nikkei had nothing but downside. When the Nikkei hit 35,000, they were completely wiped out, after which the market peaked at 39,000 and then collapsed. This is a clear example of how you can be correct on your thinking, but wiped out by an incorrect market timing call. Remember, always use stops—ALWAYS!

I warned my investors that a "10-year crash reunion" was to take place on or around October 19, 1997. Almost every one of the signs I have outlined in this book was flashing red in the fall of that year. I told everyone who would listen that a coming Asian "tiger" crisis was going to cause this big reunion smash on the DJIA just like the 1987 crash. I took my hedge funds, which were up nicely for the year, to 100 percent cash a few weeks before the October 27, 1997, smash. I saw no reason to short because I was very happy with my gains that year. The Asian currency crisis spread, and the DJIA melted down. Trading curbs were hit, and the market closed early for the first time because of the curbs on the day of the Asian crisis.

I was at my local athletic club on October 27, 1997, where reporters for the local paper were asking people if the market smash was hurting them. I told them I was 100 percent cash in my hedge fund at the time. Next thing I knew, I had a photographer taking my picture and a crowd gathering around me as I was being interviewed about the market. Once the gathering crowd realized I was just an ordinary Wall Street speculator, the excitement waned and the crowd quickly dispersed.

The next day, my picture was in the local paper, the *Bend Bulletin,* where I was quoted as being 100 percent in cash a few weeks ahead of the crash. I also was quoted as saying, "There are some good values now that prices have come down." I was right on the Asian crisis call but wrong about the 10-year crash reunion call because the market recovered and went higher. In 1999, Nasdaq had its best year ever.

That Nasdaq 1999 nonsense just shows that high can get incredibly higher even when you think it illogical and impossible. It is also another example of why a stop loss discipline is crucial to investment and trading success.

"Underwear on My Head"

Back in 1996 when the news appeared, "Failed Budget Negotiations, U.S. Government to Shut Down," the stock market was selling off hard. I had been incorrectly shorting stocks in my hedge fund looking for a break in the market. The assistant portfolio manager of the hedge fund had made a market top call I'll never forget. He said emphatically, "Ron, if the DJIA breaks above the 5,500 level to new highs, I'll put my underwear on top of my head for a full trading day." As I was losing my shirt being short as the market rallied, my assistant manager was cheerleading my losing ways. Shortly thereafter, the market raced far above his "underwear on my head" market call.

The point is that when the headline news is bad and stocks are falling, "underwear on my head" type of confidence will abound. *When you boldly call a top, you usually end up having to put a foot in your mouth or your underwear on your head.* My best call is to employ a short-side strategy and to warn that future market risk (and reward) is extremely high. How's that for a hedge!

With the Fed printing money and cutting interest rates, how high is high? I have no idea. *However, traditional yardsticks of valuation tell us that ALL investors need to look at the downside of the market as closely as the upside and position themselves accordingly.* Think of Greenspan and Bernanke as Hans and Franz, the two musclemen from the funny skit on *Saturday Night Live.* Imagine them both next to a large printing press as they inflate the money supply, saying in an Arnold Schwarzenegger–like accent, "We are here to pump-you-up" (clap). That is what they have done to create Nasdaq in 2000, real estate in 2004, and the DJIA and S&P 500 in 2007. Bernanke pumped money like never before in 2008 so look for newly created bubbles to emerge and for the strong possibility of rapidly rising inflation once the 2008 broad-based asset crash is over.

The Best Signs of a Bottom

I have already mentioned a few signs you will see at the bottom. Here, I will focus on the best indicators to know whether you are at the bottom or the top. At the bottoms of 1987, 1990, 1994, and 2003, there was one reliable and simple indicator. It was the spike in what is called the Volatility Index or the VIX. The VIX put versus call ratio is the most reliable indicator to measure fear in the marketplace. The VIX was invented by Robert Whaley of Duke University for the Chicago Board Options Exchange. The VIX can also spot market tops, but it is a much less reliable timing indicator for spotting tops. The VIX can stay down for a long time and the market can basically go sideways or even higher, so this indicator does little good for timing tops. However, when investors and traders are panicked and they are buying puts hand over fist betting the market will crash, then the VIX explodes higher.

The VIX is a great measurement of heightened fear and is commonplace to all market bottoms, whether they are cyclical or secular bottoms. Since 1995, the median VIX close has been about 22, with the majority trading between 15 and 25. On October 20, 1987, the reading hit an extreme level of 172.79. Most times, this level only needs to get near or above 50 and you know the market is near some kind of a bottom and it is time to cover your shorts and start putting money back into the market steadily. On October 8, 1998, as the effect of the Russian crisis spread all over the globe, the VIX hit 58.92. That reading was hit as the market was close to advancing to one of the biggest moves in history since Nasdaq 1999. In October of 2008, incredibly, the VIX exceeded 80. Amazing!

You will want to cover some shorts and add to the longs whenever you cross 50 on the VIX, and, again, do this slowly. Once momentum starts heading down, you are trying to catch a falling knife. As you are trying to catch the falling knife buying crashing stocks, you could get bloodied if you are too early and too aggressive. When the knife finally hits bottom, then you can get more aggressive in your buying after stocks crash and start to head up on big volume. The bigger the volume on the turn-up from the bottom, the better, as this signals market strength. You always want to average into your long and short positions, and only average up on longs. Never average down as you are trying to find a bottom. With short positions, average out your winners slowly because the market could have a long way to go down before the falling knife sticks.

As a general rule, any time the VIX reading is under 10, you have an extreme amount of investor complacency and you need to cut back your longs and increase your shorts slowly because you are likely approaching a higher-risk area in the market. *Extreme fear, evidenced by a high VIX, is very bullish. Extreme complacency of a low VIX is a yellow light of caution.* This one indicator will help you to navigate and position your portfolio wisely to increase your returns and lower your risk. The VIX indicator works perfectly to spot bottoms and can work well at tops when it is combined with the other topping indicators I have mentioned. There is no perfect indicator, so you need to know and recognize all of these flashing warning lights.

Another great indicator at spotting bottoms, and occasionally effective in identifying tops, is the Investors Intelligence survey. Investors Intelligence is a New York–based advisory service that publishes a newsletter that surveys 130 advisory firms that put out market letters. The Investors Intelligence surveys the percentage of bullish investment advisers compared to bearish investment advisers. History has shown that investment advisory firms and newsletter writers, taken as a group, are wrong most of the time. The newsletter writers became a contrary indicator, so when they are bearish, you'll want to be bullish and vice versa.

The American Association of Individual Investors (AAII) Index publishes a second report that tracks the sentiment of individual investors. These polls will almost always have a bullish bias, showing more bulls than bears even as the market is tanking. It is only at the absolute bottom when investment advisers and individual investors throw in the towel that you get readings where the bears overwhelm the bulls.

In late May 2000, after the Nasdaq and most stocks crashed, the AAII polls still showed 61.9 percent bulls and only 16.7 percent bears. These readings finally reversed near the bottom. For example, on April 3, 2001, the Consensus Inc. sentiment survey of market newsletter writers and brokerage firms reported an all-time low number of bulls, at only 10 percent. The readings continued to stay bearish even as the market turned up. It still took quite some time to put in the bottom from that all-time low bullish reading. This is why you must go slowly when probing for a bottom because you can't see the future and know how low is low. All these various indicators are easy to find and follow. I would again advise everyone to read IBD, as they highlight just about everything I have presented.

Playing Defense

An easy way to get exposure to the short side, when you see these indicators flash red, is to buy the Rydex Ursa fund. This fund will move inverse to the stock market, and it is a painless, quick way to get some quick crash insurance and protection from a falling market. In recent years, the Rydex ProFunds have made available a host of inverse index exchange-traded funds (ETFs). Because market timing is so difficult, you'll want to do this only when most of these signs of a top are flashing red. For professional investors, buying and selling options and futures on the S&P 500 and on other markets is a great way to hedge one's portfolio. If you have a long portfolio and buy put options, for example, you risk only the premium you pay for the option. The put option you bought will give you the possibility to adequately hedge your portfolio if the market corrects or crashes. The puts will rise substantially if the market crashes, and that is great hedge protection if you see the warning signs flash "sell." If you are wrong, then the puts will expire worthless and you lose the premium you paid for the option. Options and futures are very risky, but used properly, especially for hedging purposes, they are very effective. Remember, if you are long put options on the market then you win on the puts as the market goes down. If you own call options, it is just the opposite.

You can successfully "short the market" only at a top or in a Stage 4 bear market decline when the odds are heavily in your favor. *You can short individual stocks in almost any market environment because many individual stocks have their own private bear markets, even in a bull market.* Remember that shorting too early or late can crush you, so stay patient. Wait until the odds are heavily stacked in your favor before making any big plays on the short side.

Another widely used way to hedge your long positions, if you are unsure and uneasy about a stock, is to sell call options against your longs. You can earn yourself income from the sale of the calls as you wait until the market goes into a Stage 2 Advance. I see the possibility of a long sideways period in U.S. and global markets. This is where you can benefit most by either trading stocks or owning high-dividend-paying stocks because stocks basically go nowhere in a sideways market. If the stock that you sold covered calls on goes up through the strike price of your option, then the stock gets called away. You will lose your position, but you'll earn the extra income from the premium of the call option sold, which also serves as a small hedge against the long. The risk of this covered call strategy is that you don't adequately hedge yourself if the market or stock implodes, as you are protected only by the premium or credit you receive for selling the call option. If you are worried that a stock you own may fall with a market correction, then buy puts on the stock you own to more fully hedge the downside. This way, you will adequately protect yourself if the stock falls hard. However, you will still enjoy the unlimited upside benefit of your long stock if the stock rises, and lose only the premium you paid for the long put.

Again, a strategy of selling calls against your longs is best in sideways or trendless markets because you will earn the premium from selling the call, but you keep your stock. You can do this over and over again in that kind of market environment. Just make sure the number of calls you sell matches the total of the number of shares you are long. You will know you are in that kind of market by the complete contradiction of market signals flashing red and green simultaneously. The market will feel heavy, and most likely this will be after the market completes a Stage 4 Decline and everyone is numb from the fall. As Jesse Livermore would say, the tape will feel "waterlogged." The other time will be after the market has had a big Stage 2 Advance and everyone is worn out from the euphoric move as the market tops out and goes sideways for some time.

At bottoms, all the newsletter writers will be singing the same bearish tune. For example, on September 5, 1994, a special note was made to this effect from the editor of *Dick Davis Digest.* This informative newsletter had a page titled "Where the Market Is Going." Dick Davis featured about 10 different newsletter writers on the outlook for the stock market. At the bottom in 1994, the editor wrote, "The comments above are decidedly bearish. This is not a result of selecting only negative views. Rather, this bearishness is reflective of the overall sentiment among newsletter writers." The editor noted, "As a contrarian, I'm concerned by this concentration of opinion in one camp." In 1994 and 1995, everyone seemed bearish and scared. The Fed hiked interest rates for the last time in early 1995, but the market was already on its way north before the Fed officially stopped hiking rates. What the editor should have said was, "As a contrarian, I'm excited to see this concentration of bears in one camp." *A consensus bearish opinion among newsletter writers is a clear signal to go the opposite way and get bullish on stocks.*

On December 7, 1994, IBD ran a front-page article titled "Market Newsletters Form a Bearish Choir." It went on to say, "If the nation's premier stock market newsletters are right, don't expect a major rally anytime soon." That was right in front of one of the biggest rallies ever in the stock market. For example, the top-rated *Value Line Investment Survey* was recommending that investors hold 35 percent to 45 percent of their portfolios in cash, the highest cash level it has ever advised, according to this IBD article.

The point is that "everyone" is frightened at the bottom of the market—everyone except short-side traders, who enjoy profits from the decline. In 1994, the DJIA and S&P 500 closed down less than 10 percent. How much more bearish do you think investors will be when the DJIA falls 5,000 or 10,000 points? In 2008, this is precisely what the Fed feared could happen. The Federal Reserve has been fighting deflation and the prospects of a depression. They have been lowering interest rates and the government has resorted to bailouts that, combined, could create a trading bottom, but not necessarily the bottom. It typically takes about one year for the interest rate cuts to take a positive effect in a recessionary economy before it bottoms. In a depression, expect it to take much longer than 12 months and require much more stimulation and revolutionary credit creation methods to get the economy moving again. The Fed was aggressively lowering interest rates in 2001 to fight the recession, but it took until 2002 to put in the bottom, and 2003 for the market to lift off. At the market bottom in 2002, *Dick Davis Digest* had another note about the newsletter writers, saying, "The percentage of bulls hit an 8-year low." Wrong again. The bottom line is that newsletter writers and brokerage firms get bearish at the bottom. The emotion of fear always comes out at the bottom or during the bottoming process. It's just human nature.

There's another axiom that says "two tumbles and a jump," but after Nasdaq 2000, I wouldn't put too much faith in this rule. Traditionally, it has been thought that if the Fed is cutting rates, you want to be increasing longs and reducing your short positions. On September 18, 2007, the Fed lowered Fed funds to 4.75 percent and the discount rate by 0.50 basis points to 5.25 percent, and stocks exploded to new highs. A talking head on CNBC said in response, "God bless the greatest Federal Reserve in the world." Another CNBC commentator for the bull parade said, "This is so exciting." And so it goes. Once again, the Federal Reserve tried to come to the rescue of the speculators, creating the froth needed to flash signs of the top.

If the Fed gets the DJIA to recover and scream to 20,000 from excessive added liquidity, and then a 1929 or Nasdaq 2000 crash repeats, this will take the DJIA down 18,000 points to the bottom. That would compare to 12,000 points from the 2007 top of 14,000 in a "90 percent 1929 depression-like fall." The bottom line is 90 percent from 14,000 in 2007, or 90 percent from 20,000 or wherever, is still 90 percent. The higher we go and the more credit acquired, the greater the pain of liquidation. Those who do not have a short-side strategy could get completely wiped out. Again, watch the money supply and interest rates. *When the money supply gets cut to fight inflation, buckle up. Tighten the chin strap on your crash helmet and put on all your other crash protection gear, as stocks will crash violently once the money supply is cut and interest rates explode.*

Crisis Investing

Investing in the market can be like entering a war zone. It's easy to get your portfolio blown to pieces now because it's such a dangerous market environment. The surprise financial market events plus the twists and turns in the news play havoc with your emotions. Bad news can create such fear that herds of investors hit the panic button. The world's most famous trader, Jesse Livermore, once said, "There are only two emotions in the market, hope and fear. The problem is, you hope when you should fear and fear when you should hope." *If you go back to the past crises and study how the market performed from the resulting lows, you will see it is best to hope in the midst of fear.* In fact, it is best to cut short positions and deploy cash by adding significantly to long positions after stocks have crashed from a crisis.

The DJIA bottomed on October 23, 1962, on the Cuban Missile crisis, and was up 33 percent 12 months later. Two years later, the DJIA was up 57.3 percent.

After the 1973–1974 market break, the DJIA was up 42.2 percent after the market bottomed on December 6, 1974. It was up 66.5 percent two years after the low was made.

After the 1987 market crash hit bottom on October 19, 1987, it was up 54 percent from the low two years later.

After the 9/11 terrorist attack, the DJIA and S&P 500 went on to new all-time highs in 2007.

Consider these as potential headlines in future newspapers, "After the 2008 credit crisis finally crushed stocks, the market bottomed in 20XX and raced to. . . ."

Even after the 1929 crash, there was a chance to buy during that crisis and ride a rally of 48 percent in five months. But you had to get out before the market imploded to new depression lows. The DJIA had a 40.2 percent month gain in April 1933, the DJIA's biggest on record.

This biggest one-month percentage loss in the DJIA is coming soon, as the "Barry Bonds" economy has lost its juice. The next crisis will be the granddaddy of them all as we witness an unprecedented drop in the market, resulting from a likely forced cut in the money supply.

When U.S. government bonds break down or if the Fed is forced to rein in the growth of credit, get protected. You'll want to treat all rallies as opportunities to sell longs and increase shorts as the main event unfolds. Look to the 85 percent Nasdaq 2000 fall preview to see the future main event of the DJIA 85 percent crash to come.

Snowboard Dennis

Realize what we are facing will be a slow-motion version of the tech collapse. Here's a story of how a top-to-bottom market drop affects an investor.

When you are a snowboarder and you live in a town that is close to a major ski mountain, you find yourself going to the mountain as often as possible. In early 1999, I became friends with a fellow East Coaster named Dennis. He had retired and decided to manage his own money, like many investors are doing today.

Dennis and I talked often about stocks and the market. Dennis had all of his retirement account in Microsoft, Cisco, Dell, and Intel. In the latter stages of the tech bubble I was incorrectly cautious, although my hedge fund had made great returns owning technology stocks in 1995, 1996, and 1997. Unfortunately for me, I stayed nervous on technology stocks after 1997 and missed the entire blow-off top they made in 1999.

As a hedge fund manager, I was a bit humbled as novice investors like Dennis were euphoric about their gains and their newfound knowledge of the technological revolution. Dennis and others I knew threw that right back in my face as 1999 came to a close. On Christmas Eve I received a Christmas card from Dennis that said, "Merry Christmas, Ron. I hope you have a better year in 2000 like the 90% up-year I had in 1999."

My wife and I were invited to Dennis's New Year's Eve party. I told Dennis, "I think we are on the cusp of a 1929-like crash in Nasdaq and maybe you should get out and just enjoy those gains for a while." He laughed and said, "Ron, you still don't get it, do you?" Another tech bull I knew named Ken was saying the same thing, and I was getting tired of hearing it! He went on and on about the new Internet revolution and how "you bears," as he called me, are just so "clueless" to the riches to be made.

His wife told me they were excited about this new home they were building. I asked if they were building this house expecting Nasdaq 1999–type gains in the future, and she said, "Absolutely!" I told her to be safe and not to have those expectations because if I am right, they could really get hurt. A little while later, Dennis informed me that he was going to take most of his portfolio out of the four horsemen and buy the new and strongest horse, JDS Uniphase (JDSU). JDSU had become the hottest stock with new-era investors, and it was about $150 per share at the time. It was trading at an insane valuation, like all technology stocks at the time.

By the summer of 2000, the Nasdaq market, which been down about 2,000 points from the March high, was having a bear market rally at the time. When I saw Dennis, I asked how he was doing, and he said, "My portfolio is down about 35 percent or so, but this is just a small correction and the market is already on its comeback." He asked me my thoughts, and I said, "Dennis, this is Stage 1 of a bear market for Nasdaq, and this is just a normal bear market rally. When it is over, JDSU will be a single-digit stock." He chuckled. I can remember thinking that he was just dying to say, "Ron, you still just don't get it," but his confidence wasn't as high with his stocks down.

Several months later we spoke again, and now the market was off about 2,500 or so points from the highs and JDSU had been cut in half. I told him, "We're now in Stage 2 of the bear market and you don't want to see me at the final stage." I asked him how much he was down and he told me his $2.3 million account was about $1.2 million, but he still was still very confident.

When I next saw Dennis, the market had experienced another bad day, especially JDSU. I told him, "We will have another bear market rally and you need to sell some stocks and not let your account go under $1 million, because we are going to go into the final stage of this bear market decline. That will be the bottom, where you'll likely be forced to sell." He told me, "The Internet isn't going away and has nothing but explosive growth ahead, and I am a long-term investor in these stocks. Besides, Alan Greenspan is really coming to the rescue cutting interest rates aggressively."

Let's fast-forward to the exact bottom in Nasdaq in 2003. The next time I saw Dennis at our local athletic club, he was wearing a suit and tie and he had cut his hair from long to very short. He told me he'd lost everything and was leaving the area to find a job. I said, "Dennis, I truly am sorry and I will miss you." Then I said, "Dennis, if it makes you feel any better, my other dot-com investor buddy Ken just wiped out 90 percent of his portfolio in technology stocks. Many investors are in the exact same boat as you are." I was trying to make him feel better and told him how there were stories of ex-billionaire dot-com CEOs who lost everything and even stories of some that were in homeless shelters, according to the news reports. Dennis drove away, and I never saw or heard from him again.

The point of this story is its stark comparison to real estate investors from the top in 2005 to today. In 2004, real estate had all the hype and excitement of Nasdaq 1999. In 2005, real estate started its reversal similar to Nasdaq in 2000. In 2006, 2007, and 2008, the news on real estate got worse, yet there was very little fear of a 1929-style collapse. The confidence of the real estate bulls at that time reminded me of Dennis. I can imagine some minor recoveries from the very aggressive Bernanke Fed rate cuts like those Nasdaq bounces from Greenspan's rate cuts. This will only encourage the real estate bulls to take on additional levels of unproductive, speculative debt.

Real challenges face the economy and the market as the new administration comes into office. The first two years of the presidential cycle can be bad for stocks and the economy. Taxes will likely be raised, undercutting the economy as it loses its juiced-up muscle from the steroid injections of combined monetary and fiscal stimulus. Real estate will then descend into its second phase of its long bear market. This will be when the real fear starts to set in as real estate investors recognize this is not only local—it's a national and even a global phenomenon.

At the absolute bottom in real estate and for the economy, housing speculators will return to being just plain old homeowners. Investors will swear off ever buying real estate for speculative purposes ever again. They will look at the real estate bust as a wealth-destruction monster created by excessive levels of mortgage debt. This whole process may take 10 to 15 years to play out just like past long secular bear markets in stocks and gold. That will be the time to buy again. At the bottom of any market, investors will go through these three phases of pain from the top to the bottom.

"Rich Dad" Becomes "Poor Dad"

Most serious real estate investors I speak with seem confident that prices will come back. They are riding the "slippery slope of hope." I believe real estate did in 2005 what Nasdaq did in 2000 but this bear market will unfold much more slowly before it finds its secular bottom. When it is does, real estate investors and speculators alike will ask themselves why they didn't see the real estate depression coming. Many will be stuck with property flips and overpriced homes like Dennis was stuck with JDS Uniphase. Unfortunately, they will ultimately be forced to sell at the bottom as the U.S. and global economies pays the price.

This coming bottom will be unlike those in the past because it will victimize the wealthiest and most sophisticated investors (Rich Dads) as well as novice investors (Poor Dads). This is because this real estate boom was primarily fueled by the wealthiest of investors in the United States. The bad news is that unlike the Nasdaq bubble pop, which affected only a small number of technology investors, the real estate crash will affect the majority of Americans and much of the world. This could lead us into the New Great Depression of the Twenty-First Century, which could in fact become a global phenomenon, so it may instead be termed the "New Great Global Depression of the Twenty-First Century."

I can only hope that the cyclical recoveries in real estate we will likely have along this long secular bear market will give investors reading this book a chance to bank their profits and reduce their debt burdens. I hope that this depression and asset deflation call is wrong, and if it is, I still hope my warnings give every reader something to think about. The point of this book is not for me to make some big market or economic call or some gloom-and-doom end-of-the-world prediction. *This book is my attempt to get every reader to look at the downside possibilities of every investment choice they make. I also want to open your mind to the opportunities and possibilities to make bull market returns even in bear markets.*

From my own experience I know how hard it is to go from rags to riches back to rags once again. I know that excessive confidence in any investment decision, in any asset class, can bring one to his or her knees. The 2008 credit crisis is bringing many Americans to their knees. *Real estate and the U.S. economy are both skating on very thin ice, and the cracks are clearly starting to show.* Bernanke is trying to "freeze the pond" with his aggressive rate cuts by running the printing presses overtime in 2007 and 2008. If you went from rags to riches, then don't be on thin ice like most long-only investors today, or you'll find yourself back to rags quicker than you can imagine.

Start Imagining How You Can Help Save Yourself and Even Save the World

It's the year 20XX, and U.S. investors woke up Monday morning to a U.S. currency collapse that sent stocks around the globe on a freefall-like decline. The markets closed early today as trading curbs were hit and investors everywhere were riveted with fear of what will most likely follow. On Tuesday morning, markets worldwide continued to get hammered as investors panicked and sold at any price. The buyers were mostly shorts buying back their short positions and taking profits. When foreign investors woke up, they also accelerated their selling and are repatriating their assets out of the United States, which is creating a 1987-style collapse. This is occurring right at the very time when the U.S. government is struggling to prevent a capital flight to fund the enormous twin deficits and service its huge debt.

On Wednesday morning, stocks gapped down violently in a fashion now resembling the greatest crash in history, 1929. The market's selling curbs were hit and the exchanges all closed early once again. When the markets reopened Thursday, traders were faced with waves and waves of margin call selling pressure. This created forced sellers, who are finding it very difficult to find bids to hit, as so few are brave enough to step in front of this freight train of panic selling. Traders report that there is "blood in the streets" like nothing they have ever experienced. Finally, stocks complete their total and utter collapse, creating what many are calling "A New Great Depression," with stocks now down nearly 90 percent.

All that this nightmare left was the HUGE mountain of debt that stood against severely declining stocks and real estate, which many are calling "The Global Margin Call," as global markets naturally collapsed following the U.S. market crash. The fog of despair in the air on both Wall Street and Main Street was thick enough to leave investors snow-blind and paralyzed with fear and trepidation. Jobs are being cut and unemployment is soaring in what appears to be The New Great Global Depression of the Twenty-First Century. The already weak real estate market is now faced with mass liquidation as homeowners are forced out of their homes and onto the street as they mail the keys back to their failing bank. Banks that had loaned all the excess credit, force-fed to them by the Federal Reserve, are now underwater, and thousands had to close their doors.

Angry depositors lined up to get any cash they could get their hands on. Investors worldwide now realize history just repeated itself as a Depression similar to 1929 has arrived. The primary cause this time was the overleveraging of real estate and not just stocks, as was the case in the 1920s.

Everyone, from the government to its citizens, is asking, "How did we get here, and how could such a thing happen to this once great nation?" Government officials are being asked, "How in the world did you let the United States get so dependent on foreign investors to buy U.S. government bonds and let our massive twin deficits and national debt get completely out of control?" and, "How did we get so dependent on hostile foreign nations for our energy needs?"

Congress blasts the Federal Reserve for letting the derivatives market turn into a $400 trillion accident, resulting in collapsing banks across the nation. The newspapers write, "How did we get so far into mortgage debt, margin debt, auto debt, credit card debt, corporate debt, and government debt to the tune of tens of trillions of dollars? Who allowed such easy access to credit? How did our country go from the world's largest creditor to the world's largest debtor nation? Did anyone really think the Federal Reserve could just print money incessantly before the weight of all that supply would eventually collapse the U.S. dollar and foreign investors would flee? Did the government really believe our debts and deficits were just "numbers on paper" to be ignored? Today, the world learned that those "numbers on paper" were in fact numbers to be feared.

Stop Imagining and Start Acting

This book is partially a warning, but it's also a call to action that should extend beyond the scope of your personal situation. The simple math of the debt side of the balance sheet overwhelming the asset side applies to government at all levels as well as to the entire private sector. If asset prices head into a deep secular decline, then our country could be faced with devastating results.

The fact is that when asset values crash, all the debt stacked against those assets remains. Like stocks in 1929 and real estate in 2008, asset prices can fall faster than debt can be reduced. So even as debt decreases, the true debt burden increases. This is because the debt becomes an even greater percentage of net worth as asset values accelerate their fall. The difference between the remaining high debt and the reduced assets below that debt will be like a giant global margin call with insufficient equity supporting that debt for collateral. This will affect the whole world dramatically. This giant margin call will have to be met by every single one of us. It is the reason we all must have a paradigm shift in our consciousness.

We must all do our part to save our country from bankruptcy. *First, take an active role in your investments with a new strategy that addresses the downside. Next, get involved in the political process to ensure the election of politicians who understand the fiscal challenges facing our country.* Everyone can see how dangerously high personal and government debt levels have risen. If we don't start to balance our budgets and change our policies, we face a financial collapse like that of the 1930s. We must all play a part to enact change in the government's mindset as well as among the citizenry. No more reckless unproductive debt! We must have a more practical and cautious eye towards credit and credit creation within the financial system.

It is entirely possible that if our government acts swiftly we can lessen the impact from this financial crisis. Let's look to past administrations like Truman's when we had balanced budgets and fiscal responsibility. The government was able to pay down billions of dollars of wartime debt, and the country enjoyed a growing economy. If the federal government slashed all nonessential spending and restored fiscal sanity then we could use the overflow of tax money from a growing economy to buy back many government bonds in the open market. This would reduce our dependence on foreign nations to fund our debt and deficit-created consumption.

These are worthy goals that will require some short-term pain. However, the long-term gain for our children and grandchildren is well worth it. When the U.S. puts its financial house in order and starts to respect the concerns of other nations, we will once again become "a shining beacon of hope" to the rest of the world. Regaining respect from the rest of the world, as was earned by our fathers and grandfathers, would be one of our primary missions. *The time for action is now so we will have a healthy and stronger tomorrow.*

CHAPTER 11

MY BEAT-UP CHEVY AND THE 10 IRON LAWS OF INVESTING

As I wrote this book, I decided that I wanted to end it on a lighter note by telling my story. I went back through 20 years' worth of material that I had saved on the markets and my career. I am an information junkie who saves just about everything. I graduated from Cleveland State University in 1986 with a business degree in marketing. Everyone always asks me, "Why in the world did you go to college in Cleveland?" My answer is that I had a full scholarship to play Division 1 soccer, so it seemed worth it, and it was. I enjoyed the whole Cleveland State University experience. I can say one thing about the people in Cleveland: They have some of the most passionate sport fans in the nation.

As I look back over my 20-plus years in the investment business, I wonder if the next 20 years will look the way I expect. I have based my outlook on the education and experiences I've had in the past. I started out as a retail margin clerk in early January 1987 for a division of Merrill Lynch called Broad Court Capital. I can tell you that I had absolutely no clue about life in New York City and the world of Wall Street. I lived in the Park Chester's cockroach-filled apartment complex in the Bronx, commuting to Wall Street on a miserable hour-long subway ride every single day. I worked for Merrill Lynch in the day and played semiprofessional soccer for the Brooklyn Cosmos at night and on the weekends. I lived the full New

York City experience, and there isn't a better place to start an investment career than on Wall Street.

The year 1987 was a wild ride for investors as stock prices raced to new highs until the infamous "Black Monday" in October rocked world markets. The U.S. bull market was in full force after Fed Chairman Paul Volcker had wrestled the financial system back from the brink after the inflation battle of the 1970s. That victory in the early 1980s set the stage for the long and mighty boom the U.S. economy has enjoyed. Paul Volcker stepped down in 1987 and was replaced by Alan Greenspan. Greenspan immediately started off by raising interest rates to fight the inflation war that had seemingly already been won. Only five weeks into his term as Fed chairman, he single-handedly set off the biggest crash since Black Tuesday in 1929. This was only the first crash of Greenspan's controversial career as Fed chairman.

As a margin clerk, I witnessed firsthand the devastating effects of margin debt in a crashing stock market. I was amazed at the massive number of accounts that wiped out because of the resulting margin calls from this devastating crash. I was responsible for handling the retail accounts of several small brokerage firms from around the country. Many of these brokerage firms went completely bankrupt as a result of the disappearing equity. I say disappearing because one day I saw accounts with millions of dollars in equity, and the next day, Black Monday, the equity all but vanished. Greenspan's rate hikes in 1987 were like a magician waving his magic wand, saying "abracadabra," and then poof! All the paper equity was gone.

Where did the paper equity go, and how did this equity evaporation happen? When stocks crashed and market values tanked, all that margin debt remained. Margin debt, like all debt, eventually needs to be repaid, so stocks had to be sold to pay off the remaining margin debt. This forced liquidation by massive numbers of investors resulted in the great crashes of both 1929 and 1987. In a crash, selling begets more selling, as a greater number of stocks need to be sold to cover the margin requirements as prices fall. This is when *debt* truly is a four-letter word. Greenspan understood what was happening and why. The word on the street was that he called all the mutual fund bosses and told them to stop selling stocks to meet redemptions. I guess the message was that the Fed would be there to write the checks to the mutual funds to meet redemptions so they wouldn't have to keep selling stocks.

In October 1987, I remember seeing many stocks go from $12 to $3 overnight in the accounts for which I was the margin clerk. The Dow Jones Industrial Average (DJIA) dropped by only 36 percent, but most of the smaller stocks fell by 50 percent to 75 percent overnight. I remember thinking that if I bought these stocks at $3 and they rebounded in price to just half of their previous highs, that I could make 100 percent on my money. The decision to start buying was not an easy one, as everyone was in a virtual panic. The fear was like a thick fog of despair, my first lesson in capitulation. You literally had people in absolute terror screaming "get me out at any price" so they could meet margin calls. I now understood what a bottom in the stock market looked like, and it wasn't pretty. I also learned my first two Iron Laws of Investing. . . .

#1 Iron Law of Investing: When the Fed is raising interest rates, investors need to be raising cash.

#2 Iron Law of Investing: When there is fear and market despair everywhere, buy like there is no tomorrow!

After making a nice little score in the market at the bottom of the 1987 crash, I decided it was time to become a stockbroker. It wasn't as easy back then to find a job as a broker. As it turned out, the CEO of one of the brokerage accounts I handled at Merrill was in New York. He was doing a road show for a little IPO I will call SKINS Bagel Stores (SKNZ). Because I had done such a good job for his brokerage firm in the panic of 1987, the CEO invited me to come to the SKNZ presentation. When I met him outside after the presentation, I asked if I could work for his firm as a stockbroker. I remember he looked at the beautiful New York City skyline and said to me, "You mean you want to leave Merrill Lynch and this awesome city and work for my little company in Portland, Oregon?" I laughed and said yes, and I was hired on the spot. I then asked if I could bring my buddy Paul, who worked with me at Merrill Lynch, as he wanted to be a broker, too. He agreed, and Paul and I gave our two-week notices and packed for a very memorable road trip.

My First Road Trip across the United States

If you have enjoyed any of the Chevy Chase's *Vacation* movies, then you will like this story. My best friend, Paul, and I packed up my Chevy Cavalier hatchback that my sweet Mom gave me for the trip to the West Coast. Paul and I packed everything we had in the back of that little car, and that was our first big mistake. The second big mistake was putting one of those pack-a-sports on the roof of the car. The car sank about six inches after we filled that thing and the inside of my car with too much stuff. Off we went across the United States in my weighted-down Chevy Cavalier. We started out from my dad's house in Otisville, New York, and decided to take the southern route across the country as we headed to San Diego and Los Angeles to see some friends and family.

As we approached San Diego, my car gave in to all of the weight of our gear. It started to sputter, and finally it just stalled out. I had to get my friend Joe in San Diego to come tow us. We dropped the car off at a Chevy dealership and stayed at Joe's house. After a wild night in Tijuana, Mexico, Paul and I got in the patched-up Cavalier and headed to Los Angeles. This is where the fun begins.

The patch work on the car apparently did little good as we literally sputtered all the way to Los Angeles. After spending a night visiting family in L.A., we started on the final and most exciting part of our trip toward Portland. When we left L.A., the car started sputtering right away until it stalled right in the middle of a four-way intersection during early morning rush hour. The car just wouldn't start, so Paul and I got out and pushed the car out of the congestion. While we held up traffic pushing the car forward, we received quite a greeting from the early morning commuters. Horns were blowing and swear words were hurled at us from every direction. We pushed the car until we found a long stretch of road. We discovered that if we pushed the car fast enough, it would try to start, but would continue to stall. On the final try, we got the car to start and keep running without stalling. We just had to accelerate fast, and as long as we could maintain a speed above 55 mph, the car wouldn't stall.

For some unknown reason, at that speed, the car seemed to drive just fine. With a full tank of gas I drove until I started to get really drowsy and could no longer keep my eyes open, so I asked Paul if he would drive. He reminded me that if I stopped the car, we may not get it going again. We agreed that we needed to keep driving until we could get to another gas station and find a mechanic. So I came up with this brilliant idea, "Paul, I'll keep the cruise control on at 55 mph and you hop over me as I slide under you and we can switch seats as we cruise along the highway." I told Paul that I would focus on the wheel and he just needed to focus on not hitting the stick shift between us as we traded sides. As Paul and I were both halfway across, Paul accidentally hit the stick shift and we found ourselves on the shoulder of the highway careening completely out of control.

The shoulder was filled with loose gravel, and we were both holding onto the steering wheel, me underneath Paul. I realized that we needed to get the car off of cruise control as we were whipping violently back and forth at 55 mph on loose gravel. I reached down and hit the brake with my hand, which disengaged the cruise control. Immediately, the car went into an uncontrollable spin. After several full spins on the loose gravel, a barbed wire fence on the side of the highway caught the car, which was on two wheels, as it was ready to flip over. After the car sat back down on all four wheels, we both sat there completely stunned in a big cloud of dust. As the cloud cleared, we realized our pack-a-sport must have gone flying like a Frisbee into the middle of the highway, sending our socks and underwear all over I-5. All I could do was look at Paul and say, "I'm so sorry. Thank God we are alive." Now that was one heck of a ride!

After Paul and I picked up the remaining pieces of our luggage and underwear and pack-a-sport off the highway, we realized we had a flat tire on a car that likely wouldn't start. We didn't have cell phones back then, so I had to run to a diner and truck stop about three miles away. Exhausted, I asked about 30 people the same question, "Got a jack?" Once I finally found a guy willing to lend me a tiny jack for a $50 deposit, I ran all the way back to our car and changed the flat tire. Then I had to run back to town to return the jack and get my deposit back. Of course, the truck driver that lent me the jack took off with my money and was nowhere to be found.

Then it was a quick run all the way back to the car because I knew that we both needed to push the car to get it restarted. We put the car back together and after about two hours, we were able to get the car running and back on the highway at 55 mph. Little did we know what future crash event awaited us, one that made this incident look like a picnic. Just like I needed car insurance for this trip, you'll need crash insurance for your trip down Wall Street. This is why I wrote this book and developed my short-side strategy.

My Sinking Chevy and Nasdaq 2000

We stopped the car at a nearby mechanic. He told us that while we might be able to make it to Portland, we risked the car engine's blowing up. Since the car was given to me by my mom, I took the risk. The car drove horribly, reminding us of what a bad decision it was to overload my car with all of our stuff. Our new problem was that the car would aggressively spit and sputter on any major deceleration near 35 mph.

As we got close to the Oregon border, we saw a mountainous climb ahead of us. This climb was very steep, and Paul and I knew it would take a mighty toll on the car. The scary part was that the main highway had major construction going on and traffic was directed to an alternative mountain pass. This skinny, steep road had only two lanes and no shoulder, and deep ravines on both sides of the shoulders. It was a temporary road, and not one to have any car troubles on. Paul and I looked at each other in despair as we approached the base of the steep climb ahead. I looked at Paul, raised my eyebrows, and without one word spoken between us, I floored it.

I knew that my chances were "slim to none" in making this climb successfully, so I had to give it all the car had to have any chance of making it. As you can imagine, the steeper the mountain climb, the slower the car went. The Chevy really started to get burdened and decelerated to the point where we were only going about 15 mph. The car was making all kinds of crazy noises, and now we had a long line of cars trailing behind us. Traffic was heavy on the other side, so nobody could pass us. This was a real disaster in the making.

As we approached the last mile before reaching the top of the mountain pass, there was a sudden loud explosion. The car stopped, almost creating a pile-up behind us. Black smoke and oil were coming from the hood of my car, and we couldn't see a thing. Choking on smoke, I pushed Paul out the passenger side door of the car, and we rolled to the edge of a steep ravine on the slim shoulder of the road. We both lay there on the hill like soldiers under enemy fire looking up at the long line of angry drivers, wondering what the heck we should do. Then something remarkable happened.

We heard this loud, deep-pitched voice say, "Push the car down the mountainside." Paul and I both looked up as if this was a voice from God. Then we heard it again, "Push the car down the mountainside or you are going to cause an accident" in a very deep, echoing-like voice. Since this was the car trip from hell, we looked down this time. We saw this construction worker with a bullhorn working on the main highway a couple hundred yards or so below us. I looked at Paul, shrugged my shoulders, and put the car in neutral. We then pushed the car down the side of the mountain where it proceeded to fall for about 100 yards before it crashed at the bottom. I remember feeling sick, almost numb as I watched my car roll all the way down the mountainside into a mushroom-like cloud of dust and smoke. People drove by laughing as I stood there in humiliation.

Later on, after the smoked cleared, we waited for a tow truck to pull my car up from the bottom of the mountainside. As we sat there waiting, Paul and I wound up laughing uncontrollably as we thought about the whole nightmare trip across the country. At that point, we were both just thankful to be alive.

In many ways, this road trip was a precursor of the coming wild ride I would have as a stockbroker, and then as a hedge fund manager. The wild swings of the stock market whip your emotions from side to side the way my beat-up Chevy flung that pack-a-sport off the roof of my car. *After a crash is over, you are left stunned and numb until you are ready to pick up all the pieces.* This is exactly what I saw at the bottom of the 1987 crash and again at the bottom of the Nasdaq 2000–2003 crash.

Investors like my friend "Snowboard Dennis" felt exactly this way as they saw their portfolios go up in smoke. Let's make the comparison. Both my Chevy and Nasdaq put the pedal to the metal for a very steep climb. Both blew a gasket at the top, and both blew up. That long slide down the mountainside reminded me of the long slide Nasdaq had from 5,100 to 1,100. As I looked on bewildered and in shame, so did Internet investors, who watched their technology stocks go up in flames. Having been a Wall Street speculator for 20-plus years, I am an expert when it comes to crashes. However, whenever I invested or traded with stock market crash insurance or a short-side strategy, I drove my portfolio safely and protected. That's what my strategy is all about—crash protection.

My First Education Course: Crashing Stocks 101

Then I was in beautiful Portland, Oregon, and soon after, I became a stockbroker. The firm I joined up with was a small boutique that specialized in micro-cap new issue and secondary stock offerings. I was a 24-year-old punk kid stockbroker with zero sales experience and clueless about how hard it would be to make money. I was "dialing for dollars" out of the white pages of the phone book trying to sell municipal bonds for a living. I quickly found myself back to my college days eating the only meal I could afford, Top Ramen soup. This is one tough way to make a living. I found myself monthly at the bottom of the broker commission rankings at 235. That means I was number 235 out of 235 brokers in the firm in terms of commission performance for most of my first two years as a broker.

I found myself doing some crazy things just so I could feed myself and make ends meet. Fortunately for me, the firm I worked for had daily luncheons sponsored by mutual fund wholesalers. I could get a free sandwich and chips if I sat in the room for an hour listening to the wholesalers pitch their family of mutual funds. Their hope was that I would then sell those funds to my clients, which for the most part were nonexistent (clients, that is). The brokerage firm would also have the CEO of each company they were doing initial public offering (IPO) deals for, present to the brokers as well. These free lunches kept me alive, literally. The best meals were the closing parties that were thrown after an IPO deal was successfully completed. These were always "all you can eat" buffets.

At one of these events, when I didn't even have enough money for Top Ramen soup, I had a great idea. I asked the waiter to get me a clean Hefty garbage bag from the kitchen. Then my broker friends surrounded me as I filled up the garbage bag with several pounds of food. I knew I wouldn't starve that week. The term "starving brokers" is based in reality.

Another survival tactic I regularly employed created a great mystery at my brokerage firm. We had a Coke machine in the kitchen area for all the employees and a giant box where everyone was supposed to throw the empty cans. When the box was about three quarters full, or right before the Coke machine man came to collect all the cans, I would sneak into the office at night with several large Hefty bags. I parked my car in the basement of the building to make this a completely covert operation.

One time I had several extra-large bags of cans in the elevator. I was on the third floor expecting to go directly to the basement when the elevator stopped as someone hit the button on the second floor. Panic hit me as the elevator door slowly opened. I was sure I was caught. The door opened and it was the maintenance guy, who just laughed, as he couldn't even fit in the elevator because there were so many bags of pop cans. After I filled my car with several large bags, I would drive to Safeway to return the cans. At five cents per can, I was making more money returning pop cans than I was as a stockbroker.

Back at the office, I would leave just enough cans in the giant box for the Coke machine man on collection day not to suspect anything. For a while, he just thought many employees weren't putting their cans in the box. Eventually, everyone figured out somebody must have been stealing them. The firm had no idea it was one of their fine young stockbrokers stealing the pop cans to earn a living.

Playing in the Garbage Dump

Obviously, our careers as stockbrokers weren't looking all that good. It felt like our college days again, eating poorly and being far away from home. The only difference was that I was in the real world and handling other people's money. This was a difficult environment for a young, impressionable stockbroker. I was surrounded by other senior and more experienced brokers pitching low-priced stocks that all seemed to have such exciting possibilities. I couldn't take the temptation, so I started pitching bonds less and moved more to tiny micro-cap stocks.

My first stock idea was one that most of the brokers I worked with were very excited about at the time. Let's just call the company Renex Software Products (RENX). I was told that all the excitement around the office was about their great software and coming large contracts. As everyone was buying, the stock was falling. My well-meaning and honest broker friends were not worried because the word was that big news was coming. I started buying for a few clients at around $3.75, down from $7 where everyone else had started buying. My thinking at the time was with the stock cut in half, it must be cheap. This story will help you understand my next three Iron Laws.

A few weeks after I started to buy the stock, it had already drifted down to $2.75. I am now down 25 percent for my clients and I am not a happy camper. The brokerage firm decided to have an emergency conference call with the management team of Renex Software. I listened to the president of RENX tell us how they were shipping tons of product, yet they were nowhere near profitability. I knew little about their great technology, but I noticed that they were selling the product for $200 when it cost $300 to make. During the question-and-answer period with the management team, I asked a simple question, "Mr. President, I was wondering if you could explain to me in layman's terms what your product is, and what is your competitive advantage?" He said flatly, "Our product is like toilet paper, and our advantage is that we sell it cheaper than everyone else." I knew it was time to go to my new clients with my tail between my legs and advise them to sell.

That "toilet paper" comment by the CEO was completely ignored, and most of the brokers continued to average down. After a couple of name changes and reverse splits, RENX basically went bankrupt. The president of RENX was right about one thing. The stock became "toilet paper" right along with his product. This is where I learned that hope kills in the stock market.

#3 Iron Law of Investing: Never average down in "cheap" stocks, as cheap gets cheaper and hope kills.

#4 Iron Law of Investing: Have a set of timing indicators to help you buy low and sell high and always be hedged for downside protection.

#5 Iron Law of Investing: Cut your losses short so you never ride a stock all the way to zero.

The #5 Iron Law of Investing applies to every stock. Whether it's a speculative company like RENX or a top, well-respected blue chip like Enron—zero is still zero! It didn't matter that I paid $3 and others paid $7, because if you ride a stock all the way down, it's still a 100 percent loss.

There are many crooks on Wall Street trying—or should I say lying—to get people to give them money or to buy their crummy little stock. We had a company that our firm was doing an IPO for that claimed to be "one of the largest independent mobile home retailers in the United States." I remember Paul asking one of the senior brokers, "What would be a good stock to put my friends and family into?" I was standing right there, and this well-meaning broker said, "Paul, Hu*** Homes is a very low-risk, high-reward play, and it is even going to pay a dividend immediately after the stock IPO starts to trade. This might be the best idea of my career."

The company went public at $7.50 per unit. I will use the fictitious symbol of HUGELOSS for HU*** Homes. The stock started heading down quickly after the IPO, and everyone was stunned. How wrong can you go with the "largest" company in an industry group that is also paying dividends? The answer is dead wrong. About a year or so after the IPO, the company mysteriously ran out of cash. The company's president and founder, Harry Hugeloss, convinced the brokerage firm that everything was fine, so the brokerage firm did a $10 million 10 percent convertible preferred stock offering for his company. I decided that something was rotten here, so I took a huge loss in the company I had appropriately named HUGELOSS.

There were some really good and honest brokers who bought this crummy little company's story hook, line, and sinker. I remember one broker we'll call Jerry, who sold a ton of the 10 percent preferred stock to his customers. From the minute we did that money raise, the price on that preferred stock dropped about 15 percent. Then the stock and those preferred shares started to fall like a stone until the company very quickly ran out of the $10 million the brokers just raised for them.

I went to our firm's head of research to ask what had happened. She said that in her channel checks the word *embezzlement* came up. Dealers and customers of HUGELOSS said very unkind words to describe this company as "crooks that don't pay their bills." At least the brokerage firm knew where the money didn't go. Jerry's career was never the same. Paul also had seen enough after that experience and moved on to better things. I was close to doing the same thing, as this experience was horrible, but it leads me to my next two Iron Laws.

#6 Iron Law of Investing: Always diversify with large and small common stocks, long and short.

#7 Iron Law of Investing: Don't completely trust anyone's word on the street (especially CEOs of small companies), as Wall Street is crawling with snakes and crooks.

My Luck Starts to Change

For some stupid reason I continued to play in the garbage stocks. Let me give you a visual of this. One day my cell phone was on vibrate/ring mode. When it rang, the phone vibrated off my desk and into the garbage can without my knowing. I took the garbage out to the giant green dumpster outside my office. When I couldn't find my cell phone, I realized what must have happened. I had someone call my cell phone so I could hear it ring while I searched around in the garbage dumpster for it. After about 15 minutes of digging through filth, I found the phone, but I was a stinky mess.

Searching for high-risk unprofitable penny stocks is like looking in the garbage dumpster of the stock market. What I came to realize was that most penny stocks and unprofitable micro-cap stocks go down, even in a roaring bull market. This was no fun, not at all. I would sit at my desk and look at my Quotron machine and the market would be exploding higher. That green on my screen was greatly contrasted by the red stock symbols on the machine indicating that all my crummy little stocks were in fact down and at a loss for the day. I found myself hoping the stock market would be down for the day because this would be much easier to explain to my clients. It would go something like this when the market was down, "Mr. Client, our stocks just went down with the market today." When the market was up, I would have to say, "The little stocks are always slow to move up with the market, but they will eventually follow." These conversations always left me with a pit in my stomach.

One day after a long morning of watching my crummy stocks fall, I went out for a walk to ease my tension. After returning from my break, I met a beautiful woman on the elevator. I asked her what she did and she said she was an attorney in the same building I was working in. She told me her name was Susan, and all I remembered was that her last name started with the letter H. I immediately went down to the first floor of the building where a giant board listed all the companies and the employee's names. I found her firm and her name. I went back to my office to call her and I asked for Susan Howard. Susan Howard got on the phone and I explained that I was the guy who met her on the elevator. She impatiently said, "Yeah, so?" I asked her what kind of law she practiced, and she said in a slightly annoyed voice, "I am a divorce attorney." I knew this wasn't going well, so I said something like, "Susan, I am not married and I don't plan on ever getting married, so thank you very much." I hung up, relieved that the call was over, having never gotten to the point of asking her out.

Five minutes later, my phone rang and it was Susan Howard. She said kindly, "Ron, I don't think I met you today. I think you have me confused with Susan Hautala. I spoke to her about it and she faintly recalls meeting you. I'll patch you over to her now." Before I could say no, the other Susan answered the phone. I went through the same routine, and she quickly interrupted me and said, "I am on billable hours here. Are you trying to ask me out?" I said yes, and the rest is history. We fell in love and got married. My luck was changing.

Earlier in the book, I mentioned my friend Wally who had a very positive influence on my life. In 1990, he volunteered to do a sales course called "The Psychology of Selling," created by Brian Tracy. I was motivated because it was a free course, and a free lunch would be provided. Brian Tracy is an unbelievable speaker and self-help expert. His course, taught to me by Wally, changed my life. I learned about selling techniques and, most importantly, about goal setting. I had an "aha" experience during this course.

The sales course helped me go from number 253 to multiple months as the firm's number one producer. I was promoted to assistant sales manager and trained other new brokers. I was again promoted to vice president of syndicate, where I got to work directly for one of my mentors in the business. In Syndicate, I learned about selling IPOs and secondary stock offerings to other stockbrokers. The brokerage firm I worked for syndicated some great deals that I was fortunate enough to work on. Several of these companies are still around, and two of the companies I helped syndicate were two of the best performing IPOs in the history of the firm.

Traveling around the country with these CEOs, raising money for their IPOs, was fun. The syndicate expense accounts are large, so I stayed in the fanciest of hotels and lived large doing IPOs and secondary stock offerings.

Hot Deals and Stock Promoters

My first hot deal was an IPO disaster, but at least I wasn't in the syndicate department yet. This was with a company I will call PS Auto Centers; let's give this company the fictitious symbol of PITS. The deal was supposed to be a "hot deal," meaning that it was a very oversubscribed stock offering. The reason was because there was a small-time stock promoter we will call Art, who was going to run the stock from the IPO price of $10 per share to $100 per share. PITS was a quick-stop auto center like Jiffy Lube. At the free lunch presentation that I, of course, attended, PITS management projected opening 200 of these PS auto centers. At the time they had only three of them, and all three were losing money, so these projections were a bit overhyped, as was their story.

I participated in the IPO with 10,000 shares, with the idea that I would flip it in a few days at a premium, where the stock was no doubt going. The day the deal started to trade, it opened at $10.50 per share, a very small premium to the $10 offering price. Immediately, the stock dropped to $9.75 per share and I told my clients to sell, and we did. Before long, the stock got cut in half. At this point, the small-time promoter Art does a conference call and convinces everyone he's getting big buyers together. He would say things like, "I am going to run the stock up." The firm decided that they would help "clean the stock up" and took down a huge block of shares at a big discount to the market. The brokers were given permission to take down a big piece of this block in their "bag account." The "broker's bag" was an acceptable practice back then and was a separate account with the broker's rep number, where he can hold stock until he retails it out of his bag account into customer accounts.

In this particular case, the broker held PITS at $4.50 per share. Then he would retail the stock to his customers at the market price of $5, making a 50-cent profit. Plus, he would add a commission on top of that. It was almost too good to pass up, but I did because I believed the stock was headed deep down into a very dark pit. In theory, this was a very profitable strategy for brokers because they could hide their cost from the customer and do it as a net trade and even hide the commissions. In reality, however, things can backfire, and they did with the PITS stock takedown.

The stock started to get pummeled soon after the brokers took the shares down into their "bag." Now the stock was $3.50 per share, so they all had a quick 20 percent loss in the bag account. The brokers had Art, the promoter, telling them not to worry as he had big buyers coming in soon to, supposedly, "run the stock." The stock ended up being a giant anchor tied to these poor brokers' ankles as it sank toward zero.

As PITS sank into a deep financial pit, they merged with an insurance company, of all things. Then, these two merged companies bought a bagel company and merged the three together. So now we have a bagel company, an insurance company, and an auto center combined into one company. I am not sure what the new combined company strategy became. In my mind I imagined a customer driving up to one of the PITS auto centers to order a bagel while his car was being worked on. The company then could try and sell the customer an insurance policy while he was eating his bagel.

The Start of the New Era

As time progressed, I decided that I wanted to do something else. In 1993, it looked like the industry was heading in a new direction. The basic choice that stockbrokers were faced with at the time was whether to be an asset gatherer or an asset manager. My friend Dan attended a hedge fund conference and came back full of enthusiasm, saying, "Absolutely! This is the way to go." We took most of 1994 setting up the fund, and our goal was to start by January 1, 1995, in time for a new bull market. One of my favorite market timing indicators was flashing a bear market signal in late 1993 and throughout 1994. The Dow Jones Utility Average (DJUA) was in a severe sell-off. Whenever that happens, bonds and then stocks are soon to follow the DJUA down. Sure enough, 1994 was a bear market year for most stocks.

#8 Iron Law of Investing: When the DJUA falls into a Stage 4 Decline, sell all bonds and start selling stocks short. If you don't feel comfortable shorting stocks, then cut back severely on long positions and raise cash.

After launching the hedge fund on the first trading day of 1995, I had a preset goal of 3 percent gross returns per month. I hit that return goal precisely in 1995, and came reasonably close the following two years. Previously, I told you that I slipped badly in the oil patch bear market in 1998 for about a 20 percent loss. In 1999, I started shorting heavily about four months too early. I still managed a barely profitable 1999, but I was so bearish about the market and the economy that people could hardly stand to be around me. In 1999, I kept saying that Nasdaq and the DJIA would repeat 1929, and we risked a severe recession or even a depression once the Nasdaq bubble blew.

I got some redemption in 2000, however, buying puts and shorting Nasdaq stocks. In 2001, I had to mark down and write off the remains of all my private adventures, so 2001 and 2002 where tough years as I searched for a bottom. The fund, however, enjoyed big gains in the 2003 and 2004 bull market move after I identified the inverse head-and-shoulder bottom in the market averages and by having some concentrated big-winning long positions.

In February 2003, I sent out a letter to all my investors stating that Nasdaq had repeated 1929 Dow in duration as well as in percentage terms. The March 2000 top to the March 2003 bottom of 35 months was the same exact amount of time in 1929 from its top to bottom. The 80 percent drop in Nasdaq was close to the 1929–1932 drop of 89 percent, but most Internet and telecom stocks fared worse than stocks in 1929. I got bullish and positioned my fund aggressively long, and as a result, my fund had two big winning years. Then the unthinkable happened.

Never Again

#9 Iron Law of Investing: Never break any of your investment rules.

In 2005, I made a terrible mistake. I had correctly ridden a particular stock from $2 per share up to a huge gain. After this stock peaked out at $7 from $2 where I originally bought it, the stock fell back to $5. I thought I could buy the stock back below the higher prices where I sold it, as the company's "business was on fire." I figured that the big institutions that had just bought a slug of this stock in a private placement deal would make a goal line stand at that $5 per share price. I went in for a quick trade and took a concentrated position, looking to make a half-point move on a bounce and then sell once again. The stock went from trading like water to an absolute drought of no volume. It was as if someone turned out the lights and the volume practically evaporated to nothing. The stock had a slow motion collapse from $5 to $2.60 per share. It was the strangest thing; it really hurt my fund, and, like magic, my equity was cut in half.

#10 Iron Law of Investing: Never put more than 10 percent of your portfolio in any one stock pick, and no more than 25 percent of your total portfolio in micro-cap stocks.

Fortunately, I was not trapped on margin with this loser stock or I would have done a Victor Niederhoffer move and wiped out completely. I decided to call around the street to see if I could figure out what was going on with my loser stock. One analyst who covered the stock told me I was "screwed," as the big hedge funds in this stock were trying to unload. The problem was that there was no one who wanted to buy the stock because everyone thought "something was wrong."

I decided to do all I could for my fund and my investors. I had every liquid penny of my own money in the hedge fund, as I believed that was the right thing to do, and up to that point it had been. Then the company came out, and as one analyst described it, "they barfed up a bad quarter." The bad news was out. Obviously, someone had been tipped off to the earnings miss. As the word got out, the stock collapsed even before the bad news hit the wire.

The only solution at that point seemed to be to try to engineer a sale of the company and create a take-over bid so I could get the heck out. I was trapped in this little illiquid stock, and I needed to get out. I found a perfect company to buy my loser stock and immediately flew to Minnesota to talk with management. They laughed at me when I first sat down, saying, "Ron, you wasted your plane fare if you came all the way here to have us buy that little garbage company." I reminded them that they promised to give me 30 minutes if I showed up, so they agreed.

This Minnesota outfit was concerned about the CEO of the loser company I was trying to convince them to buy. I told them that since he didn't own much stock, they could just oust him, and I laid out how strategic a purchase this was for them. Three or so hours later, they were asking me how to help them put together an acquisition deal. I tried to put this deal together in a friendly fashion and quickly arranged a meeting of the two companies' management teams. Unfortunately for me, the CEO of the loser company sabotaged any potential of a deal. Later on, I made new plans and I told this company's management that I was going to "take matters into my own hands."

I found a large NYSE-listed company that would be a perfect strategic fit to buy my loser stock. I introduced the two management teams and tried to put this deal together in a friendly fashion. The truth was that I wasn't bullish on the stock at the time, but it did trade over a million shares per day, and it was liquid. If I could trade my illiquid stock at a premium for this liquid name, then I'd be home free and I could get us all out.

I showed up at the scheduled due diligence meeting in 2005 right before I attended the "Minyans in the Mountains" retreat. This NYSE-listed company gave me the standard tour and, you guessed it, a free lunch. The public relations guy handed me a couple of the company's newly released products, patted me on the head, and sent me on my way. Before I left, I put my plan B into action. I found the secretary and asked her to give her boss a letter I had written. I asked her to let the CEO know I was disappointed not to have been able to meet him since I had traveled all the way from Oregon just to hand him my letter. She agreed.

Three weeks later and still no call had come from this CEO. My thought was that he either hadn't read it or had thrown it in the garbage can. I was running out of time because the loser stock I owned was on to me. In fact, they put out a press release saying that at their next annual meeting they wanted shareholders to approve a "rights offering" the management team put into place. They said in the press release that they feared someone was planning on trying to take the company over (me) and the rights plan would thwart those efforts.

They were correct because the management didn't have a majority ownership, so without a "rights plan" they were susceptible to a hostile takeout. They knew I was on to that fact. I had three weeks until this vote would take place at the annual meeting. I was sure the vote would be passed because small shareholders usually approve these kinds of votes when management tells them it's a good thing to do. It wasn't looking good for me. I knew if this "rights plan" went through, my shareholders would likely force me to liquidate, and that could mean a near wipeout.

I decided to go to a secluded park to think about the whole thing. It was very early in the morning when I left the office to go to the park. I sat by a quiet spot near the beautiful Deschutes River in very deep thought. I knew time was short and an unsolicited takeout of my loser stock was my only possibility of salvaging my fund. I decided to say a prayer that went like this, "God, if my letter is sitting on the CEO's desk, will you please nudge him to pick it up and to call me, PLEASE." A couple of hours later that very same day I went back to the office and my secretary left a note on my desk that said, "The CEO just read your letter and he wants to talk to you immediately." When I called him, he said, "Ron, for some strange reason I decided to pick up your letter today and read it. I think you are absolutely right—let's put a takeout plan in place."

This CEO told me that several months earlier he and his chief financial officer had visited the management team of my loser stock, and he said they threw all the information in the trashcan as they walked out the door. He said, "Ron, we couldn't stand those guys." My proposal pointed out that it was partly because of the management team of my loser stock that the stock was trading at a nice discount to its true asset value. I told him he could eventually fire all of them, and that alone could increase the value of the company. We agreed to a swap of his NYSE-listed shares at a 40 percent premium for my loser stock.

The next day Jim Cramer from CNBC told the world to buy my NYSE-listed stock, but now the deal was far less attractive as the acquiring stock rose substantially. This was because the price of the transaction was to be based on the close of business the day before the deal would be announced. When Cramer recommended the NYSE stock as a "buy, buy, buy," it skyrocketed, and the next trading day the deal was announced. I was a hero for about four weeks. People called me from all over the country congratulating me because it came out in public filings that my fund did the swap deal that set up the announced takeout deal. One broker friend called me up and said, "Ron, you freed us poor shareholders from the CEO the way Bush freed the Iraqis from Saddam." At this point I felt pretty good, but, unfortunately, we were on a 90-day lockup with the newly acquired shares. I couldn't sell the new shares for 90 days after the transaction for regulatory reasons. My 10-week stint as a hero was about to come to a crashing end.

Right about the time the lockup ended, I received a "short report" regarding our new stock. This report was spread all over the street and the NYSE stock we had just acquired was getting mauled on tens of millions of shares. The problem was that I couldn't fully disagree with the short report in that the stock was arguably overvalued and could go a lot lower. The stock wound up giving up much of the 40 percent gain we had gotten in the exchange. I was forced to sell our position because that was my goal, to get my investors liquid. Plus, it looked like the new stock was set to do its own swan dive off the cliff, so I pulled the ripcord and took the hit. After this nightmare of unfortunate and unexpected events, each of which came completely out of the blue, I decided to close down my fund. It was a bitter pill to swallow.

Interestingly enough, that second deal with the NYSE company wound up breaking down as well. That company wound up dumping the loser stock for which we had swapped. Even more interesting is the fact that if the CEO of my loser stock had pursued the first Minnesota company deal, we would have had a grand slam home run. That Minnesota stock went from $6 per share when I visited them to $21 about a year or so after my visit. We could have swapped our loser stock and made a pile on the new stock as it advanced to $21.

In December 2007, the CEO of my loser stock was trying to close on a new buyout deal to get his shareholders $4.60 per share in a cash deal. The $4.60 new deal looked like a pittance compared to the potential "four-bagger" if he had pursued my Minnesota deal. Believe it or not, that new buyout deal blew up as well for my former loser stock. The loser stock was trading at a big discount of $3.25 only days before the $4.60 per share cash deal was supposed to commence. The stock then announced that the new buyer changed his mind and my former loser stock went from $3.25 to $1.00 overnight and now looks like a table-pounding buy opportunity. Even more ironic is that the Minnesota company's stock that ran to $21.00 per share, imploded to $1.50 per share because they didn't make acquisitions like the one I presented to them. I am not shedding any tears for that company either.

The CEO of that Minnesota company wound up selling $15 million worth of his stock from $10 on up to $20 per share. He is now back buying his stock at $1.50 to $2.00 per share. It sure pays to be an insider with privileged information to sell high and then go back and buy low. *Remember—follow the smart money, the informed money.*

The moral of the story is: Never—and I mean never—break your investment and trading rules or you'll wind up regretting it. Most of my fund investors appreciated the massive amount of effort I put forward to get the fund liquid after getting trapped. I can honestly say that in 20 years in the business, this series of events provided the best lessons I have ever learned. It was also the most painful. It validates all the investment rules given throughout this book. It helped me fortify the best strategies that I acquired over two decades of trading and to outline the short-side strategy in this book.

Whatever investing or trading philosophy you have that works, stay with it. I just want to encourage everyone to look at incorporating some crash insurance by having a short-side strategy with positions on both sides of the market. Come visit me at my web site, www.RonCoby.com, and together, let's navigate through the dark economic clouds that are forming on the horizon to a safe landing versus a crash landing. In my final chapter, I will show you how I put everything together. So far I have told you why I believe all investors will need to have a new strategy as well as a new mind-set as the markets and the U.S. and global economy goes through a long period of adjustment. In the next chapter, I want to show you how I discovered an incredible new tool for effective timing of stocks, bonds, currencies, metals, and commodities to effectively execute on this short-side strategy.

CHAPTER 12

FINDING THE GRAIL: THE CHAPTER THAT DEMANDED TO BE WRITTEN

When I originally wrote *Discover the Upside of Down,* the book didn't have a Chapter 12. At the time I didn't think it needed one. However, the subsequent economic events of the last few months changed all of that. As you will quickly understand, there really was something missing.

So consider this a bonus—a chapter that demanded to be written. In effect, it's a continuation of the last chapter, as my "old beat-up Chevy" turns into a brand new Hybrid built for the new millennium. At the risk of being accused of self-promotion, I offer you "the rest of the story."

The Quest

After reading about my 20-plus years of wild market adventures, you might think of me as a Wall Street version of Indiana Jones. Many of these market experiences can be likened to Indiana fighting off dangerous situations and battling the bad guys, but in the concrete jungles of Wall Street. Like the famous scene of the boulder chasing Indy down a tunnel, I have had stocks roll me over and absolutely crush me, but somehow I have always found a way to keep my market adventure alive. The good news is that instead of discouraging me, it has forced me to find the upside of down in the markets, and even more importantly, in life.

My most recent adventure reminds me of *The Last Crusade,* where Harrison Ford as "Indy" hunts for the Holy Grail. I say this because I, too, have been hunting for a trading grail, a system to aid in successful timing of the market. I have been searching my whole career to find that extra edge in investing because timing can make or break you. Your analysis can be absolutely dead-on correct about the direction of a stock's move and even the market's direction. But if you are early and/or late in buying and/or selling, you may not only miss the bulk of the move, you may end up losing money.

Perhaps the best news in this entire book is that I can say, "Eureka! I have found it!" As a result of the crazy sequence of adventures over the past year or two, I have recently stumbled upon the best timing system I have ever seen. I believe I have discovered "The Grail" indicator to best execute the short-side strategy for my clients.

Before I tell you what it is and how I found it, let me address a very important fact about how to reduce portfolio volatility, which is critical for the tumultuous times I see ahead. There is a real benefit to investing in noncorrelated markets, which has been documented by Nobel Prize–winning researchers. Their findings reveal that by investing in markets that move independently from one another, a portfolio is less volatile and over time achieves superior returns. My version of this is best accomplished by investing on both the long and short side in multiple stocks and in diverse global markets, as well as in various commodities. As you have read, I refer to this as having a short-side strategy where the goals are increased returns, reduced risk, and low volatility.

As I have stated repeatedly, no one can see the future, so everyone must be concerned with risk management. This is why you need a short-side strategy addressing both the upside and downside. For proper portfolio positioning, let the market guide you and adjust your positions, long and short, accordingly. Resist betting everything on one market prediction or even listening to those "prophets" who claim to know with 100 percent certainty that a crash (or boom) lies dead ahead. Instead, learn to react intelligently to price movements for risk management. A wise saying is, "No one can predict which way the wind will blow, but you can learn to adjust the sails."

You don't want to be fully short or in cash for that certain crash ahead, if instead the country goes into an inflationary super boom. You must be flexible and nimble and ready to act when new fundamental and technical data warrants a change in position. I've given you numerous principles, but specific timing for buying, selling, and shorting is crucial to making money.

Every investor needs specific guidelines to help identify when market trends are about to change. Such a sensible trading strategy points you in the right direction, but even then it is often difficult to know when to pull the trigger. Adding precise timing signals to the mix is what is needed to give you the courage to buy low and the confidence to sell high and vice versa on the short side.

This kind of timing indicator produces the additional benefit of removing emotions that sabotage investing: fear, greed, and pride. When it's time to sell or buy because your indicator says sell or buy, you do it. *Fear is afraid to buy low. Greed is unwilling to sell high. Pride makes you ride losers.* By sticking with the discipline of a short-side strategy and proven timing signals, you are no longer ruled by your emotions. No longer do you see yourself as a failure when a trade fails because you are just following your risk management discipline and your buy/sell signals.

To make money in the market you must buy low, sell high, cut your losers, and ride your winners. The beauty of stocks, bonds, and commodities of all kinds is that you can do this in two ways: Buy low and then sell high, or sell high first and then buy back lower later. Both are part of my short-side strategy. Either way, you still need to know when you are high and heading lower, or low and heading higher.

This is the profound weakness of many, if not most, speculators, money managers, and investors: poor timing, overtrading, and too much confidence in the fundamentals of a trade. It is because I have struggled with these same issues that I have long sought to find "The Grail," an indicator or market timing system that would greatly reduce these weaknesses.

The Discovery

My recent travels led me to Medford, a small town in southern Oregon. It was there that I met a fellow seasoned market veteran, Denny Lamson. The amazing thing is that Denny had created a market timing indicator he actually named "The Lamson Grail™"! Along with my discovery of The Grail came the discovery of a very interesting man.

Besides being an excellent money manager, Denny is a true twenty-first century renaissance man. He is an awesome singer with some excellent recordings of his music. Denny is into art and is a partner in a company that markets the finest European bronze sculptures in existence today. Denny has been a stockbroker and a branch manager for two different major brokerage firms. He is a CTA (Commodity Trading Advisor) with Vision Financial Markets, an RIA (Registered Investment Advisor), and now a partner in Coby Lamson Capital Management. The point is that Denny is a bright, experienced, mature, and patient man, all of which helped him manage money and aided in the discovery of The Lamson Grail market timing indicator.

At our first meeting, I felt like I was looking in the mirror as Denny related his story. He told me of his own Wall Street adventures and how he spent hundreds of hours and tens of thousands of dollars over several years developing a market timing indicator. As he demonstrated his system, I was astonished at the incredible accuracy of the buy and sell signals it has made on stocks and commodities of all kinds over the past five years. The adventure Denny has had creating The Grail is itself a fascinating story, one I plan to share with you in my next book. To learn more about how the Grail works and to view some of the featured grail charts, visit www.Cobylamson.com.

Denny and I quickly became close friends and formed Coby Lamson Capital Management. Our firm is using The Lamson Grail to execute my short-side strategy managing money for clients in stocks, commodities, currencies, and metals. With "The Grail" we have a proprietary market timing indicator for a smoother ride through volatile times. Maybe now I can be like Indy in *The Temple of Doom* and help protect my clients from the probable economic doom that both Denny and I unfortunately see ahead. You can also visit my web site at www.RonCoby.com and learn more about how we manage money utilizing The Grail to execute our short-side strategy.

My Acre of Diamonds

You may have heard the famous story "Acres of Diamonds" told by Russell Conwell. This is my shortened adaptation of the story of a farmer in India who set off to find his fortune in diamonds. He sold his farm and left on his quest.

Meanwhile, back at the farm, the new owner had a visitor, an old priest who noticed a sparkling black rock on the new owner's mantle. The priest picked up the stone and asked him where he had found it. The man said, "There are hundreds of them in the sands behind the house." The priest replied, "Do you know what this rock is?" The farmer said, "No, what?" The priest replied, "This is a diamond of enormous value." The farmer took the priest to the back of the farm and there literally were "acres of diamonds." In fact, it became the Mines of Golconda, the most magnificent diamond discovery in the history of mankind.

There are at least two lessons we can learn from this story. First, know what you are looking for. A diamond in its rough form doesn't look at all like a finished diamond. Second, know where to look. The grass isn't always greener elsewhere. The original farmer set off to find his fortune without ever looking right in his own backyard.

The question we all need to ask ourselves is, "What and where is my acre of diamonds?" The Grail is the set of tools that are the diamonds I have discovered. This technical indicator is the most incredible short-term and long-term market timing system I have seen in my two-plus decades in this business. Before I met Denny, I was just like the Indian farmer looking for diamonds in the wrong place. But when I met Denny and saw his system "sparkling on the mantle," I immediately knew I had found an "acre of diamonds."

Our goal is to help investors through the difficult and volatile years ahead using my short-side strategy coupled with The Lamson Grail market timing indicator. Here is why we will need all of this and more as we brace for the years just ahead.

The Years Just Ahead

George Bush is leaving the White House with one of the worst approval ratings of any U.S. president. He is also leaving the new administration with some very difficult challenges. These include a very costly war in Iraq, a potentially nuclear Iran, jihadists in nuclear Pakistan, stagflation, exploding debts and deficits, and the real estate depression, to name just a few.

Add to the mix the sobering fact that new presidents tend to make the most difficult and unpleasant economic decisions like tax hikes or spending cuts early in their first term. This is one reason why the first two years of a presidential cycle, in this case 2009 and 2010, might be volatile and very challenging times for the market.

Following the initial settling-in period, the Obama administration will hope to get the economy back on track by his fourth year, just in time for reelection. This often-repeated cycle creates surges of volatility and uncertainty as stocks go boom, then bust, and then boom and bust again. The only way to protect yourself and profit from both the ups and the downs is to have a short-side strategy utilizing tactical asset allocation and diversification into multiple, noncorrelated markets.

To put it another way, you must have a preservation of capital strategy to deal with the forces of deflating stocks, markets, and economies. You must also have a preservation of purchasing power strategy as paper money continues to erode in value. This is why Denny and I have created a money management platform deploying a short-side strategy that implements The Grail's precision tactics.

Dreams Do Come True

If you haven't figured it out yet, I'm an optimist who just happens to believe the stock market and the U.S. economy are in for a long period of adjustment. I prefer the term *realist* and, of course "the Short-Side Strategist" to describe myself and my outlook. However, since I'm flexible enough to go both long and short in spite of this bearish view, I consider myself a new breed of bear. I'm no "bull in a bear suit" that professes gloom but in practice only goes long markets and stocks. Rather, I'm a new breed of bear, one who clearly sees the very real dangers ahead and uses a tactical strategy of investing and trading on both sides of any market, long and short.

My Wall Street hero is the legendary trader Jesse Livermore primarily because of the motivating influence the book *Reminiscences of a Stock Operator* had on my career. I admired the tenacity he displayed in this great market book and his ability to make a comeback from devastating market losses. I set out to write a financial book that incorporated many of the characteristics of the greatest market books ever written by him and other Wall Street icons. I noticed that most of the very best books were published by John Wiley & Sons, including two written about Jesse Livermore and his life. When I got a call from John Wiley & Sons telling me they wanted to publish *Discover the Upside of Down,* a long-held goal and dream had come true. Wow! The most respected and prestigious publisher of investment books, that published books for so many of those I admire, agreed to publish my book. I almost cannot believe it. I feel honored that they have published it and privileged that you have taken the time to read it.

In summary, I want to remind you that no one, absolutely no one, can see the future. The U.S. and global economies might be heading into an inflationary super boom as the bulls predict, rather than the long period of economic contraction that I expect. Either way, why fear the downside, when there are risk management strategies and profit opportunities in down markets? If you are a U.S. dollar and stock market bear, there's no need to get all your money out of the country and live in fear. Whether it is in the markets or in your life, always remember to look up and *Discover the Upside of Down.*

Hopefully, I have given you the tools to safely navigate through the turbulent times that have already begun. The storm clouds are darkening in real estate and the U.S. economy, so it is high time to hunker down and get prepared.

The good news is that after the bearish trend disappears over the horizon, a new secular bull market will rise once again. At that point, I'd like to write a book entitled *Nothing but Upside: Stocks, Bonds, and Real Estate.* Thanks for reading. I hope this book will help you reposition your investments wisely by incorporating some form of my short-side strategy.

Good luck and God bless.

EPILOGUE

THE SPEED OF CHANGE

While 21 years of experience went into producing this book, the bulk of the original writing took me about six months. However, I spent most of 2008 changing many of my forecasts and rewriting them as past events for the 2009 John Wiley & Sons book launch. The pace at which so many negative events have unfolded is stunning.

Looking back on 2008, Bear Stearns collapsed; Indy Mac Bank and Fannie Mae were taken over by the federal government; Lehman Brothers filed for bankruptcy, the U.S. dollar came very close to collapsing; and real estate is still on the verge. Oil hit $145 per barrel and then abruptly reversed back to under $70. Gold touched $1,000 before reversing course and heading lower. China's market went boom and then quickly got cut in half. Commodity prices and the price of just about everything have been all over the board.

Stocks finally gave in to all the negative news and progressed from a normal 10 percent correction to a full-fledged bear market decline. The market has had violent up and down swings throughout the year. I am sure that most long-only investors who read this book can certainly see the benefits of hedge protection, as well as the profit opportunities from shorting weak and falling stocks.

To fight the bear market, the Federal Reserve has been doing all it can to keep the economy from imploding. The Fed cut interest rates with Greenspan-like speed to fight the real estate bust. Unfortunately for Ben Bernanke, it's getting harder to reinflate deflating asset bubbles and to get the economy back on track. To many it would appear that the Fed is "pushing on a string" and is losing the battle as the massive accumulated debt strangles the burdened U.S. economy.

As we have seen, the financial crisis and the resulting bear market in the United States is like a speeding train careening off the tracks taking all the passengers, that is, the rest of the world, right along with it. With quite a bit of air coming out of the global markets, especially China, the question is like Nasdaq 2000, will this be the first phase of a Chinese market crash? Or will it be more like the 1987 crash/correction and see China heading back to new heights as the majority of investors still believe? Look back to my Snowboard Dennis story to see how the next two phases in China's decline are likely to unfold.

The soaring price of oil drove crude and oil stocks to blow-off tops where every speculator thought it had nowhere to go except up, right before oil stocks crashed.

Real estate is playing out exactly as I discussed in Chapter 2, "Boomtown to Ghost Town." Even if the Fed can manage a good inning or two, I still hold to the view that real estate's extra-inning game will end in loss for the real estate perma-bulls. The real estate market has a long period of adjustment ahead even if the Fed can engineer a few bullish intervals.

In case you are still not aware of what has been going on in the minds of those in the Federal Reserve, let me remind you. The Fed is fighting off the potential of a massive debt contraction cycle that would lead to the New Great Global Depression of the Twenty-First Century. They see a real possibility of a 1930s-style economic calamity. However, this time the calamity is being primarily caused by the slow-motion crash in real estate values. This deflation fight with excessive liquidity by the Fed has fueled inflationary pressures. You know what comes next from reading the book.

If the Fed can create another false economic boom, which can only be built on an even higher mountain of debt, then I strongly urge every reader to take advantage of whatever small window may open to get your financial house in order. *I would also suggest that you share with those you love the reasons why you are taking such drastic actions as reducing mortgage debt, getting off margin, and minimizing all other debt.* Debt truly is a four-letter word especially in tough economic times, so take advantage of whatever bounce the Fed can give the economy with their aggressive interest rate cuts and other "heroic measures."

I want every reader to understand that I do not advise any nonprofessional to trade stocks on his own in this coming new era of volatility. However, I have given you some important tools and strategies if you choose to take on the risk. This is especially true of shorting stocks. Don't do it on your own unless you are devoting the necessary time to your account using strict stop disciplines, and unless you get the necessary education to fully understand the risks of shorting and using margin. Anyone who seriously wants to short stocks must read the best books on the stock market, the economy, and shorting. The best book on shorting stocks is by William O'Neil, *How to Make Money Selling Stocks Short* (McGraw-Hill, 1988). Another book I would highly recommend is *Empire of Debt* by Bill Bonner (John Wiley & Sons, 2006). These books will reinforce why shorting needs to be part of any investment strategy going forward.

My suggestion is that investors get a seasoned stockbroker, professional money manager, or investment adviser who employs strategies that address the downside of the marketplace as well as the upside cyclical moves. They must utilize either tactical asset allocation strategies like I discussed in the book or shorting as an investment tool for protection and profits. I would be very careful of those that use long-only strategies where only rising markets and rising stocks can yield profits. Most investors have now likely seen the logic for having a short-side strategy as markets around the globe are correcting and individual stocks are crashing. Watching these markets having violent moves up and down should convince you that the days of buy and hold are dead and gone. A more proactive strategy of buying low and selling high or the reverse (shorting) is needed in this new era of extreme market volatility.

I want to leave you with another thought, my final note. The true upside of down is that it is in the tough times of life that we have an opportunity to grow as human beings. Life can be so hard. Many lower- and middle-class Americans are truly suffering from the rising costs of living and the stagnation in the economy. Every day, they struggle to put food on the table for their children and to pay their bills. They are faced with rising fuel, food, health care, and tuition costs. Their homes and stocks, if they own any, are falling in price. *When everything you own is going down and everything you need for existence is going up, you have serious stagflation in the economy.* If my outlook is correct, and I pray that it isn't, more people in America and from around the world will fall onto extremely difficult times. The upside of down times is that you are forced to look beyond yourself and to dig deep within your heart, mind, and soul for answers.

When it's all said and done, there is way more to life than investment profits. Faith, family, and friends will help you get through any kind of tough times you will have to deal with. My heroes in life are those men and women who can take tragedy and turn it into triumph and those who turn personal pain into gain for themselves and, more importantly, for others. It is those who fall hard but find a way to pick themselves back up that I admire and who inspire me the most in life. I am confident that this period of economic contraction will end and that a new era of growth and prosperity will unfold. We humans are tough, and I believe the world is starting to see that we are all in this together. While we will get through this tough economic period, why not make the suggested changes so that you have a possibility of experiencing the upside of down versus getting upside down in falling stocks, bonds, and real estate? In the financial analysis, I will leave you with this thought: Though the world and its markets will be ever-changing, the short-side strategy will endure.

GLOSSARY

American Depository Receipt (ADR): A stock representing a given number of shares in a foreign corporation. ADRs are bought and sold on U.S. markets and are traded in U.S. dollars.

Bear: A stock market bear is an investor who believes the stock market is set to fall into a bearish trend or is about to crash.

Bear Market: A prolonged period of declining stock prices accompanied by widespread pessimism and fear.

Bid; "Hit the Bid": A bid is an indication by a trader, dealer, or investor of a willingness to buy a stock. It is the price an investor can sell a stock to a broker/dealer.

Book Value per Share: A measure of the net worth of each common share.

Broker/Dealer: A person or firm in the business of buying and selling stocks.

Bull: An investor who believes a stock or market will rise.

Bull Market: A prolonged period of rising stock prices accompanied by widespread optimism.

Business Cycle: A natural pattern of alternating periods of economic growth and stagnation.

1st Stage: Expansion (Boom)

2nd Stage: A Peak (Top)

3rd Stage: Contraction (Decline)

4th Stage: A Trough (Bottom)

Call: An option contract giving the owner the right to buy a specific amount of an underlying stock at a specific price over a specified time period.

Call Writer or Selling Calls: An investor who receives income or a premium and for a certain period of time has the obligation to sell the underlying stock at a specific price at the call buyer's discretion.

Correlation: The extent to which two securities or markets move together.

Cyclical: Referred to in the book as the shorter-term movements in stocks and markets.

Deflation: A persistent and general fall in the level of prices in the economy. This book often refers to deflation of asset prices like stocks and real estate.

Depression: A prolonged period of contraction in the economy, generally considered to be six consecutive quarters of declining GDP.

Derivatives: Futures, options, forward contracts, and other investment vehicles in which the value depends on another securities value.

Discount Rate: The interest rate charged by the 12 Federal Reserve Banks for short-term loans made to member banks.

Diversification: A risk management approach that mixes all kinds of various securities and investments in a given portfolio to reduce the impact of any one security or investment in the portfolio.

Dividend: A distribution of a company's earnings in the form of cash or stock.

DJIA: The Dow Jones Industrial Average is the most widely used market indicator, consisting of 30 very large and actively traded stocks.

DJUA: The Dow Jones Utility Average is a market consisting of 15 utility stocks. This indicator is often used as a leading indicator to anticipate future moves in interest rates and stock markets.

Expansionary Monetary Policy: A monetary policy widely deployed by Alan Greenspan and Ben Bernanke where the money supply is greatly expanded with the intention of fighting deflation. Aggressively lowering interest rates is part of an expansionary monetary policy.

Federal Funds Rate: The interest rate charged by one bank lending federal funds to another bank.

Federal Reserve Board (The Fed): A seven-member group that directs the operations of the Federal Reserve System led by a Federal Reserve chairman who leads the decision-making process. The president appoints the chairman and Congress approves, but the Fed reports to Congress.

Fundamental Analysis: Fundamental analysts measure intrinsic value of a stock and study overall economic climate, industry conditions, and the financial condition of a company or market.

Hedge: A strategy used to reduce the risk of an adverse price movement such as shorting stocks or selling calls. A hedge fund uses hedging strategies.

Hedge Fund: A private investment partnership for high net worth individuals. Hedge funds use various investment strategies to hedge against market downturns. Most hedge funds go long stocks as well as deploy shorting as an effective hedging strategy.

Inflation: A persistent and measurable increase in prices across the board in the economy. Inflation has been evident in commodities of all kinds in the early years of the new century. Asset inflation is where the values of stocks and homes are inflated primarily from excess credit creation and wild speculation.

Investment Adviser: A person who makes investments on behalf of another and charges a flat fee or a percentage of assets managed.

Long: The term used to describe owning a stock.

Money Supply: The total stock of bills, coins, loans, credit, and other liquid instruments in the economy usually stated as M1, M2, and M3. (Greenspan discontinued reporting of the M3 aggregate in 2006.)

Nasdaq: The National Association of Securities Dealers Automated Quotation System consists of over 3,500 over-the-counter stocks. Nasdaq 2000 is referred to in the book as the stocks on the Nasdaq Composite Index that crashed from early 2000 and ended in early 2003. The Nasdaq Composite Index is a market-weighted index of all common stocks traded on Nasdaq.

Scale-in, Scale-out Seller: A disciplined trading approach where one slowly accumulates or sells a stock position versus buying or selling the full position all at one time.

Sell Stop Order: A sell order to protect a long position or limit a loss. It is entered at a price below the current price and is triggered when the market price goes through or touches the sell stop price.

Short: When an investor borrows shares of stock from a broker/dealer and sells them in the market, he/she is said to put on a short position. One hopes to buy the stock back later at a lower price. Sell first (a short sale) and then buying the shares back later is called the buy to cover. Shorting can be an effective profit and protection tool in a bear market when used in a responsible way. Irresponsible shorting is called "naked shorting," which is shorting without legally borrowing the long stock to go and sell short. This is a highly unethical practice not recommended in this book.

Short-Side Strategy: A short-side strategy deploys various investment tools like shorting and other hedging techniques for risk control and incorporates strict trading disciplines like stop losses. A short-side strategy deploys tactical asset allocation using both fundamental and technical analysis for proper equity exposure in bull and bear markets. A short-side strategy addresses both the upside and downside of the marketplace versus long-only buy and hold strategies. A short side strategy looks to invest in noncorrelated markets to reduce volatility and risk. The goal of a short side strategy is to buy low and sell high as well as to short high and then buy back lower. A short-side strategy requires one to recognize that a new approach to trading and investing is required in this new era of volatility and systemic risk.

S&P 500: A value-weighted index of 400 industrial stocks, 40 financial stocks, 40 utility stocks, and 20 transportation stocks.

Stagflation: A period of economic stagnation combined with rising inflation and rising unemployment. Stagflation can take on various degrees of intensity. A period of mild stagflation is when asset prices, like stocks and real estate, fall even as inflationary pressures like commodities rise, along with prices across the board. Eventually, stagflation can lead to a severe recession with rapidly rising unemployment combined with mass inflation, or a period of intensified stagflation.

Stop Order: A customer order that becomes a market order when the market price passes a specific price. A mental stop is the point you have determined in your mind that you will take a loss on a stock.

Technical Analysis: A method of determining future price movements using stock charts by studying past prices and volume. A pure technician strictly focuses on price and is unconcerned with the fundamentals and fundamental analysis.

INDEX